VAGRANT KINGS

DAVID STERN, KEVIN JOHNSON, AND THE NBA'S ORPHAN TEAM

R.E. GRASWICH

street press
A COMMUNITY WRITING & PUBLISHING CENTER

Graswich, Robert Edward

Vagrant Kings: David Stern, Kevin Johnson and the NBA's Orphan Team
R.E. Graswich

ISBN: 978-0-9898209-3-6
LCCN: 2013918830

1.Stern, David, 1942—. 2. Basketball commissioner—United States—Biography.
3. Johnson, Kevin, 1966—. 4. Basketball player and mayor—United States—Biography.
5. Sacramento Kings basketball franchise—United States—History—20th Century.

Design: Seth Watkins. Typeset in 10.5/14 Adobe Garamond

First Edition

To Betty, William and Bob,
for the faith

Chapters

Preface: In Sacramento, Dying May Be Redundant

On September 16, 2011, a few days after returning home from Tennessee, where he exchanged wedding vows with Michelle Rhee in a rainy outdoor ceremony, Kevin Johnson, the mayor of Sacramento, was on a speakerphone with David Stern, the commissioner of the National Basketball Association. The conversation was similar to many discussions by the two men. The topic was a new arena for Sacramento.

Stern wanted to know how Johnson would pay for the arena, and how much money the city of Sacramento would contribute. Stern was looking for a big number. He was obsessed with taxpayer contributions for arenas. His goal was to maximize the public funding and reduce the dollars expected from the owners of the Sacramento Kings. Stern was an expert in arena financing and Johnson was an amateur. But the commissioner was determined to help the mayor build a new facility in Sacramento, no matter what it cost the city.

In this way, Stern's position toward Sacramento was paradoxical. He was keen to see the city keep its NBA team. Yet he needed assurance that Sacramento was willing to pay for the privilege. Nobody rides free in the NBA.

There were other cities and easier paths, but Stern was patient. Without a new building, without substantial arena funds from the city, the Kings would move away, leaving California's capital without a major league sports franchise. David Stern didn't want that. The commissioner, more than the mayor, more than the people who owned the Kings, more than almost everybody other than the region's most passionate basketball fans, wanted the Kings to stop their wanderings and find a permanent home in Sacramento.

To make that happen, Stern was prepared to risk his reputation and test the loyalty of his employers, the 30 NBA franchise owners, to save one of the worst teams in pro basketball for one of the smallest, poorest markets in major league sports. Before the Kings, Sacramento was a place where the biggest athletic event was an annual charity football game between police officers and sheriff's deputies that drew 30,000 fans in the late 1970s.

David Stern worked more than a decade to save the Kings for Sacramento. As he entered the final months of his 30 years as commissioner and prepared for retirement in February 2014, Sacramento would be his exit act, the place where the stage goes dark and the audience sits in silence for a moment, realizing that the NBA has come of age and the maestro has gone, having resurrected the league in 1984 from its drug-addled carnival days to become an institution that stands for something other than good times and fast living.

As he secured his legacy, Stern led the NBA owners to turn down a $100 million bonus offer to move the Kings. In not taking that money, the NBA proved it was willing to protect its most vulnerable community, Sacramento. Stern used three words to describe this moment. He called it, "The appropriate outcome."

SACRAMENTO, population 466,488 in 2010, was a modest market for the NBA, but David Stern was spiritually invested in the city. He blessed the Kings' move from Kansas City as a young, new commissioner in 1985, and approached Sacramento with an intensity that suggested a moralistic line in the sand. His faith was rewarded as the Kings sold out 17 of their first 28 seasons in Sacramento, an NBA record. If the league could not protect a small, loyal and exposed market, what could it protect? What good was it?

Stern christened two arenas in Sacramento, first a temporary facility in 1985 with only 10,333 seats, then a permanent structure in 1988, capacity 17,317. Shortly after 2000, the commissioner began to put aside other duties to personally lead the task to replace the 1988 arena. Time was running out. In 2008, Johnson was elected and Stern found himself with a unique ally, a former NBA all-star guard in the Sacramento Mayor's Office. By winning his election and becoming mayor of his hometown, Johnson proved pro athletes could have second chapters, lives of substance after the cheering stopped.

There was a complication. Johnson despised the Kings. He hated dealing with them. It was an old grudge that dated back decades. One day in 2012, when I worked for Johnson as Special Assistant, he asked me how many times he had defeated Sacramento during his playing days with the Phoenix Suns. I did some research and returned to his office a few minutes later. "In 12 years, your record was 37 wins, 11 losses," I told him. He shot me a dirty look and said, "Are you sure they beat us 11 times? That doesn't sound right." Kevin needed to be reminded of his domination over the Kings. A 37–11 record wasn't domination enough.

THE PHONE conversation between Stern and Johnson that day in September 2011 did not go well. Stern was bristly. He felt Johnson was stalling about the city's financial participation in the new arena. Stern pushed Kevin, wanting to know exactly how the mayor was going to produce big public dollars for the project. Johnson couldn't tell him. The mayor didn't know.

Exasperated, Stern asked a final question about potential user fees charged to Kings fans. "Thank you," Johnson said. "You've ended my honeymoon." Joel Litvin, the NBA's president for operations, laughed in the background and said, "Congratulations." The commissioner had the final word: "Sorry to be a prick. That's my role. If there's going to be a prick, there's only going to be one."

In the history of Sacramento, David Stern might be the only person of real stature who wasn't disdainful toward the city, didn't turn his back and walk away. Sacramento is littered with the memories of remarkable people who stayed for a while, got bored or restless or tired or ambitious, and left.

John Sutter, the Swiss adventurer who founded Sacramento in 1839 and owned the site where gold was discovered in California, left for Pennsylvania. William Tecumseh Sherman, who helped survey Sacramento's street grid in 1848, left for Atlanta, among other places. Leland Stanford, who was one of four Sacramento merchants who organized the transcontinental Central Pacific Railroad, started a university in 1885 to memorialize his son. The school would be located at his ranch in Palo Alto, 118 miles from Sacramento.

More recent history was no different. The author Joan Didion left for New York. The newspaper columnist Herb Caen left for San Francisco, where he wrote the line, "In Sacramento, dying may be redundant." The actor Tom Hanks attended college in Sacramento and left for Hollywood.

Ronald Reagan came from Hollywood, moved into a sumptuous home on a lovely street in Sacramento, served as governor, and left for a better address in Washington, D.C. Another Hollywood transplant, Arnold Schwarzenegger, disliked Sacramento so much he often commuted about 700 miles each day, round trip, to avoid spending the night.

THEN THERE was Kevin Johnson. Born and raised in the downcast Oak Park neighborhood of Sacramento, he left for college, made almost $30 million playing basketball and came home, a nesting instinct that appealed to David Stern.

In January 2013, Stern and the NBA owners were given an unprecedented opportunity. A group that included Microsoft CEO Steve Ballmer, one of the nation's wealthiest men, wanted to buy the Kings for a record price and move the team to Seattle. The sale and relocation required league approval. In NBA history since 1949, just one similar transaction had been rejected. And that was because the prospective investors had questionable balance sheets. There were no questions about the Seattle balance sheets.

But Ballmer and his team made a strategic gamble. They tried to move fast, too fast, and miscalculated the NBA's internal politics. Instead, the NBA favored a partnership led by Vivek Ranadive, a native of Mumbai, India, who made a fortune in Silicon Valley. Ranadive vowed to keep the Kings in Sacramento.

Commissioner Stern wasn't allowed to vote with the Board of Governors, but his influence on behalf of Sacramento, intervention that began when the team landed in California in 1985, was consistent, persuasive and decisive. Thanks to David Stern, Sacramento finally had something that wouldn't leave: the Kings, who by coincidence were the most transitory team in U.S. sports history, America's vagrant franchise.

MY ASSOCIATION with the Kings began in 1984, when the team was still in Kansas City. My employer then, The Sacramento Bee newspaper, knew the franchise was moving to Sacramento. The paper assigned reporters to cover every aspect of the Kings franchise. I was sent to Oakland to cover the Golden State Warriors, preparing readers for comprehensive NBA coverage. By 1987, I was the main reporter attached to the Kings, and covered them on and off as a columnist until 2007. Much of my reporting was negative. The Kings were an awful team for most of that time. When people asked why I was so negative, I pointed to the scoreboard.

New arenas were always desirable in the NBA. Team owners could make more money in a new building. And they could spend that money on improving their franchise with superior, expensive players. Team owners were pleased when taxpayers covered the costs of arenas.

There were many proposals to build new arenas for the Kings. I became a specialist in finding weaknesses in the plans. I followed the money, which always led to mountains of taxpayer dollars. After working in radio and TV for a few years, I joined Kevin Johnson's mayoral staff in 2009 as Special Assistant.

Three months later, Johnson became convinced that Sacramento needed a new arena to keep the Kings, despite his disdain for the team. He assigned me to help with the arena project. "A lot of people think I'm crazy for letting you work on the arena," he told me. "But it's smart to have a guy who knows how to kill an arena on our when side when we go to build one."

I learned it was far easier to kill an arena than build one. And I learned other things. I came to appreciate the emotional connection between the city and its only major league team, a connection that stretched across the franchise's long-distance history, which began in the 1930s in the dreams of a Rochester, N.Y., high school basketball star named Lester Harrison.

He founded the team and owned it over three decades. As a reporter, I had the opportunity to speak to Harrison a few years before his death. In time, I met people from Cincinnati and Kansas City and Omaha who shared a connection with Kings fans in Sacramento.

Every pro sports team has long-distance fans, but no team could match the Kings for fans whose far-flung towns once claimed ownership of the same franchise. Only one team comes close to having covered so much ground, the Atlanta Hawks, who played in four cities. Three of those moves took place in six seasons, 1949-1955. The Hawks are sedentary compared to the Kings.

TWO DAYS after the NBA rejected the Seattle move Kevin Johnson held a pep rally in the lobby of Sacramento City Hall. He introduced local politicians and business leaders and thanked the community for not giving up. He said the fight for the Kings was "about not letting somebody take something away that wasn't theirs." For Johnson, it wasn't about the Kings. It was about Sacramento. The team and the city were interlaced.

Having followed the Kings for three decades and threaded their history back almost 90 years, having reconstructed the moves and the teases and near misses and breakdowns, I knew the NBA made the right decision when it reached, as Stern said, "The appropriate outcome." The Kings could not have been taken away by someone like Steve Ballmer, who would pay any price, even a crazy price, for a beaten down, itinerant NBA team.

No, Ballmer and his friends in Seattle didn't deserve these vagrants. Seattle needed something that sparkled. By contrast, Vivek Ranadive, who came to the U.S. with almost nothing, was fine with the idea of taking something battered and broken, something that often failed, something he could possibly—somehow—fix with hard work and enthusiasm and brains and luck.

The Kings never sparkled. They rarely succeeded. They had no luck. They were a team for the millions of average and easily forgotten people who endured life and moved around and found no shame in being eliminated in the second round of the playoffs. At least we made it that far, these people would reckon; it could have been worse.

As former Los Angeles Lakers coach Phil Jackson once said, "I do feel sorry for Sacramento. It's tough to be good losers." In 2013, Jackson would agree to join the Kings' front office, but only if the team relocated to Seattle.

This is the story of the Kings and their search for a city that would make a home for them. It's a story made vital by the connection between two people who bet their legacies to anchor the franchise, David Joel Stern and Kevin Maurice Johnson. In a sense, their partnership began in 1966. That year, David Stern, newly graduated from Columbia Law School, was assigned as a lawyer to the NBA. And in Sacramento, Kevin Johnson was born.

David Stern knew the Kings were the perfect team for Sacramento, a city accustomed to supporting losers. He knew that Sacramento, easily overlooked and ignored, would love to welcome the vagrants in, to make them a suitable home, fix them up and pray they didn't wander off again.

How all of that came to happen is the story that follows.

Chapter One:
A Distant Memory

Kevin Johnson is a Christian man, pious and reverential in houses of worship and not given to indifference toward coffins. This explains why Kevin waited in the doorway, his back warmed by sunlight, his face bathed by red light filtered through stained glass windows at Saint Rose Catholic Church in Roseville, California, on August 27, 2012, the day they buried his friend Tom Friery.

I arrived 30 minutes early and saved a seat for Johnson in Row 3. With the funeral about to start and Kevin not present, I looked back at the door and finally saw him, the mayor of Sacramento, standing in the light. He would not enter the church until the casket was rolled down the aisle and locked into place for the Mass of the Resurrection. The coffin, draped in white linen on a retractable stand with wheels, began to move after a nod from the parish priest, the Very Reverend Michael O'Reilly.

Tom Friery had been Johnson's first, most loyal and possibly only friend within the bureaucratic hierarchy of Sacramento City Hall. He was the retired city treasurer. From the Treasurer's Office, Friery directed the financial instruments and debt structures of Sacramento for 35 years, earning among municipal officials a reputation for prudence not weakened by his inclination toward civic pride. Friery loved his work. He was good at it.

When he was not at work, Friery would think about sports. He was a fan with diversity. Football, basketball, golf, he loved them all. That was one reason he was drawn to Kevin Johnson. Other than a joy of sports, the two men had nothing in common. Friery, age 69 at his death, lived 19 miles from Sacramento in a carefully engineered suburban community with meandering streets, green grass and taupe tile roofs. He was pleased with his home's proximity to a golf and tennis country club. On the day he collapsed and died from a heart attack, Tom Friery was in a Northern Nevada hotel room with his wife, preparing to play 18 holes.

Kevin Johnson, born March 4, 1966, didn't like golf. He preferred the asphalt of cities to suburban greenery. When it came to sports, he was the rare U.S. elected official who could speak from the perspective of having been there, not as a fan but as a star. When a pompous city council member, Robert King Fong, once tried to impress colleagues with a sidebar about his recollections of basketball games witnessed at Madison Square Garden and Boston Garden, Johnson interrupted and reminded Fong that the mayor, too, had been in those glorious buildings, not as a fan but on the floor, at center stage, running the show for the Phoenix Suns. Fong blinked and fell silent.

For Johnson, the game was basketball. His accomplishments reached almost to the pinnacle, one step short of the grandest achievement possible in the National Basketball Association. In 1993, as the starting point guard for the Suns, Johnson had the memorable and humbling experience of playing against Michael Jordan and the Chicago Bulls in the best-of-seven NBA championship series. Johnson and the Suns lost in six games.

Two decades later, when people would ask about the difficulties associated with a tricky political issue, Mayor Johnson would say, "It's really not that big of a deal compared with trying to guard Michael Jordan in the NBA Finals." The line always brought a laugh. No other politician in America could steal it. Best of all from Johnson's perspective, it was absolutely true.

Over the next two decades, Johnson would measure every challenge against a yardstick made when he was 27 years old and playing against Michael Jordan in the Finals. Johnson would do many things: start an after-school program, open charter schools, fight with teachers' unions, face questions about his relationships with teenaged girls, receive and misspend large amounts of federal grant money, start a real estate development company, pay fines for violating city building codes, get elected mayor, try to change the governance system, and spend four years trying to keep the Kings from moving away from Sacramento. He would consider those insignificant compared with matching up on Jordan. For the rest of his life beyond 1993, Johnson's toughest challenge was a memory.

Kevin Johnson was an athlete. And like many athletes, civilian life out of uniform, after the cheering stopped, never quite measured up. How could it? Kevin performed surprisingly well against the more experienced and talented Jordan. It was during other parts of the series, as Johnson's teammates tried to handle Jordan, when the Suns struggled to calibrate their adrenalin and let the champs run away for easy baskets and victory.

The 1993 NBA Finals ended when Chicago forward Horace Grant knocked the ball from Kevin's hand as time ran out. Johnson wanted to win the game with a dramatic, heroic shot. His ambition was denied. The Bulls won 99-98. They were the champions. Johnson was not finished thinking about dramatic, heroic shots.

He continued to try spectacular moves, "Moon shots," he called them, as he faded away from basketball and into real estate development, education and politics. More often than not, the ball would be knocked from his hand as time ran out. Ambition denied. He kept trying.

THE SERIES against Jordan and the Bulls was a high mark for Kevin Johnson and, by geographic extension, for Sacramento, his hometown. Sacramento is a community proud of its athletic stars, but for reasons of coincidence and habit, most of those stars have been baseball players.

Athletes such as Dusty Baker, Larry Bowa, Johnny McNamara, Jerry Manuel and Steve Sax came from Sacramento and made their fame in baseball. Kevin played baseball, too. He signed a professional contract with the Oakland Athletics after graduation from Sacramento High School. He soon abandoned baseball to concentrate on basketball. Although Sacramento had almost no presence among the ranks of NBA hometown cities, Johnson's decision to switch sports, outdoors to indoors, summer to winter, was the right choice.

His accomplishments in basketball, which included 12 professional seasons, three NBA all-star games and the championship series against the Bulls, served as testimony to his work ethic, determination and ambition. Success was all the more remarkable considering that he stood barely 6-foot-1 and was frightfully skinny the day he presented himself to the NBA draft in 1987.

It would be difficult to exaggerate the physical limitations Johnson had to overcome in his path to NBA stardom. Consider another skinny young 6-foot-1 guard, Bob Cousy, who was intentionally ignored in the 1950 college draft by Coach Red Auerbach and the Boston Celtics. Auerbach thought Cousy was too small. Many things changed in the NBA between 1950 and 1987, but some things stayed the same. Pro basketball was a game for big men.

As draft day approached for Johnson, many NBA teams were intrigued by his quickness and leaping ability. They were concerned about his size, outside shooting ability and West Coast pedigree. His college experience was with the University of California, Berkeley, which, while renowned for academic research, highly selective enrollment standards and political protests, was not a basketball dynasty.

On draft day 1987, Kevin and his family rented three motel rooms alongside a freeway in Sacramento and invited friends over to watch the proceedings live on TV from New York. The very best players were flown to New York to attend the draft in person. The fact that Johnson watched from a Sacramento motel room indicated his status as a skinny 6-foot-1 point guard from Cal.

Kevin and his family had no idea what would happen. Six teams skipped him before the Cleveland Cavaliers called Kevin's name with the No. 7 pick. The 10 highest NBA draft picks are considered elite. The moment should have been glorious for the young man from Sacramento, with Commissioner David Stern stepping to the microphone to announce the draft pick and calling out Johnson's name. Boos were heard in the Felt Forum at Madison Square Garden, where the draft was held, and in taverns across Cleveland. Stern had a pained expression on his face after he read Johnson's name.

Back at the motel, Kevin was devastated, not by the distinction of being No. 7 (he was very proud of that number) and not by the booing or the commissioner's reaction, but by the insult thrown down by one of the teams that ignored him: his hometown club, the Sacramento Kings. Kevin was the best college basketball player in history from Sacramento. But he wasn't good enough for the Sacramento Kings, who held the No. 6 choice that year.

As if to intensify Johnson's humiliation, like laughing in his face, the Kings drafted a player of almost identical proportion, potential and position, Kenny Smith, from the University of North Carolina, which was a basketball college, Michael Jordan's school. Adding to the insult was the fact that the decision to draft Smith over Johnson was made by an NBA legend, Bill Russell, the Kings' new coach.

Russell should have known how good Johnson was at Cal. Berkeley borders the city where Russell grew up, Oakland. And Russell should have known what drafting Kevin Johnson would have meant to Sacramento and the Kings. Russell chose Kenny Smith anyway.

As years passed and Johnson surged beyond Kenny Smith on the basketball court, the snub of draft day 1987 was not forgotten. At particular low moments from 2009 to 2013, after Johnson had been elected mayor and was trying to build a new arena for the Kings, he continued to make references to the decision to draft Kenny Smith over the skinny point guard from Sacramento.

By then, Bill Russell was long retired and the Kings' ownership had changed twice. It didn't matter. "The Kings are still the same team that drafted Kenny Smith with the No. 6 pick," Kevin would tell me. Draft day 1987 was a psychological iceberg for the point guard from Cal.

HE WAS not the first person frustrated by decisions made by the Sacramento Kings. The Kings were forlorn, a wreckage on the highway of professional sports. They were habitually underfunded, cursed and foolish in their decisions, repeatedly under threat of sale, owned and managed for purposes that often had little to do with basketball.

Commissioner Stern was among the few people who cared about the Kings despite the grief they brought him over the decades. Stern would do everything possible to end the team's wanderings in Sacramento, to honor the loyalty that the Northern California Valley region blessed upon America's Vagrant Kings.

In the modern history of American pro sports dating from World War II, the Kings had no equal in professional basketball, baseball, football or hockey. No professional sports team moved among as many cities as the Kings. They were the nation's itinerant team, like a tumbleweed that wore the labels of five cities under two nicknames while blowing across the United States before landing in Sacramento in 1985.

By early 2013, the Kings were prepared to move again, this time to Seattle as a replacement pet for the empty kibble bowl left by the SuperSonics. The former Seattle NBA franchise packed up and relocated to Oklahoma City under a new name in 2008. Now a wealthy group of investors, far richer than anybody in Sacramento, had targeted the Kings as a quick, easy trophy.

It made sense for Seattle to go after the Kings. Many pro sports teams moved between cities once, maybe even twice, but the Kings were built for mobility. In city after city, wherever they landed, the Kings' ownership arrangements were temporary and transitory. Their financial footing had the firmness of sand. There was always talk of new suitors and other cities. The Kings were born disposable, convenient and available.

The Kings were accustomed to being used as leverage points in real estate deals and other business matters, but a jump to Seattle would have been different: a kidnapping intended to heal a city's emotional loss.

Seattle really didn't need the Kings, not like Sacramento needed them. Seattle suffered no shortage of entertainment. The city was represented in the NFL, Major League Baseball, Major League Soccer and top-level college athletics. Yet some people in Seattle never got over the SuperSonics' death, especially after the relocated team advanced to the NBA championships in 2012. The franchise wore the Oklahoma City Thunder logo and lost to the Miami Heat in five games.

Seattle NBA fans knew it should have been their team playing Miami. Among the most bitter was Microsoft CEO Steve Ballmer, who offered to buy the SuperSonics in 2008 and claimed he would spend $150 million to dress up Seattle's old Key Arena. In 2012, Ballmer decided he wanted to adopt a new team. He was not a man accustomed to being turned down. The price was irrelevant.

The prospective Seattle team's quality and history were also irrelevant. Certainly, Ballmer would not have confused the Kings with championship contenders. Not only were they the most migratory sports franchise in history, they were among the biggest losers. Since the formation of the NBA, the franchise had won just one title, in 1951. That year, playing under its original NBA name, the Rochester Royals, the team defeated the New York Knickerbockers 79-75 in a decisive Game 7 at the Edgerton Park Sports Arena in Rochester to take the championship.

RECOVERIES and turnarounds and resurrections could happen quickly in the NBA, with a lucky draft pick or an inspired trade. Most teams had their ups and downs. Not so the Kings, who since 1951 bounced between awful and mediocre. Since the early 1950s, the basic condition of the franchise was the stooped shoulder, why-me posture of abject failure. The Kings were always hoping for better luck next season.

There were brief, tantalizing exceptions, moments when a breakthrough victory seemed certain, only to disappear. A grand tease came in the Western Conference Championships of 2002, but quickly crashed down on the Kings in the penultimate Game 6, when Sacramento lost to the Los Angeles Lakers 106-102 at Staples Center. It was one of the most controversial playoff games in NBA history. As usual, history didn't have a trophy for the Kings.

That particular Game 6 included 40 free throws by the Lakers and only 25 by the Kings. There were mysterious fouls whistled against Sacramento in the late minutes. Conspiracy theorists included former presidential candidate and consumer watchdog Ralph Nader, who publicly demanded an investigation, and former NBA referee Tim Donaghy, who told a federal court the game was fixed.

Under Commissioner Stern's direction, the NBA convened a special investigation into Donaghy's allegations. Former federal prosecutor Lawrence Pedowitz ran the inquiry. Donaghy made many accusations about a variety of NBA issues. The Game 6 controversy was just part of the examination. Pedowitz devoted eight of 133 pages to the Kings' fate. He found no evidence to prove the game was fixed.

The investigator identified 15 erroneous or overlooked foul calls by the referees, eight of which favored the Lakers, seven of which helped the Kings. The three refs, Dick Bavetta, Bob Delaney and Ted Bernhardt, were portrayed as incompetent in Game 6, but not conspiratorial.

Pedowitz told the media in a conference call, "We took a hard look at this; it was clearly not a well-refereed game. There were a lot of errors. But if you look at the types of errors that were going on, Bavetta's errors were quite well balanced, that there was no occasion he was strongly favoring one team over the other. With regard to Delaney's errors, he only had a few. We tried to describe to you in there what the basketball operations people who looked at the refereeing saw. We tried to explain to you how a referee can always miss a call. One thing I know you understand, if you go to a game and you try to make calls yourself from the stands, even if you're close in, it depends on what your perspective is, where you are."

And Tim Donaghy had credibility issues. He was convicted of taking payoffs from gamblers and betting on other games. In Sacramento, where the Game 6 defeat and series loss were still being discussed in bars and patios a decade later, Donaghy's words, credible or not, were considered a sermon on the outrages of a corrupt system.

The series against the Lakers was the Kings' best performance in almost 50 years. Of course, Sacramento was the loser. The Kings' official history summarized the legacy without adornment. "The franchise's glory years are now a distant memory," it said.

Chapter Two: Would Have Been Real Problems

The Sacramento Kings would not have been playing the Lakers in 2002 without the work of City Treasurer Tom Friery. The Lakers would have been playing the Nashville Kings or Anaheim Royals.

In 1997, the team's owner, Jim Thomas, a Los Angeles real estate developer and former IRS lawyer with wavy gray hair and a tight smile, threatened to move the Kings unless he received a loan from the Sacramento City Council. Thomas had seen the team's balance sheet implode as he sought to make payroll and win games in the NBA without the ability to sell hundreds of luxury suites, club-level boxes and corporate "founding partner" sponsorships that are the gold standard of pro sports.

Thomas owned the Kings' home arena, then called Arco Arena, but the status of the facility as a privately owned-and-operated events center meant Thomas and his partners were responsible for upkeep and improvements. The owners could not afford the upkeep because they were scrambling to make payroll. Those factors made Jim Thomas unlike most NBA owners, whose teams played in buildings owned and maintained by taxpayer-supported public entities.

The economic disadvantages of private arena ownership for Thomas and the Kings were significant. While Thomas briefly had a spigot of operational dollars from partners such as Eli Broad, the Los Angeles billionaire who held a minority stake in the Kings, wealthy benefactors grew tired of cash calls and divested themselves of basketball, leaving Thomas mostly on his own.

In late 1997, with cash running out and the Kings losing $5 million per year, Thomas resorted to the type of legalized extortion that became familiar to sports fans and cities across the U.S. in the late 20th Century. Without a cash infusion from the city, he said, the Kings would have no choice but to move to a more generous community, a place like Nashville or Anaheim. Thomas was careful to avoid making specific threats to relocate, but he made it clear Sacramento would soon find itself without an NBA team if financial help wasn't granted by the city.

The figure of $73 million was agreed upon. City Treasurer Friery went to work crafting a deal. He was the perfect man for the job, devoid of cynicism, eager to keep the Kings in Sacramento, protective of the city's resources. Friery and City Attorney Samuel Jackson produced what they believed was the perfect instrument: a series of 30-year bonds backed by the good faith and credit of the city of Sacramento general fund. The bonds, they hoped, would lock the Kings into Sacramento for the next three decades and beyond. The city would be a pass-through agent, selling the bonds and shoveling the bondholder's money to the Kings. Municipal participation helped lower the interest rates.

With an insurance policy to guard against default, Friery and Jackson devised language that would require immediate and full settlement if the Kings moved before the bonds were paid back, plus prepayment penalties. As collateral, the city added its name to the deed on Arco Arena and 86 acres occupied by the building and parking lots. They staked a $25 million claim on the team. "I won't say anything is ironclad," Friery said. "But it's pretty darned close. The team would basically have to get kicked out of the NBA through league contraction to put the city in a position of exposure." The city council nervously agreed to the deal, and approved the bond sale 5-3 as an overflow audience of Kings fans at City Hall cheered.

Friery was so confident of his work that in 2003, he signed a letter agreeing to subordinate the city's loan position behind $35 million the Kings were quietly borrowing from the NBA. The letter legally placed Sacramento in line after the NBA if the Kings went bankrupt.

The city council didn't learn about the subordination letter until 2010, when Friery and Jackson were both retired. By then, Friery was helping Kevin Johnson finance a new arena. The retired treasurer told me why he agreed to subordinate the city's loan. "It was within my authority as treasurer, and it was the right thing to do," he said. "Otherwise, the NBA would not have loaned them the money they needed to keep operating, and there would have been real problems."

FOR KEVIN Johnson, the problems became very real in October 2009. He had been mayor for only 10 months, elected not just thanks to his celebrity status, but for his ability to convince the city's business leaders that he was one of them, an entrepreneur, willing to take risks, philosophically separated from other elected officials in Sacramento. The other politicians tended to emerge from the bureaucracies or government service industries that dominated life in California's capital.

Johnson was very different. Since leaving basketball in 2000, he built a small real estate development company and nonprofit charter school system in Oak Park, the rough, neglected neighborhood of his childhood. He was not a lobbyist, consultant, legislative policy wonk or civil servant, like many other political leaders in Sacramento.

His election came at a time of challenges in Sacramento. City government faced a $200 million deficit and unemployment was headed to 12 percent. Johnson carried the portfolio of an old-school citizen politician, the type of person who had been largely absent from the city council for decades. He was a businessman, a registered Democrat but ideologically a moderate Republican, hard charging, progressive-minded, forever talking about accountability. Which meant he would be viewed with suspicion in a city where liberal values, entitlements and public-employee unions dominated local politics.

As mayor, Kevin tried to downplay his sports background. He wanted to dazzle the city with his new image as a chief executive officer, a natural born CEO. He would upgrade the city's outdated, small-town style of government, a system that worshipped tedious collaboration, back room relationships and process over action and rendered all nine council members, including the mayor, as equal partners.

Johnson wanted to do many things. Create initiatives to bring real-world business practices to the factions within the arts and cultural communities. Provide safe, cheap housing for thousands of people sleeping in doorways, cars, in parks and along the two rivers that framed Sacramento. Teach all children to read at grade level. Create an army of volunteers. Push Sacramento into the ranks of emerging cities, with ideas borrowed from Portland, Denver, Charlotte, Phoenix and Austin. And attract attention by bringing his friends to Sacramento, celebrities like Magic Johnson, Robert F. Kennedy, Jr., Alice Waters and Wynton Marsalis.

Eventually, Johnson would add one more plank to his agenda. He would end the speculation that the Kings were ready to move away. He would do this by generating support for a new downtown arena, something that had been talked about for a decade but was never accomplished because of indecisive public leadership and bizarre, destructive actions by the people who eventually bought the Kings from Jim Thomas, the Maloof family of Albuquerque, N.M., and Las Vegas.

Talk from the mayor's office about arts, homelessness and volunteerism was greeted with eye-rolling skepticism by the city council. All but three of the eight council members fought against Johnson's election. One of Kevin's three supporters, Sandy Sheedy, withdrew her support two months after Election Day, saying Johnson didn't know how to make friends. The new mayor was moving too fast, was too imperious and not inclusive. He didn't understand how things worked at City Hall. He wanted to grab power for himself, not sustain the status quo.

As for the topic of a new arena, even Kevin's friends told him to keep his mouth shut about that. The issue was toxic among Sacramento political leaders who loved the Kings but saw a publicly owned arena as an entitlement for millionaires. "Everyone told me not to take on building an arena," Johnson said. "The common thinking was, if the Kings want a new arena, they can build it themselves. We have more important problems in Sacramento."

Philosophically, Johnson didn't like the idea of taxpayers building a new arena for the Kings. He didn't want to assume responsibility for saving the Kings. They were still the team that drafted Kenny Smith at No. 6. His time as an NBA player had taught him lessons unknown or ignored by other local politicians, especially lessons about the business practices of the NBA.

Johnson knew the Maloof family would not pay for a new arena. He knew the Maloofs were not above trying to leverage their position or scheming to move to another city. He didn't trust the family. But he understood he could not stand by and watch his city's only pro sports franchise quit Sacramento while he was in the Mayor's Office. That would be some legacy. Former NBA all-star elected mayor; NBA team leaves.

And there was something else. Commissioner Stern, the man who looked so surprised when Kevin Johnson was drafted in 1987, had become Sacramento's champion. Since shortly after 2000, Stern fought to keep the

Kings in Northern California. He hoped to anchor the team and never preside over another relocation. Kevin had absolute respect for Stern, plus a sense of fear. The mayor could not let the commissioner fight the city's arena battle alone.

One day in September 2009, a news alert popped up on the phone carried by Joaquin McPeek, Mayor Johnson's press secretary. The alert said the National Collegiate Athletic Association would no longer bring its men's basketball tournament to Sacramento because of the inferior condition of Arco Arena.

McPeek forwarded the message to Johnson, then raced up to the fifth floor at City Hall and knocked on the mayor's office door. "Did you see this?" McPeek asked. Johnson had not read the message. "I told him about the NCAA and he almost flew out of his chair," McPeek said. This was bigger than the Kings, the mayor realized. This was about Sacramento. It was about Kevin Johnson's legacy.

Johnson ordered his staff to craft a speech that defined the crisis. Something like this: A regional cultural and sports venue was needed downtown to celebrate the region's rich economic and sociological diversity. Without a modern events center, Sacramento could not be considered one of America's emerging cities.

He decided to form a "blue ribbon" task force of community leaders to bring an appearance of credibility to the process. He spent the next several days with his staff, writing task force names on poster-sized sheets of paper stuck to the walls of the fifth-floor mayor's conference room at City Hall. I was among the group. We skipped lunches, stayed late, ordered pizza and sodas. Soon names on yellow stickers covered the walls and empty pizza boxes sat stacked on the trash.

The first "blue ribbon" name was retired City Treasurer Tom Friery. No doubt, the group agreed. Tom would be an obvious task force member. Financial expert. Institutional knowledge. Respected at City Hall. Yes, we need Tom for sure. Kevin Johnson wrote, "Tom F" with a thick black Sharpie and circled it with a red marker.

THREE YEARS later, as Tom Friery's body lay inside its coffin at Saint Rose, Father O'Reilly announced he would sing "Ave Maria." Seated in Row 3, Kevin Johnson popped an Icebreaker mint into his mouth. He had been reelected for a second term against token opposition. He was bored with his job. There was no new arena and no prospect for one.

The Maloof family had walked away from Sacramento's best arena proposal, a plan designed with unprecedented cooperation and financial help from the NBA and Commissioner Stern. The Kings were awful. Ticket sales had collapsed. The Maloofs had talked to city officials in the Las Vegas suburb of Henderson, Nev., and Virginia Beach, Va., about moving the team. They would soon have secret discussions to sell the Kings to a hedge fund manager from Seattle, Christopher Hansen, whose partner was Steve Ballmer. The Kings were in play. Worse, the Maloofs seemed determined to move the team, as if to punish Sacramento.

News reports about the Kings and their uncertainty with the Maloofs and Stern and Johnson prompted many prospective investors to phone the Mayor's Office for information about buying the team. One call stood out. It was from Roger Craig, the former all-pro running back for the San Francisco 49ers. I remembered Roger from my sports writing days and was happy to call him back on Johnson's orders.

Craig worked for a Palo Alto company called Tibco Software, founded by Vivek Ranadive, an electrical engineer who was fascinated by the idea of eliminating time lags whenever information is processed and distributed. Ranadive loved action in real time. And though he grew up in Mumbai, India, and didn't watch basketball as a youngster, Ranadive had learned to love the game.

In 2009, he earned a measure of proud notoriety when The New Yorker magazine writer Malcolm Gladwell profiled Ranadive, lauding his success at coaching his daughter's youth basketball team. Gladwell called Ranadive "relentless." Since then, Ranadive had become a minority partner in the Golden State Warriors. He was the first person from India to own part of an NBA franchise.

On the phone with me, Roger Craig was coy. He told me he knew someone from India who wanted to buy the Kings. He couldn't mention the person's name, because of his association with another NBA team, but wanted to know how best to approach the Maloofs and discuss a new arena with city officials. I figured out later Craig's investor was Vivek Ranadive. I knew nothing about the man. I couldn't even pronounce his name. I thought it would be wonderful if a Silicon Valley genius like Ranadive could somehow take over the Kings.

I had several conversations with Roger, all fairly useless to him. I gave the latest news, always discouraging, and told him how refreshing it would be to have somebody smart and rich running the Kings. I said it was impossible to deal with the Maloof family, but that the city was ready to contribute money to a new arena. All we needed was for the Maloofs to go away. The family's exit was long overdue, I said.

As Roger Craig looked for a critical path to victory, I wasn't the best person to provide an inspirational speech and three-step instructions. I was too frustrated by the Maloofs' behavior to give detailed advice to Roger. But we liked each other and promised to stay in touch, just in case.

Kevin Johnson wasn't doing much better. Nothing had changed during his first term as mayor. The governing structure of Sacramento was frozen in 1921, leaving Johnson with no more power than a council member. Thousands of homeless people were bedded down in doorways, in cars and along the rivers. The arts community was going broke.

Kevin was so frustrated by the lack of progress that he took to calling Sacramento by a code name: "Clipperville," after the habitually underachieving Los Angeles NBA team. "The Clippers couldn't run a layup drill," he said. "They would bump into each other. I hated to play them. You would either get into a fight or get injured. Sacramento is Clipperville." By the same definition, he could have called his city "Kingsville," but that would have been pushing his luck.

Inside Saint Rose Catholic Church that August morning in 2012, Father O'Reilly, a pure, sweet tenor, filled the hall with Shubert's first note of "Ave Maria," the song requested by Tom Friery's family. The priest's voice was beautiful. I looked down Row 3, and realized the mayor of Sacramento wasn't paying attention. His body was shifted away from the priest. His left hand cupped a smart phone. As Father O'Reilly lingered over each sweet note, Mayor Johnson tapped away at the tiny keys, answering emails.

Chapter Three: We Got A Franchise

The games were social events, places for prominent community members to strut and be seen. People dressed for the occasion. Coats and ties for men. Dresses and heels for women. Most tickets were sold as full-season subscriptions. General admission seats were almost impossible to buy.

The arena made no concessions to luxury. Stripped of its signs and banners, it was little more than a four-sided shell of a building with a high roof, expansive hardwood floor and wooden risers surrounding a basketball court. Fans practically sat on the court. Fire exit doors were only a few feet behind the basket. The lack of frills didn't matter. The community loved the place.

Absent the coats and ties, the description would fit Sacramento, circa 2002. In this scenario, the starched, white collar audience of business owners, corporate managers, civic leaders, husbands and wives, children and friends were gathered in another place and time, in postwar Rochester, N.Y., circa 1948, at the Edgerton Park Sports Arena, two miles north of downtown.

Today, Edgerton arena is gone, pulled down six decades ago, with nothing to mark the location but sports fields and tennis courts and memories long faded. "You'd see people with diamonds and fur coats sitting in the front row, some of the ladies knitting," the 6-foot-9 Rochester star center, Arnie Risen, recalled years ago.

The neighborhood around the old building site near Dewey Avenue and Backus Street has aged not much better than the demolished arena. In early 2013, urban Rochester was home to the least valuable residential real estate in the state of New York. A two-story, white clapboard home built in

1900 with wraparound porch, five bedrooms, two baths and 2,400 square feet located one block from Edgerton Park could be bought for $27,900 in 2013, about 95 percent cheaper than similar property in Brooklyn, 340 miles away.

Between 1950 and 2010, the city of Rochester shrank by 113,000 residents. One-third of its population disappeared. The story of Rochester's middle-class exodus could be told in the depressed residential prices around Edgerton Park and the site of the old basketball arena, home of the team that would become the Sacramento Kings.

The cratered economics of Rochester real estate were relevant to Kevin Johnson, though Johnson didn't know it. In public forums, when Mayor Johnson would make his argument for taxpayer support of a new arena for the Sacramento Kings, he would always start by saying the goal was bigger than basketball. The goal was economic. The mayor understood how resentment could easily be provoked among ordinary, middle-class residents when politicians talked about public subsidies for pro sports.

Cops would be laid off and fire stations closed in Sacramento after Johnson was elected mayor in 2008. Essential-service reductions would make it difficult to ask taxpayers to divert hundreds of millions dollars into a new arena for millionaire basketball players and their billionaire team owners.

Johnson needed a way around the obvious complaint about welfare for millionaires. He needed a path to pitch the arena without stirring resentment and rejection. He turned to his friend Chris Lehane, a San Francisco political strategist and crisis management expert whose early jobs after Amherst College and Harvard Law School involved creating communications plans for President Bill Clinton and Vice President Al Gore.

Instructed by Lehane, Johnson built a sleek public relations campaign for the new arena. He created a message. And he fed that message, daily, weekly, constantly, until the words were baked into the community's narrative.

Johnson injected data from economic development studies and job projection models. He explained how a new arena would put 4,000 people to work, not just on the construction site, but also in operations and maintenance of the new building. He stopped calling it an arena and embraced the ecumenical title "Entertainment and Sports Complex."

He described how an estimated $7 billion of investment would be generated by the Entertainment and Sports Complex over the next

30 years, stimulating the rebirth of downtown Sacramento, which had withered since the late 1960s when many businesses and shoppers moved to the suburbs.

The economic development argument was straight from Lehane's playbook, tested and proved in other communities.

The economic message resonated with many voters because it was accurate, as projections go. "Always make it about protecting the taxpayers and creating jobs," Lehane said. "Never talk about how much it's going to cost." Johnson didn't cite Rochester and its economic calamities, but a comparison would have been appropriate. If nothing else, Sacramento did not want to become like Rochester, the city that gave birth to the Kings and lost them.

IN THE YEARS after World War II, the city of Rochester had no strategist like Chris Lehane. The city did have Lester Harrison, a Rochester native who graduated from East High School in 1923 and decided to create his life around basketball. Harrison played the game and adored it. In the years that followed his departure from East High, Les and his brother Jack invented the basketball team that would evolve into the Sacramento Kings.

The Harrisons established a model that would endure for seven decades and grow in value from $25,000 to more than $500 million. It would become the most transient franchise in the history of U.S. professional sports.

In those early years in Rochester, the Harrison brothers drew the pattern that would define their basketball team. They lobbied the political leaders of Rochester to replace the Edgerton Park Sports Arena. The building was too small and unadorned for major league sports, the brothers said. They wrestled with the ambitions of their fellow basketball team owners, who placed the financial demands of big city arena operators ahead of concerns from the small market men. They fought against negative perceptions of their town. They were frustrated by players who didn't want to perform in the backwaters of Western New York, on the low hills near Lake Ontario.

They won two championships and helped set the cornerstone for the NBA as founding members. They made money and lost money and watched the audiences dwindle. And they did something that would serve as a doomsday solution for the franchise. When nothing else seemed to work, they packed up and moved.

Les Harrison died two days before Christmas in 1997 at age 93. His longevity allowed him to see the NBA from its birth to its finest hour, when David Stern transformed the league from a second-rate distraction to a tightly managed, phenomenally successful global entertainment bulldozer. Harrison saw what happened in between, the years of contraction and Western expansion, the rivalry between Bill Russell and Wilt Chamberlain, free agency, the merger with the American Basketball Association, the descent into drugs, the empty seats in all those arenas and the million-dollar losses on the books.

Harrison was not around to help Kevin Johnson resolve the arena problem in Sacramento. Kevin was still playing for the Suns when Harrison died. The old man would have understood what the mayor was dealing with in 2013. The issues hadn't changed much from the Rochester days.

Of course, Harrison would have loved Kevin Johnson. Point guards carried the keys to the basketball kingdom for Harrison and his generation of coaches, men who believed that the essence of Dr. James Naismith's game was found in the leadership and generosity demanded of point guards. Centers, forwards and shooting guards were role players, utility men who hammered nails. Point guards were the artists who created the vision.

The old man never lost track of the Kings, even when they landed in Sacramento. Shortly before his death, he tried to contact the person who owned the team at the time, Jim Thomas, to offer some advice. The Kings were struggling on the court and at the box office. Harrison wanted to share his ideas.

He was ignored by the Kings, despite his legacy and status as a founding member of the league, enshrined in the NBA Naismith Hall of Fame. Had he lived long enough to see Johnson elected, Harrison no doubt would have called the Mayor's Office to discuss the troubles associated with new arenas and franchise relocations.

The conversation would have been fascinating, basketball guy to basketball guy, separated by 80 years.

MANY THREADS were consistent between 1930s Rochester and 21st Century Sacramento. And some things were different. Professional basketball was not promoted for its ability to generate jobs and economic development when Harrison started out. The game was sold as entertainment, a way to escape the drudgery of the house and socialize in a warm building among friends on frigid winter nights.

In larger cities, arena owners used pro basketball to keep the lights on and sell tickets, beer and peanuts when the typically more popular local hockey team was skating in another town. City people in the industrial East preferred pro hockey to pro basketball in those days.

Basketball was growing. The game became a popular activity at the high school and college levels in the 1920s and 1930s, especially in smaller cities and towns in the Midwest and East Coast. Those early patrons saw the beauty in Dr. Naismith's YMCA character-building activity. They saw the spiritual benefits of social order, cooperation and self-sacrifice. The peach baskets first used by Dr. Naismith in 1891 were gone, but that original sense of the game explained why Les Harrison loved to play and longed to coach. Harrison's style was a pure brand of basketball. Athletic, disciplined players who followed orders, worked hard and helped teammates climb to victory. That was basketball.

As the popularity of amateur basketball spread across America from rural communities to city schools, churches and clubs in the 1920s and 1930s, the pro game assumed a more sinister, theatrical niche in big cities. In the brick walkup apartment and steam pipe environment, pro basketball was not necessarily a YMCA game, but a wrestling match and bloody endurance test.

Several promoters set wire cages around the court. They created an atmosphere that encouraged brutal play and rowdy behavior by fans. The caged-sport image stuck to basketball for decades. In the 1970s newspaper sportswriters described high school basketball players as "cagers" when descriptive variation was required, without understanding the negative origins of the reference.

Away from major cities, civic minded local business owners with an appreciation for marketing, men such as Fred Zollner, who owned an engine piston manufacturing company in Fort Wayne, Ind., began to sponsor pro basketball teams built around former local high school and college stars who might be operating drill presses on the factory floor.

Public entertainment opportunities were precious in smaller communities. So company-sponsored teams like the Zollner Pistons and Anderson Duffey Meat Packers were appreciated in towns like Sheboygan and Oshkosh, Wis., Fort Wayne and Anderson, Ind., and Rochester. When David Stern took over as NBA commissioner in 1984 and focused on the marketing side of the game, he was honoring the promotional vision of Fred Zollner and friends.

Before there was an NBA, pro basketball teams would hire the best local players and barnstorm around the countryside in car caravans, the trunks filled with ball bags and uniforms. They built rivalries with nearby communities. They played in high school and college gyms and National Guard armory field houses. Some of the most popular barnstorming teams featured African American players, notably the Harlem Globetrotters and Harlem Renaissance Five, who performed a vibrant, technically advanced version of the game, filled with quick cuts, sharp passes and pivots, for white audiences.

The Globies and Rens of that era were serious, highly skilled basketball players, but they found it financially advantageous to amuse their audiences with clowning props and ball tricks. White crowds expected the jester stereotypes, especially after an insurmountable lead had been built. By the 1950s, the Globetrotters were more popular for their tricks than their basketball talents.

In Les Harrison's basketball world, a sporting entrepreneur could thrive. There were no heavy-handed leagues to make needless rules or siphon away profits. Games were physically rough and slow paced. Baskets were scored with two-handed set shots and layups. There was no shot clock. Clubs with the best passing guards and toughest defenders won.

It was basketball the way Harrison liked it, the way Naismith intended. If a team had a benevolent corporate sponsor, players would receive regular paychecks. Less generous managers would pocket the corporate funds and let players argue over gate receipts, after expenses were subtracted.

By 1937, deep into the Great Depression, the cheap winter's night entertainment provided by pro basketball was popular enough so three corporations, Goodyear, Firestone and General Electric, decided to organize a league with nine teams based in towns around the Great Lakes. Players shifted among tire casing machines and welding equipment to the basketball court. They called it the National Basketball League.

The new NBL intrigued Les Harrison. He recognized there might be some benefits to organized leagues. They could help build credibility and rivalries among fans, bring structure to a chaotic scheduling process and assist with financial stability by pooling gate receipts and orchestrating reciprocal games. Harrison likewise appreciated the independence of barnstorming schedules, which gave the owner-coach the ability to make private arrangements with sponsors and opponents.

The perfect setup for Harrison would be the right league with the right structure. Since the 1920s, Harrison had been chasing his passion, building and coaching independent basketball teams for the barnstorming circuit, always on the move in his bulky double-breasted suits and radical comb-over straining to hide his bald spot. He entered community basketball tournaments, which were popular between the wars, put on first-class shows and often throttled his opponents with tough, disciplined play. He kept an eye on the NBL.

HARRISON KNEW the game and had an eye for talent. His coaching skill—he had been an outstanding player at Rochester East—was exceptional for his era. By the time Prohibition ended in 1933, Harrison found a way to match his basketball ambitions with the promotional objectives of the revived liquor industry.

He convinced the Seagram's whiskey distillers of Montreal and Ebers Brothers, a Rochester liquor wholesaler, to sponsor two separate pro basketball teams, the Rochester Seagram's and the Rochester Ebers. Both teams would be owned, managed and coached simultaneously by Harrison. Brother Jack Harrison, a Rochester lawyer, managed the books. In their spare time, the Harrison brothers ran their father's fruit and vegetable company. Soon, Les Harrison devoted more time to basketball and less to fruit and vegetables.

By World War II, the Harrison brothers and their basketball teams were among the few entertainment opportunities available to Rochester residents. Les Harrison, stretched to his limits by the responsibilities of running two teams, merged Ebers with the Seagram's in 1943 and moved the games into Rochester's largest indoor sports venue, Edgerton Park Sports Arena, with 4,200 seats. The building was named for Rochester's early 20th century mayor, Hiram Edgerton, a courtly building contractor made distinctive by his short, pointy white beard.

The new arena held a unique and sorrowful place in sports history. It was originally part of a children's prison, the Western House of Refuge for delinquents, criminals and orphaned and homeless youth under the age of 16. It was a place unimaginable today.

The Sports Arena was designed as the prison Drill Hall, where young inmates received physical punishment and military-style training. The main building, a gothic red brick structure four stories tall, was filled with 400 boys by 1852, soon after its opening. There was little education beyond carpentry and blacksmithing lessons. Boys were beaten. They were required to work under contract labor agreements. Day after day, they made buggy whips and furniture and marched in the Drill Hall.

Conditions became so notorious that in 1884, the New York State Assembly conducted investigations into the House of Refuge. Legislators demanded reforms, including the end of forced labor and physical punishment. The prison closed in 1902 and was made into a park. Much of the old prison was demolished, but the Drill Hall was spared and turned into a sports arena in 1941. During World War II, portions of the park were blocked off with fences and housed German and Italian prisoners captured by Allied troops in Europe.

This is where the basketball team that became the Sacramento Kings would savor its greatest victories. The franchise never had a happier home, or a home with a more sorrowful story.

Les Harrison was determined to present a first-class basketball product. He faced a significant marketing challenge from the biggest newspaper in town, the Democrat and Chronicle.

The newspaper was the flagship of the Gannett Company, whose corporate headquarters were on Exchange Boulevard in Rochester. The chain's conservative chief executive, Frank Gannett, disapproved of liquor and was not impressed by a basketball promoter using a Gannett newspaper to publicize a whiskey company and liquor distributor. Gannett didn't want his sports pages filled with stories about the Seagram's and Ebers basketball teams.

Harrison understood. He wanted his teams to be respected and to receive free publicity in the local newspapers, which would build credibility and sell tickets. Harrison folded the two teams into one and changed the identity. Gone were the names Seagram's and Ebers from the jerseys of Rochester squad members, replaced with a dry title: Rochester Pros.

The name was new, but Harrison continued to receive sponsorship money from the Montreal distiller and liquor wholesaler. The Pros scheduled games against the best touring teams in the country. The turnstiles at Edgerton arena began to click for the Harrison brothers. Many games were sold out, validating the owners' faith in the city, the sport of basketball and themselves.

THE SUCCESSES of the Harrison brothers and the Pros were noticed across the Great Lakes by the men who ran the National Basketball League. World War II was over. Soldiers, sailors and airmen were coming home. America needed new, better class family entertainment. An NBL franchise was offered to Rochester in 1945, with the promise of putting the city on the map as a member of the top professional basketball league in the U.S. Membership would be a real investment. The franchise would cost the Harrison brothers $25,000, or about $350,000 in 2013 dollars.

The brothers asked Seagram's and Ebers for financial help, but the liquor sponsors could not see much value in paying additional franchise fees for something they already sponsored. The Harrison boys decided to gamble. "My brother and I mortgaged everything we could get our hands on, and we got a franchise," Les Harrison told the Rochester historian Kevin Cook.

The NBL franchise was awarded to the Harrisons, and Rochester joined the big leagues. Les Harrison decided that as a big league city, Rochester needed a team with a more imaginative name than Pros. He organized a community contest to christen the new NBL team and offered a $100 victory bond to the winner.

Richard Paeth, 15 years old, took the prize with a crowning alliterative image. The name he invented was the Rochester Royals.

Chapter Four: One Of My Few Mistakes

Moving into the big leagues paid dividends for the brothers Les and Jack Harrison. With capacity audiences at Edgerton Sports Arena, the Royals tore through a 24-10 record and won the NBL championship in 1946, the team's first year in the league. The championship series made it clear the Royals were formidable. They swept the Sheboygan Red Skins in three consecutive games.

Les Harrison's gifts were displayed at the box office and on the basketball court. With a roster that included an esoteric clutch of future stars, including Otto Graham (football), Del Rice (baseball), William "Red" Holzman (basketball) and a young actor named Chuck Connors (television), the Royals were winners. They reached the NBL finals for three consecutive years, success the franchise would not repeat over the next six decades.

Harrison didn't limit his energy to the NBL. He scheduled as many exhibition games as possible at Edgerton, adding barnstorming matches on nights between NBL contests. "We must have played 100 exhibition games," Holzman recalled. Two years after joining the NBL, the Royals were earning about $40,000 a year for the Harrison brothers. NBL teams split their gate receipts, allowing the Royals to make money wherever they played.

So successful were the Royals that the Harrison brothers made plans to eliminate general admission tickets and focus on season ticket packages. With a sales narrative worthy of future major league marketing directors, the Royals announced they were doing the community a favor by providing season tickets, removing the need for fans to stand in lines outside

Edgerton Park Sports Arena on brutally cold winter nights. The Harrison boys could drive to the bank and deposit their ticket receipts before the arena doors were unlocked.

The NBL was making Les and Jack Harrison prosperous, but the Rochester promoters saw new horizons. They had the best team in the best pro basketball league in the U.S. But there was another league, a richer league, the Basketball Association of America, run by big city arena owners to cover the nights left vacant by their traveling hockey teams. The NBL had the top players. The BAA had the money.

Walter Brown, who owned the Boston Garden, formed the BAA in 1946, appointing Maurice Podoloff, an arena operator, lawyer and hockey executive from New Haven, Conn., as president. Podoloff, who emigrated from Russia as a child, ran the American Hockey League. He was able to link the Basketball Association of America with Boston Garden, Madison Square Garden in New York, Maple Leaf Gardens in Toronto, Chicago Stadium, Baltimore Coliseum, Cleveland Arena, Detroit Olympia and St. Louis Arena. The arenas were true major league buildings that dwarfed Rochester's old children's prison Drill Hall.

The BAA arena owners and hockey men knew how to freeze water and sell tickets, but they didn't know basketball. (And they didn't know the consequence of laying wooden basketball floors over ice rinks. Several BAA games were halted when the ice under the court melted.) BAA teams had serious bankrolls and big arenas, but they couldn't compete for talent against the basketball-pure NBL.

For wealthy BAA owners, the solution was found in a series of mergers that brought the best NBL teams into the BAA. Les Harrison and the Rochester Royals moved to the BAA in 1948, along with the Fort Wayne Pistons, Minneapolis Lakers and Indianapolis Jets.

Mergers were in fashion, a solution to the financial savagery created by too much competition. So a grand merger of the NBL and BAA began to make sense. Harrison was at the table on August 3, 1949, in a room at the Empire State Building, when Podoloff set into place the cornerstone of the National Basketball Association. The NBL and BAA completed their full merger that day, reconfiguring themselves as the organization known as the NBA. The Russian hockey man Podoloff was named president.

Two years later, the Rochester Royals were the NBA champions. It was a schizophrenic title series. The Royals won the first three games against the New York Knickerbockers, but lost the next three games. Facing humiliation and defeat before 4,200 fans in the old Drill Hall, the Royals won the decisive Game 7 after Bob Davies was fouled by Dick McGuire under the basket with 44 seconds left. Davies sank both free throws to break a 75-75 tie. The Royals closed out the series with a layup by Jack Coleman for a 79-75 victory on a glorious Saturday night at Edgerton Park, April 21, 1951.

Royals guard Bobby Wanzer would take a special gift away from the Drill Hall that day, a keepsake from Les Harrison. "I remember he had a set of gold cufflinks, and he promised them to me if he won. And he took them off and gave them to me," Wanzer said.

A memorable date: April 21, 1951. As of 2013, the franchise had not participated in another championship series since that remarkable night in Rochester.

The Kings would not play in another NBA Finals, but at least they stayed in the NBA. History would guarantee no such happy fates for many of the original 17 teams. The Chicago Stags and St. Louis Bombers folded in 1950. The Indianapolis Olympians survived until 1953, when the NBA dwindled to eight teams. The survivors were a hardy group. The Celtics, Knicks, Lakers, Pistons, Warriors, Hawks, 76ers and Royals comprised the league in 1953-54, but mid-20th Century resilience did not mean success in Rochester.

With fastidious rules about the home team keeping 100 percent of the gate money and a prohibition against barnstorming exhibition games, the NBA began to strangle the Harrison brothers. The Royals had an impressive team, led by the $25,000 per year center, Arnie Risen, and two quick, adroit guards named Bob, Wanzer and Davies.

Without gate splits, however, large crowds in Boston and New York did nothing for the Royals' balance sheet. And with barnstorming team exhibitions banned, no longer could Rochester fans pay to see games between Harrison's home team and the Harlem Globetrotters.

THE GAME WAS evolving, pushing Les Harrison further from center court each year, forcing him to massage his temples and watch his tough, no-nonsense defenders get brushed aside by opponents who deployed a style that muscled the ball inside. The NBA officially brought a stop to Harrison's plodding, guard oriented Victorian strategies in 1954, when the 24-second shot clock was plugged in. The Rochester roster that seemed so formidable in 1949 was a collection of middle-aged men by 1954.

The geezers began to lose. Under NBA rules, teams had exclusive rights to draft college stars within their geographic reach. There were no strong college basketball programs near Rochester. Harrison still had his eye for talent. He acquired Maurice Stokes and Jack Twyman in 1955, but the founder relinquished the coaching chores to his star guard Bobby Wanzer, proving that the team's success was more important than the owner's ego.

The Royals continued to lose. Fewer fans bought tickets. Many nights, barely 2,000 showed up. The people who did present themselves at Edgerton Park were not the same genteel crowd that cheered the Royals a few years earlier. When the Minneapolis Lakers were shoving the Royals around one night, a fan threw a knife at Lakers center George Mikan as he protested a foul. The blade missed its target but left an impression. "No sooner am I within about a foot of the ref than I see a knife go by me and it sticks in the court," Mikan said.

Burdened with so many empty seats and unruly fans, Harrison blamed television, a new entertainment option that kept decent people in their living rooms on cold nights. He blamed the exodus of middle-class city residents to the suburbs, which brought significant changes in the economic demographics of Rochester. He blamed the arena, arguing that a major league city deserved something better than a refurbished Drill Hall for juvenile prisoners.

At least there was a solution to the last complaint. In 1955, a new $8 million sports auditorium, Rochester War Memorial, with 8,000 seats for basketball, opened with great civic pride and hope for Harrison and his city.

Rather than salvation, the new building verified the Royals' inability to sell tickets. Wide swaths of empty, unsold seats were visible on NBA game nights. It wasn't just TV's intrusion and the suburban exodus that kept people away. A newly established hockey team, the Americans, drew double the audience of the Royals. In 1956, Harrison said he lost $23,600 on the Royals, his fifth consecutive year of negative results.

His financial model was disintegrating, but Harrison still had hope. The 1956 NBA draft arrived and the Royals held the first pick. There was little question about whose name should be called with that No. 1 pick: University of San Francisco center Bill Russell.

Yet the Royals did not draft Russell. They passed on him and drafted Sihugo Green, a Duquesne University guard who would be immortalized in trivia as the basketball player taken ahead of Bill Russell. The Boston Celtics ended up with Russell, and one of the great legacies in American sports was born.

The fine-print details of what really happened between Russell and the Royals has been lost to history and buried within selective memories. Harrison said, yes, of course he was aware of Russell's talent, but on the night he scouted Russell, at a college all-star game in New York, the center was awful. "We found out later that he knew were watching him and he did poorly so he wouldn't end up in Rochester," Harrison said.

Another story, this one told by Red Holzman, claimed Russell was offended when Harrison brought an African American Royals player, William "Dolly" King, to help persuade Russell that the Rochester franchise was supportive of black athletes. The Holzman story would be difficult to accept.

Dolly King was 40 years old at the time, a basketball legend. A former Harlem Rens star, King joined the Royals in 1946 and was the first African American player in the National Basketball League. It's unlikely that the young, untested Bill Russell would have been offended by a recruiting visit from the iconic Dolly King. (And unlike later NBA stars, Russell did not insist on playing in a big city. His first choice was the Minneapolis Lakers, the league's best club.)

The upcoming Melbourne Olympics were another concern for any team drafting Russell. The basketball portion of the Games would not end until December 1. Russell had committed to play for the U.S. team in Australia, making him unavailable for the first 20 or so games of the 1956 NBA season.

Finally, there is the story that Russell demanded $25,000 from Harrison, knowing the dollar figure was the same amount paid to Risen, who, unlike Russell, was not African American. Only two other players (both white) had $25,000 salaries: Minneapolis center Mikan and Boston guard Bob Cousy. Other versions of the money story inflated the demand to $50,000, with leverage being supplied by the Harlem Globetrotters, who coveted Russell and ultimately offered him $32,000. (Russell was tempted by the Globetrotters but leery of their brutal travel schedule.)

Presumably, Russell would have known the Royals were losing money and that Harrison could not afford a $25,000 rookie of any color, much less a rookie center from San Francisco costing $32,000 or $50,000.

At this point, the stories converged and the truth was scattered into pieces. The most likely reasons why the Royals bypassed Russell were Harrison's philosophy and his balance sheet. He still believed guards were the key to championship basketball. He considered most centers (other than Mikan and Risen) overrated, and didn't want to risk bankruptcy with an unproven center from San Francisco. Of course, he was wrong. "It was one of my few mistakes," Harrison said years later. The 1956 draft would not be the last time Bill Russell would leave a negative impression on the franchise born by Les Harrison.

WITHIN A YEAR, Harrison was calling promoters in other cities, searching for better market conditions, discussing the potential relocation of the Royals. He was devoted to his hometown of Rochester and tried to find local investors. Rochester turned its back on the Harrison brothers' basketball team. "We were really selling out the place at first," Les Harrison said. "Everyone wanted to be there. Then we moved to a bigger place and started losing, and people stopped coming. We didn't have any choice but to sell." Beyond a collection of about 2,000 loyal fans, the NBA was a sideshow near the shores of Lake Ontario. The glory days were over.

Harrison spoke with two businessmen in Kansas City, Marty Marion and Milt Fishmann, who offered him a job at $25,000 per year if he moved the team to Missouri. He rejected the offer and focused his search on the large cities of Ohio. He met with civic leaders in Cleveland and Cincinnati. He was impressed by Cincinnati Gardens, a monumental limestone and brick edifice on Seymour Avenue that would seat 11,000 for basketball.

Built in 1949 for $3 million, the arena was designed on plans for Maple Leaf Gardens in Toronto. The Cincinnati market was in the heart of high school and college basketball country, Southern Ohio and Northern Kentucky. Two Royals players, Jack Twyman and Dave Piontek, attended college in Cincinnati. They knew the region and assured Harrison the Royals would be a perfect fit there.

Harrison had heard enough. He announced the Royals were moving to Cincinnati on April 3, 1957. The explanation was addressed in a statement that would serve as a prescient manifesto for Harrison's wandering franchise over the next six decades:

"From a survey made, it was evident that the trend of the National Basketball Association is to larger, major league cities with a potential draw of approximately 1 1/2 to 2 million people. In addition, it is necessary to include in the successful operation of a team the radio and TV financial market. The city of Rochester, with its excellent facilities and attractiveness, however, failed to come within the scope of these qualifications."

With those words, the most migratory team in professional sports made its first move. And Rochester, despite its excellent facilities and attractiveness, was erased from the NBA map forever.

Chapter Five: A Gross Miscarriage Of Justice

Mayor Kevin Johnson was running late, stuck in a meeting. He hated being late. Especially on this day, the day he was scheduled to greet one of his heroes, NBA legend Oscar Robertson, at Sacramento City Hall.

As Johnson's Special Assistant, my job was to look after visiting celebrities. I had never met Robertson, who was then 73 years old. I was familiar with his basketball accomplishments and the stories circulated by generations of sportswriters, tales about how difficult the man could be, how surly and monosyllabic he could turn at the slightest annoyance.

I figured an honest approach would work best. I introduced myself and told Robertson we would have to kill some time waiting for the mayor. Friendly and relaxed and dapper in a navy blue suit contrasting with his thick white hair, the man I met was nothing like the prima donna described by sportswriters. Robertson settled onto the couch along the back wall of the mayor's private library on the fifth floor of City Hall. He didn't care about Johnson's tardiness. "This is nice," Oscar Robertson said as he looked around the room. "I don't think I'll want to get up from here."

Robertson was enjoying a day filled with appreciation. First there would be a ceremony in the City Hall lobby, where he would say a few words to the 50 or so fans and media gathered beneath a giant replica of his No. 14 Cincinnati Royals jersey. That night, he would attend an NBA game and help the Kings present a trophy for community involvement and leadership, the "Oscar Robertson Triple Double Award."

The date, April 20, 2012, was an important anniversary for Oscar. Fifty years earlier, he closed out the 1961-62 NBA season with an average of 30.8 points, 12.5 rebounds and 11.4 assists for the Royals. His production in those three essential categories has never been matched.

On that sunny morning, I figured out what the sportswriters failed to see or decided to ignore when they spoke critically of Oscar Robertson. He was an accomplished sportsman who transcended the frivolity of sports. Robertson wasn't surly or suspicious. His sin was honorable. All he wanted was to be taken seriously.

Chatting in the mayor's library, we got along fine. He asked about Johnson's attempt to build a new arena for the Kings, a three-year effort whose most recent chapter had been slammed shut seven days earlier by the Maloof family at a press conference in New York. "It's a shame. I know how hard Kevin's been working at this," Robertson said. "It would be devastating for the city to lose the basketball team."

Robertson knew about cities losing basketball teams. His adopted city, Cincinnati, lost the predecessor to the Kings in 1972, when the team was still called the Royals. Robertson was traded to Milwaukee two years before the Royals moved to Kansas City, but he suffered along with Cincinnati basketball fans when the NBA team packed up and left. "You'll notice the league still hasn't come back to Cincinnati," he said.

Oscar Robertson loved Cincinnati. He was raised in Indianapolis, but Cincinnati became his home during his college years at the University of Cincinnati. The Royals drafted Robertson as a territorial pick, a hometown hero, in 1960, after he helped lead the United States to a gold medal in basketball at the Rome Olympics. Before his retirement in 1974, Robertson's accomplishments stretched well past his triple-double season.

He became leader of the NBA players union. He waged monumental courtroom fights over free agency. His litigation gave players more control over their services, leading to higher pay and greater prominence and credibility for the NBA. "They still call that part of the collective-bargaining agreement the 'Oscar Robertson Rule,'" he said. After retirement, Robertson launched businesses in various fields, from office document management to cleaning supplies.

And he did other things. He wrote an autobiography and a book on improving one's basketball skills. He raised money for charities. He donated a kidney to his daughter Tia when the autoimmune disease lupus caused her kidneys to fail. His approach to these matters was straightforward. "I'm no hero, I'm just a father," he said after the kidney transplant. Which may explain why some people saw him as aloof and distant in a game that rewarded exaggeration and self-promotion.

Kevin Johnson pushed open the door to the library and rushed to greet Robertson. Johnson loved playing host to celebrities. He believed his ability to attract famous people to Sacramento, if only for a hug, handshake and press conference, was more important than his legislative work as mayor. "This is the kind of stuff they really don't get around here," he said.

The two retired NBA all-stars, separated by almost three decades but aligned in their determination to be something larger than retired NBA all-stars, rode the city council's private elevator to the lobby and joked through a media session. Johnson made dramatic emphasis of Robertson's triple-double season. "Do you know how hard that is? A whole season of triple-doubles!" he said. "It's unbelievable! It's hard to even imagine it today!" Robertson said he wished he could have played against Johnson, explaining how he would dominate Johnson by forcing him left, where right-handed players can be less effective. "I noticed that about him watching him on TV," Robertson said.

They were loose and relaxed. After the press conference, Johnson rushed to another meeting. Robertson wanted to return to his hotel to rest for the Kings' game that night. A car and driver waited near the back entrance to City Hall on H Street, along with a dozen autograph seekers waving memorabilia for Robertson to sign. I wanted to lead Robertson, forcing him to the left, past the outstretched arms and Sharpie pens. He waved me off. "It's no problem. I'll sign them," he said.

Robertson worked his way through the crowd until one fan, a professional collector holding basketball cards enclosed in plastic sheets, all destined for eBay, said, "Why are you so grumpy, Oscar? How about a smile for us?" The tone was sarcastic and smug, borderline nasty. Robertson stopped and glared at the man for several seconds. I expected Robertson to say something. He looked like he wanted to say something. But he was silent. He handed the pen to another fan, walked to his car and disappeared without another word.

CINCINNATI WAS like that for the Royals, filled with light moments of promise and fun, followed by frustration, disappointment, sorrow and departure. After just one season in Cincinnati, Les Harrison decided the move from Rochester in 1957 was a mistake. The hopeful market analysis offered by Harrison's two Cincinnati players, Jack Twyman and Dave Piontek, was wrong. Harrison averaged only 3,700 tickets per game his first season, leaving the team with more empty seats at Cincinnati Gardens than the Royals suffered at the new Rochester War Memorial.

There was no obvious reason why people didn't rush to buy Cincinnati Royals tickets, but public skepticism over the NBA as a second-rate product would be a reasonable conclusion. The Reds baseball club dominated the market, having been a member of the National League since 1876. The Bengals would not begin play in the American Football League until 1968, a decade away. A minor league hockey team, the Mohawks, competed directly against the Royals and had a winning record. The Mohawks struggled at the box office and folded in 1958.

For Harrison, it was bad enough to lose money in his hometown. Now he faced negative cash flow in his adopted city, 500 miles from Rochester. He began to contact potential investors, asking if they wanted to buy an NBA team.

Harrison found two prospective buyers. One represented a group of Washington, D.C. business owners who would take the team to the nation's capital. The other was an old friend from Rochester who, belatedly for Harrison, thought it would be nice to return the Royals to their original outpost near Lake Ontario. The Rochester offer was slightly better, $250,000, a 10 percent premium over Washington. Basketball fans in Rochester learned of the proposals. They petitioned the NBA to bring the Royals home.

As Harrison waited for the NBA Board of Governors to meet and approve the return to Rochester, a third group appeared, this one from Cincinnati, cobbled together by Ohio business interests, claiming they would turn the club into a community owned enterprise. The price matched Rochester's $250,000, an NBA record. The lead investor was Thomas E. Wood, a Cincinnati insurance executive.

The NBA Board of Governors, who despite their lofty title was simply Harrison's fellow team owners, advised him to keep the Royals in Cincinnati. The NBA owners had visions of a true national league with teams, sponsors and network TV audiences in big cities across America. They weren't interested in returning to a backwater like Rochester.

And they knew real potential awaited the Royals in a young star named Oscar Robertson, who would graduate from the University of Cincinnati in two years and join the team as a territorial draft pick.

Pressured by his NBA colleagues, Harrison sold majority interest to Tom Wood and the Cincinnati group and went home to Rochester.

The Royals, born as the unique personal property of a visionary basketball man, a team with a legacy dating from the barnstorming days of the Great Depression, would on that day begin an existence of operational instability and managerial incompetence. The instant Harrison gave up control, the Royals stopped being one man's dream. They became a commodity.

THERE ARE no public records to establish exactly what happened next. The official franchise history published by the Sacramento Kings covers the next nine seasons with one sentence relevant to ownership: "The team was moved to Cincinnati in 1957, where one year later it became a public corporation." The reason for the opacity can be explained by the presence of one person, Louis Jacobs, who ran a company called Sportservice from the second floor of a chaotic suite of offices at 703 Main Street in Buffalo, N.Y.

Jacobs, called Louie by his friends, was in the concession business. A large part of his success was built on his willingness to loan money to struggling sports franchise owners in exchange for silent equity in the team and long-term concession rights. Louie was always there with cash for team owners when the bankers shook their heads and walked away. Louie shook his head, but never walked away. Les Harrison matched the profile of a sports owner primed for Louie's benevolence.

Harrison would have followed a well-worn path to 703 Main Street in 1958. Baseball franchise owner Bill Veeck worked his way through four teams (Milwaukee, Cleveland, St. Louis and Chicago) with help from Louie. Veeck admitted that any time he had financial challenges, "I did what any man of minimal intelligence would do. I took it to Louie Jacobs."

Les Harrison had more than minimal intelligence, but he was hurting financially and looking for investors. Les and Louie certainly would have known each other from Western New York sports and arena operations. Louie was in the right place to help.

His Sportservice was part owner of the Cincinnati Gardens. The Royals' low attendance was hurting concession sales. Louie operated on the principle that the only thing worse than poor attendance was zero attendance, which would have been the result on 35 or so darkened nights if the Royals fled Cincinnati.

Louie Jacobs handed out astonishing sums of money to his sports partners around the country. One associate described an encounter with Louie that illustrated the turnaround time for a loan. "Anytime you want more than $3 million, give us 24 hours' notice. Any less than that sum, we'll get you immediately." The type of money needed by Harrison and the Royals would have been crumbs for the Jacobs operation, requiring nothing more than a phone call and an agreement for certain considerations down the road, such as equity in a money-losing team.

Louie touched all corners of sports and entertainment. He was beloved by the men who ran Major League Baseball and the NBA. Many of them borrowed cash from him. Which meant league headquarters would not necessarily have troubled Louie for paperwork on his transactions, even when the deals involved ownership positions.

As for Louie, he preferred to listen, not talk. He didn't like lawyers and was rarely seen to write things down, though everything was written down somewhere. Property title research on an arena in Rhode Island once discovered a Sportservice concession contract that lasted 99 years, with stipulations on the stipulations. Sportservice even locked up the earth beneath the building. Above ground, Jacobs claimed his operation was simple. "We're in business to sell peanuts," he said.

THE JACOBS operation began in 1915, formed by Louie and his brothers Marvin and Charles. As children, they sold peanuts and newspapers on Buffalo streets. Their breakthrough came from selling candy in a Buffalo theater. Louie joked that he realized concessions were a good business when the profits from his theater candy counter exceeded the annual salary of the president of the University of Buffalo.

By 1960, Sportservice controlled food concessions at ballparks in New York, New Jersey, Maryland, Ohio, Illinois, Wisconsin and Michigan. Within 10 years, they would operate in 39 states with connections to 24 major league baseball, football, basketball and hockey teams, 50 racetracks, 300 theaters and hundreds of bowling alleys. The company had approximately 70,000 employees. Louie paid special interest to racetracks. The gambling part of racing intrigued him.

The brothers invested in everything that moved. The goal was to sell peanuts around the clock. When no events existed and their arenas stood dark, they made up events. They invented the arena ice show, featuring comedic, handsome men dressed as hobos and beautiful, virtuous women in very short skirts, all gliding around on skates. The ice extravaganzas evolved into the Ice Capades and Ice Follies, which filled arena seats for 50 years and blazed a Zamboni path for Disney On Ice.

In the 1950s, when Louie took over after the retirements of his brothers Marvin and Charles, the company managed a breathtaking feat. It sold food in the clouds by providing meals for the burgeoning airline industry. Airports became a key sales point for Sportservice, starting with Washington National. The platinum Jacobs touch went global in 1960, when Sportservice became the official food concessionaire for the Summer Olympics in Rome. Oscar Robertson, polishing his star image at the Rome Games, would have smelled if not digested Sportservice food in Italy that summer.

Cincinnati was an important pin on the Jacob brothers' map. Louie was among the original investors in Cincinnati Gardens in 1949, and by 1963, he owned 40 percent of the brick and limestone arena, with an option to take majority control. He put his son Jeremy in charge and created a new company called Emprise, an amalgamation of the words "empire" and "enterprise," which would hold real estate acquired by Jacobs.

The year 1963 was significant. Tom Wood, the insurance man and original Cincinnati investor with Les Harrison, died in April. His family wanted to sell its share of the Royals and the Gardens. A prospective new partnership stepped forward. Jake Brown, who was the attorney and advisor for Oscar Robertson, and Warren Hensel, a business associate of Jake Brown's and a basketball fan.

A deal was reached with Louie, whose primary interest was peanuts, not basketball. The Jacobs organization would claim the Gardens. Brown and Hensel would own the Royals. The disparate pieces seemed aligned. Brown and Hensel took over the Royals. They pushed out the coach, Charley Wolf, and replaced him with young Jack McMahon.

Brown and Hensel were running the team. Louie was selling peanuts. But doing business with Louie was never quite as simple as peanuts. Mysteriously, the team's sale wasn't formally recorded. Louie possessed vital documents, hidden in a place known only to Louie. Somehow, the paperwork managed to disappear.

Louie had connections with Maurice Podoloff and the NBA owners. He began to lobby the owners, stalling the final settlement of the agreement. "Arguing against his own deal," Robertson wrote in his autobiography. "Pepper Wilson, our general manager, would make a half dozen phone calls just to figure out who his boss was." Louie Jacobs prevailed, as usual. He paid the Wood family $420,000 for another 40 percent of the Gardens and 56 percent of the Royals. "And for all intents and purposes, the franchise lost its last chance of having ownership that actually cared about winning and losing," Oscar Robertson wrote.

The Royals, who in the vision of their founder had been foremost a basketball club and secondarily a product designed to fill arena dates, were now an arm of the Gardens' concession business, a platform to help Louie sell more peanuts.

THE ROYALS were still a good basketball team. Robertson validated his status as one of the NBA's great young players, assisted in 1963 by the arrival of another popular territorial draft pick, Jerry Lucas, from Ohio State. The Royals reached the NBA semifinals in 1963 and 1964, but lost both times to Bill Russell and the Boston Celtics. (Si Green, the man the Royals drafted over Russell, was by then on his fourth team. He retired with the Celtics.)

The priorities of Louie Jacobs were driven home at the 1963 series against Boston, when the Royals were forced to move their Eastern championship games away from Cincinnati Gardens and into the Field House at Xavier University. Hedging his bets, Louie booked a circus into Cincinnati Gardens for the week of the NBA semifinals. He didn't think the Royals were good enough to survive that deep into the playoffs. He couldn't risk leaving the Gardens empty with all those peanuts to sell.

The circus proved precisely where the Royals existed in the chain of the Jacobs' business priorities: right behind the elephants. Max Jacobs, Jeremy's brother, became chairman of the Royals and helped oversee a generational transition after Louie died in 1968. The old man passed away at his desk at 703 Main Street in Buffalo, buried in the middle of a transaction, exactly as he predicted he would go.

The Jacobs family was constantly alert for new territories. The Royals were pressed into duty as a scouting party. Games were scheduled against NBA opponents in prospective basketball markets, cities such as Indianapolis, Omaha and Cleveland. Going on the road was probably a good thing for the franchise. Things were not going well in Cincinnati.

As the 1970s arrived, the Emprise holding company and the Jacobs operation began to veer into serious trouble, thanks to Louie's fascination with gambling. The organization was under federal investigation for conspiracy to gain ownership of the Frontier hotel and casino in Las Vegas. Named with Emprise were several Mafia figures.

Federal prosecutors established that Louie Jacobs was very familiar with Las Vegas. He loaned money to Moe Dalitz, a bootlegger, gangster and one of the pioneers of the Vegas gambling industry, to buy the Stardust hotel and casino in the late 1950s. (Another person who helped arranged loans for Dalitz and the Stardust hotel was Jimmy Hoffa. He steered Teamsters Central States Pension Fund dollars into the casino.)

A federal jury in Los Angeles convicted Emprise in the Frontier ownership affair in 1972. The fine was $10,000, peanuts for Emprise, but the felony conviction cast a black shadow across the Jacobs' holdings. Sports leagues, including the NBA, made moral probity a key in the narrative they presented to fans. It was hard to sell that story when one of your teams had associations with gangsters.

Making matter worse for Jacobs, members of the House of Representatives and the U.S. Senate began to ask questions about the family's involvement with the Cincinnati Royals. The timing of the questions was bad for the NBA, which was trying to avoid federal antitrust problems in its merger with the upstart American Basketball Association.

Senator Sam Ervin made the Royals and their owners a potential target. "Not only was Emprise found guilty, but a necessary ingredient of that guilt involved intimate business dealings with known racketeers," Ervin said. Those were chilling words to NBA Commissioner Walter Kennedy, a former Harlem Globetrotters press agent who replaced Maurice Podoloff as the league's chief executive in 1963. Kennedy was forced to do something about the Jacobs' NBA interests.

The commissioner declared the league would "reopen our inquiry of the Jacobs family and determine their qualifications to operate an NBA franchise." Jeremy Jacobs called the Los Angeles conviction "a gross miscarriage of justice." Justice was done.

Within the year, the gross miscarriage would push the Jacobs family out of the basketball business in Cincinnati. The Royals would be sold to a group of Kansas City business owners. For the NBA and its vagrant franchise from Western New York, Southern Ohio was a territory that promised success but delivered only headaches and heartache. Thanks to Louie Jacobs, a pattern of migration would continue for Les Harrison's vagrant team from Rochester.

IN CINCINNATI, the franchise began to demonstrate a sad tendency, the capacity for tragedy. The Royals closed their first regular season in Ohio with a game at Minneapolis on March 12, 1958. That night, the Royals' remarkably athletic star forward, Maurice Stokes, raced to the basket. He was blocked by another player, tumbled over the opponent's back and crashed to the floor. The incident was routine, with one problem. When Stokes fell, his head struck the hardwood floor.

As the crowd of 2,300 leaned forward to watch, the 232-pound, 24-year-old sat up on his knees and clutched his head for a moment, then collapsed. He was revived with smelling salts. In the tough-guy style of the era, Stokes went back into the game. Three days later, flying home with the Royals after a playoff match in Detroit, he became disoriented. "I feel like I am going to die," he said before passing out. An ambulance met the plane in Cincinnati and carried Stokes to the nearest hospital, Saint Elizabeth's, across the Ohio River in Covington, Ky.

Seizures and coma followed. Stokes was paralyzed, the motor controls of his brain permanently damaged. What followed over the next 12 years was the most inspiring story of public friendship between two sportsmen in American history.

Jack Twyman, who joined the Royals with Stokes in 1955, became his friend's legal guardian and financial benefactor, organizing charity events to raise money for medical expenses, even teaching Stokes to communicate with eye blinks. Twyman said he only did what needed to be done when hospital staff asked for signatures on insurance forms. "I was the only one there, and decisions had to be made," he said. This devotion to his friend would be the hallmark of Jack Twyman's life.

Stokes recovered enough to smile and make public appearances, typically seated in his wheelchair. He died in 1970 at age 36. Twyman lived to age 78 and continued to raise money for charities until his death in 2012. "He gave me a lot more than what I have given him," Twyman said.

Maurice Stokes and Jack Twyman, basketball men to the end, lived out their days in Cincinnati, a city that would have no future in the NBA.

Chapter Six: Left To The Professionals

The sad fate of Maurice Stokes and the focus by Louie Jacobs on peanuts marked a change in fortunes for the Royals. Dark clouds gathered over the team in Cincinnati. The clouds chased the franchise across America.

Fans would buy tickets and fall in love with the team, but that love would be manipulated and not returned. For the next two decades, the manipulation was overseen by a minor sports figure named Joe Axelson, who was hired by the Royals shortly after Louie's death to run the franchise on behalf of brothers Jeremy and Max Jacobs. Oscar Robertson described Axelson as "a guy nobody had ever heard of."

Axelson replaced General Manager Pepper Wilson, the able and respected front-office man brought on board by Les Harrison in 1957. Axelson had a modest background, even for a guy nobody had ever heard of. He played high school basketball and baseball in his hometown of Clinton, Ill. His interest in sports came from his father, Joe, Sr., who coached high school teams in central Illinois for 38 years and taught young Joe the maxim of deflected responsibility. "My father used to say, 'The only thing wrong with coaching is the players,'" Axelson said. The younger man would live by those words.

Young Joe graduated from Northwestern University with a journalism degree and went to work on the weekend sports desk at the City News Bureau of Chicago, a no-nonsense training ground for reporters. He served in the Army in the 1950s and coached military basketball squads.

He bounced around as sports information director at Georgia Southern College and refereed high school and college basketball games at night. He became assistant executive secretary for the National Association of Intercollegiate Athletics, a group focused on small college sports. He found another job as tournament director for the Bowling Proprietors Association of America. The provenance wasn't platinum, but in the bowling world, the ambitious Axelson would have connected with Louie Jacobs' organization, which ran concessions at hundreds of bowling alleys. One day the Cincinnati Royals came calling for the hungry publicist.

Joe Axelson's real talent was salesmanship, his ability to make other people trust and believe him. There was no evidence of anything else. Axelson excelled at boasts laced with humility. He would tell people he read four novels per night, then lament about his weight while admitting he gained 100 pounds since his baseball playing days. He once looked a reporter in the eye and said, "I think I know as much about talent and what it takes to win in this league as any man alive. But I also know that it involves chemistry and a lot of luck."

In Cincinnati, young Max Jacobs would become a prototype member of the Axelson fan club, with admiration based on big talk and skills never quite demonstrated. Asked how he got the job of general manager for the Royals in 1969 despite a thin resume with no major league experience, Axelson said, "I liked what I was doing, so I turned them down. I think that intrigued them, and then they made me an offer it would have been insane to refuse." That was Axelson: chemistry and a lot of luck.

To help sell tickets and create instant credibility for the team and its rookie general manager, Max Jacobs and Axelson brought in the retired Celtics legend Bob Cousy to coach the Royals. They paid him the extraordinary salary of $150,000 with a three-year contract. "I did not anticipate re-entering basketball so soon," Cousy said. Unlike Axelson, Cousy was big-league talent, a guy everybody had heard of.

The son of a New York City taxi driver, Cousy had been raised in the Upper East Side of Manhattan, when the neighborhood was filled with hard-nosed immigrants from Eastern Europe and Ireland. Cousy was neither. He was French. He came to the attention of Celtics fans during four outstanding college seasons at Holy Cross, 35 miles from Boston. His acquisition by Celtics coach Red Auerbach was a story wrapped in basketball lore.

Auerbach didn't like Cousy. The coach thought the 6-foot-1 point guard was too small for the NBA. Despite his local popularity, Cousy was not worth drafting, Auerbach insisted. Cousy finally signed with the Tri-Cities

Blackhawks, who played in Moline, Ill., in 1950. Before the season began, the Chicago Stags folded, forcing a dispersal draft of their talent. League President Maurice Podoloff ordered the Blackhawks to give up Cousy if they wanted their first choice among Stags players. It would only be fair, Podoloff said. Give up Cousy? Done, the Blackhawks responded.

As the dispersal draft reached its final three players, teams began to argue about the details. Podoloff, the Russian hockey man who often ran out of patience with his NBA team owners, became fed up. He took three pieces of paper and wrote one name on each scrap. The papers were thrown into a hat. The hat was passed around.

Hands gingerly removed Podoloff's folded scraps. Celtics owner Walter Brown went last. He was stuck with the paper that held Cousy's name. Bad luck, Boston! The Celtics were forced to accept a short, unloved guard who would become one of the best players in NBA history, a man whose peripheral vision allowed him to make passes behind his back without turning his head. Cousy has large eyes and a uniquely narrow face, a face for basketball.

Which is not to say Cousy had a head for NBA coaching by the time he reached Cincinnati. He made headlines, but that was about it. High strung and nervous, he complained about the erosion of team discipline compared to his playing days, imposed $50 fines for infractions and clashed with his men.

With Axelson at Cousy's side, the Royals made bizarre trades, including deals that launched Oscar Robertson to Milwaukee and sent Jerry Lucas to the San Francisco Warriors. Relying on the magical powers of chemistry and luck, the Cincinnati chess masters dismantled a tough, competitive team and wrecked the Royals in a matter of months.

THE MANAGERIAL infamy of the 1969-70 Royals was not limited to player swaps. Cousy decided to suit up and play point guard in seven games, despite his age (41) and seasons away from the game (six). He made 10 assists in 34 minutes of action, proud stats for a 41-year-old retiree, hardly worthy of an NBA legend.

Cousy and Axelson did manage to identify a future star, Nate "Tiny" Archibald, in the second round of the 1970 draft. But they almost missed Archibald in pre-draft evaluations at a Memphis motel, confusing the basketball player with a bellman. All of this would lead Oscar Robertson to create an unforgettable image in his autobiography when he described the Royals' new general manager: "Axelson didn't know a basketball from a pumpkin."

The decision by Axelson and the Jacobs brothers to hire Bob Cousy in Cincinnati was questionable for another reason. Cousy was a Boston legend and Royals fans hated the Celtics. Cousy represented the enemy. Red Auerbach once chased a Royals fan, gas station attendant Eddie Finke, into the stands at Cincinnati Gardens after Finke heckled and spat at the Boston coach. The incident touched off a brawl.

Royals' fans enjoyed lighting cigars to mock the cigar-smoking Auerbach whenever the Celtics lost in Cincinnati. At one such game, a fan ran to the sideline and blew cigar smoke in Auerbach's face. The offender was a woman, so Auerbach didn't punch her. But he did grab the cigar from her mouth.

As the 1970s began, Joe Axelson had more important concerns than the rivalry between Cincinnati and Boston. With the federal conviction and Congressional investigations closing in and the NBA unhappy about the attention on the Royals, the Jacobs family instructed Axelson to move the team and sell it. The time had come for another new start.

There was at least one compelling financial reason to move. In Kansas City, a new arena was being planned to replace the American Royal stockyards pavilion. The Jacobs' organization intended to run the concessions at the new building. The basketball team, with its felonious ownership connections, was a complication. Concessions were more lucrative than team ownership. The decision to relocate and unload the team would have been relatively easy for the family.

So Kansas City, which had been among the places that received consideration from Les Harrison in 1957, beckoned again. Axelson announced the relocation at a press conference on March 14, 1972. He managed to praise one community and insult another in the same breath. He said Kansas City was "a great basketball city. Cincinnati is not."

And Cincinnati didn't really argue the point. A small crowd watched the final game at Cincinnati Gardens on March 24, 1972. The New York Times ran a two-paragraph story under the headline, "4,022 See Royals Go."

Years later, Axelson told reporters he had been studying the Kansas City market since 1969. Shipped to Milwaukee from his beloved Cincinnati while these maneuvers were underway, Oscar Robertson was furious over the deceptions by Axelson and the Jacobs family. "I was put through a year of hell because someone wanted to sell hot dogs," he wrote in his autobiography.

Axelson had business contacts in Kansas City from his NAIA marketing days. The metropolitan Kansas City region might not have been large enough to support an NBA team, but the Midwest offered potential. The Cincinnati Royals played three games at Omaha Civic Auditorium in 1970 and six more in 1971. Attendance was promising if not spectacular, ranging from about 3,100 to 8,000.

Missouri and Nebraska sports fans loved high school and college basketball. They might be persuaded to buy into the pro game. With a flourish characteristic of Axelson, the franchise simultaneously moved to two cities, Kansas City and Omaha. The Royals were rebranded as the Kings to maintain their royal heritage in a community where Major League Baseball already claimed title to the Kansas City Royals.

The Omaha flirtation was more gimmick than business plan. The real target was the new Kansas City building, a $3.5 million facility called Kemper Arena, which would open in 1974 with 17,000 seats for basketball, more than twice the size of old Municipal Auditorium in Kansas City and Omaha Civic. The Kings played 15 games at Omaha in 1972 and 14 the next year. Axelson scratched Omaha from the name in 1975, but the Kings played a handful of games in Nebraska every season until 1979.

Also purged from the franchise was the Jacobs family. On May 29, 1973, within a year of moving west, Axelson found nine Kansas City investors willing to buy the Kings for $5 million. The key partners were a lawyer, Robert Margolin, and Paul Rosenberg, who ran a printing and graphics firm. Leon Karosen, who owned a clothing manufacturing company, would take controlling interest. As luck would have it, Axelson would be made a partner in the new Kansas City ownership group.

The NBA had obtained national reach with teams in Seattle, Portland, Los Angeles, Phoenix and San Francisco. In the center of America, the Kings went nowhere fast.

Bob Cousy was pushed into retirement in 1973 in the midst of an 11-game losing streak. The Kings had an impressive shot-blocking center, Sam Lacey, but balanced improvement would not appear for another four years, when the Kings won the Midwest Division on the strength of two young players, Otis Birdsong and Scott Wedman.

The 1980-81 season ended with the Kings battling their way into the Western Conference finals. Unable to score more than 89 points, they lost to the Houston Rockets in four games. The Kings weren't much of a team, but they were tough on defense. And defense didn't easily translate into ticket sales.

Curiously, the Kings' success came when Joe Axelson left the franchise on special assignment to create a new marketing plan for the NBA in New York. Before he departed, Axelson tried to make the deal of his lifetime. He sought to lure Earvin "Magic" Johnson out of Michigan State University as a freshman and dress him in a Kansas City Kings uniform. "I was ready to sign him for a little over $1 million for four years, but I could not convince the owners to do it," Axelson said. Johnson signed with the Lakers after his sophomore season and never gave the Kings a second thought, except when playing against them.

Axelson spent three years at league headquarters. When he returned to Kansas City, the Kings resumed their decline. "We believe that ownership should leave professional sports to the professionals," Karosen said, explaining why Axelson was brought back in 1982. Oscar Robertson's reaction to those words was not recorded.

KAROSEN AND HIS partners were respected business leaders in Kansas City. Like Les Harrison, however, they lacked the financial capacity to absorb persistent box office losses and pay for the best players. There were other impediments to brisk ticket sales. Despite its national platform and Joe Axelson's marketing plan, the NBA was burdened with drug scandals that did not play well with the public, especially in Middle America.

Utah Jazz player Terry Furlow died in 1980 after driving his car into a freeway utility pole near Cleveland under the influence of cocaine and Valium. Phoenix star Walter Davis missed 27 games in 1981 after binging on cocaine and alcohol. Over the next several years, NBA stars Micheal Ray Richardson, Lewis Lloyd, Mitchell Wiggins and Duane Washington would be suspended or temporarily banned from playing for violations of league drug policies.

The usual suspect was cocaine. The 1980s would be rich and transformative years for the league, with the arrival of David Stern in the Commissioner's Office and the talents of Magic Johnson, Larry Bird and Michael Jordan. The rivalry between Johnson's Lakers and Bird's Celtics would become a national attraction. Jordan would create his own universe. But the NBA's party habits hurt the undercapitalized teams in smaller markets. When the 1980s began, the league was in trouble.

One key decision-maker in place to fix the problems was Stern, the son of a New York City delicatessen owner. Stern joined the NBA as an outside lawyer fresh from Columbia Law School in 1966. After passing the bar, Stern was hired by Proskauer Rose Goetz Mendelsohn, a New York law firm well known for dispensing legal advice to sports leagues. He handled the NBA desk until 1978, when Commissioner Larry O'Brien, the NBA's third leader after Maurice Podoloff and Walter Kennedy, hired Stern as general counsel.

O'Brien put the smart, young, ambitious lawyer in charge of the league's core property: the NBA's image. Stern took over public relations, marketing and TV contracts. It was the most important job in the building.

Several teams were on the brink of bankruptcy. Major corporations, whose advertising dollars greased the gears of pro sports, saw the NBA as a netherworld of narcotics, crime and chaos. "If you had 30 minutes with a prospective sponsor, your first 20 minutes were spent trying to convince him that the players weren't all on drugs," said Steve Mills, an NBA executive in the early 1980s. David Stern brought control to the chaos. In 1984, the owners made him commissioner.

In Kansas City, the drug scandals and the Kings' mediocrity, plus the presence of Major League Baseball and the NFL, gave residents little reason to buy season tickets and corporate sponsorships for pro basketball. The franchise was losing about $1 million per year, too much for the ownership to absorb. Gone were the team's easy money days, when Louie Jacobs needed just 24 hours' notice for any transactions over $3 million.

This time, the solution would not come from peanuts or an office in Buffalo. It would come from California and a place called Sacramento.

There, a young man who helped run his father's contracting and construction business believed that community pride and many millions of dollars in profits could be generated by using major-league sports to leverage municipal planning decisions. The young man envisioned a huge real estate gamble fueled by sports.

He favored infrequent haircuts, blue jeans, flannel shirts and tennis shoes. He chain smoked cigarettes and drank coffee by the gallon. He was convinced he could transform the Sacramento real estate market, if only he could get his hands on a big-league pro team, even a bargain-basement loser.

He formed partnerships, put together a credit line and scouted for a franchise to buy. The NBA seemed perfect. It was easy to break into and cheaper than Major League Baseball or the National Football League. The struggling Indianapolis Pacers sparkled as a target.

Then Gregg Lukenbill heard about the Kansas City Kings.

Chapter Seven: We Foresaw The Reality

Five days before Christmas 2012, Westcore Properties, a San Diego real estate investment company, paid $600 million for 110 buildings in Sacramento, Indianapolis and St. Louis. The buildings, which comprised 11.1 million square feet, were not monuments of design and innovation.

They were warehouses, distribution centers, low-rise office buildings and call centers, structures built near freeways. Anonymous boxes with walls made from prefabricated concrete tilted into place, the buildings had vast open floors, high ceilings decorated with insulation pads, truck loading docks and rows of industrial lights. They featured small tinted-glass windows, when they had windows at all. About half of the Westcore transaction involved properties within two miles of the arena where the Sacramento Kings would play.

The Westcore acquisition was unusual for two reasons. It was the largest industrial real estate transaction of 2012 in California. And it represented the estate of one man, Joseph Benvenuti, who died at age 91 on May 30, 2012, and whose vision for his empire was brought to focus by the Kings.

Thirty years before his death, Joe Benvenuti was busy buying thousands of acres of farm fields inside the northern city limits of Sacramento, property with no value for short-term development, zoned for agriculture and vulnerable to floods. The land was called North Natomas, after the Maidu Native American word "Natoma," meaning "upstream."

In the late 1970s, after listening to a pitch from a hopeful young real estate contractor and developer named Gregg Lukenbill, Benvenuti set in motion a strategy to speed development in North Natomas. The concept would build around Lukenbill's dream and Benvenuti's access to money.

The idea was to establish a major league sports team in the midst of newly acquired farmland, with the understanding that in exchange for bringing the team to Sacramento, the developers would be allowed to build warehouses, homes, apartments, office parks and distribution centers on the farmland, on a fast-track schedule. One community benefit would pay for the other. Or so the pitch went.

In theory, the plan would allow a seamless transition from farm town to major-league city. It was the magnum opus of Benvenuti's career, a real estate game played across a broad public stage where everybody would take certain risks.

The Kings would change their image as a money-losing, second-class franchise and become a political sledgehammer and NBA winner. Sacramento would expand its destiny and join the ranks of big-league cities. Benvenuti figured to end up the biggest champion of all, financially speaking. When he died and his children sold his property to Westcore, he was proved right. He was not just the biggest winner; he was the only winner.

Under the rules of the game, Sacramento would get an NBA team. Benvenuti, Lukenbill and their associates would get expedited civic entitlements on thousands of acres for development. Benvenuti would throw in an arena. He would pay for it and own it, no cost to taxpayers. Before they finished, Benvenuti and Lukenbill would build two arenas, temporary and permanent. By the time Benvenuti died, approximately 55,000 people would live in North Natomas, up from zero when he started buying land in the area.

In 2012, the North Natomas community bustled with strip malls, stucco-sided homes and apartments with tile roofs and community gyms and swimming pools and traffic congestion. Property values rose and crashed. Between 2006 and 2012, two out of every five homes in North Natomas received foreclosure notices. Residential housing values fell about 45 percent.

As for the permanent arena built for the Kings in 1988, it was falling apart by 2012. Patches were visible on the exterior where stucco had fallen away. The unique, planned community envisioned by Lukenbill and Benvenuti did not exist. The dream had devolved into suburban sprawl and volatile property values. But the real estate game, defined as a strategy for riches, had spun enough gold to carry the Benvenuti legacy for generations.

Joe Benvenuti was a real estate speculator, but he wasn't the first to play the game in North Natomas. The true pioneers were Lukenbill and his friend Frank McCormack, who bought 435 acres of farmland near the point where two of America's grand highways, Interstate 5 and Interstate 80, intersected. The price was $2.3 million, about $5,300 an acre. The year was 1978. Lukenbill was 24 years old.

The land purchase wasn't an act of impetuous youth. Lukenbill was young and he could be impetuous, but he had patience and discipline and a huge ballast of courage, matched by recklessness. He wanted to build a new town on his acreage and connect that town to Sacramento, which would blossom with astonishing speed, he believed, once the right people were in charge and the proper cultural attractions—major league sports—were present to drive development and growth. Like many dreamers, Lukenbill lacked just one important element: money.

The 435 acres represented a huge risk for the young man, a gamble he could not sustain without financial help. His angel investor was Joe Benvenuti, who saw the simplicity of Lukenbill's plan to use pro sports as leverage for real estate development.

Benvenuti quickly began buying more property around the Lukenbill acreage. Together with another developer, Bob Cook, a Lukenbill friend named Steve Cippa, Benvenuti's children and a regional thrift bank known as Sacramento Savings and Loan, the partners formed something called the Sacramento Sports Association. Run by Lukenbill and Benvenuti, the Sports Association would control 4,100 acres in North Natomas soon after 1980.

EVERY CITY had stories about land speculation. In Sacramento, gamblers made bets on property values in the Gold Rush of 1849. But never before in Sacramento history was the greasy guts of land speculation so obvious, so public, that local newspapers and TV stations covered the property development drama with intensity typically reserved for serial killings and kidnapper trials.

One day in 1985, Gregg Lukenbill made headlines simply by showing a reporter a property tax bill. The bill was for $53,000. It was related to some of Lukenbill's North Natomas land. The news report that followed showed how the path to riches in the real estate game was strewn with troublesome obstacles such as property taxes. "We're going through the agony to build sports facilities," Lukenbill said. "I would venture a guess that we are $15 million in the hole right now." Future homeowners in North Natomas would feel his pain as their property values crashed.

The public nature of Lukenbill's complaint, the fact that he and Benvenuti and their partners played their game in plain sight and on TV rather than twisting arms or making political deals in back rooms at City Hall (which they also did), made some people angry. Most angry of all were residents of older, established neighborhoods in Sacramento, people who believed concrete and asphalt spread across North Natomas would overwhelm the city with unmanageable growth.

They thought Lukenbill and Benvenuti didn't care about culture and quality of life but just wanted to make a quick buck. Appropriately for a developer working under the glare of public spotlights, Lukenbill never denied he liked money. He wanted to get rich the right way, he countered, by making his community even richer than himself.

In many California communities in mid-20th Century, people who advocated cautionary growth policies were a lonely tribe. They were passionate in their beliefs and hoarse of voice because, despite their pleas and binders filled with data and warnings about traffic and pollution and instant ghettos, nobody in charge would listen.

Sacramento was a different place in 1980. People did listen to concerns about growth, important people, including the mayor, Anne Rudin, a retired nurse from Philadelphia whose political passions included nuclear disarmament, gay rights and smoking bans. Rudin wanted to see major league sports come to Sacramento. But she sympathized with her neighbors who were concerned about massive suburban developments replacing farmland.

Rudin wanted to build a firewall between the tantalizing lure of major league sports and the incendiary question of land use. She was angry that Lukenbill and his friends were connecting the two, like the carrot tied to the stick.

While Lukenbill believed pro sports would inspire the community in its march toward growth, Mayor Rudin saw sports tearing Sacramento apart over land-entitlement policies that had no business being linked to basketball. "The sports issue and the land use issue have both been (confused) from the very beginning," she said. "That has clouded some people's vision, making everybody's job very difficult."

The people with the most difficult job, politically at least, were the nine members of the Sacramento City Council. Lukenbill and Benvenuti didn't believe the council had the backbone to do what a progressive city should do, which in their opinion meant opening North Natomas for development. They worried that council members (or at least a majority, five of them), led by Rudin, would bifurcate the question of major league sports and development, not understanding that one could not exist without the other.

Under Lukenbill's scenario, real estate entitlements would generate the millions of dollars needed for basketball, hockey, football or baseball teams and their facilities. There was no other way to raise the kind of money required for sports. Such were Lukenbill's fears that in 1979 he managed to place an initiative on the Sacramento ballot that would override the council's authority to make zoning decisions in North Natomas. Lukenbill wanted voters to directly make the rules in the real estate game.

His ballot measure failed. Voters, convinced that zoning and entitlements were best left to professional planners and elected representatives, chose to maintain the traditional process, with committee hearings and City Hall staff reports and back room lobbying and passionate public testimony and whimsical soliloquies by council members and dramatic roll-call votes by the city council. That's how municipal policy decisions were made in Sacramento. It was all about the process.

DESPITE HIS ballot measure and reluctance to place his future in the city council's hands, Lukenbill appreciated the bureaucratic process. He understood his critics and his supporters (he was, after all, from Sacramento) and believed the city authorities would ultimately act in Sacramento's best interests, which happened to be his best interests. "Most of the people who have been against us come from big cities," he said with a nod to Mayor Rudin. "They think growth is going to create Philadelphia slums, Boston slums, tremendous traffic problems, urban blight. Those people often say they're not against sports. They're against growth. But it you're against sports, sports creates a positive image for the community. I think a positive image will make more people want to come here."

To increase the certainty that the weight of public and political opinions would fall on his side, Lukenbill and his partners needed a deal closer, something big, tangible and alive to create deep civic passion around the land-use debate. Lukenbill had spent years telling the community how Sacramento would benefit from major league pro sports. He would talk until his voice wore out. Now he needed action. The solution, he decided, was to light out from Sacramento, backed by financial support from Joe Benvenuti, and bring home a trophy: a real big league team.

His first preference was baseball. Lukenbill loved the rich baseball history of Sacramento, the 1950s home plate from the local minor league ballpark nailed to the wall at Joe Marty's bar on Broadway, the roster of local kids who fought their way to the major leagues.

The original 435 acres in North Natomas bought by Lukenbill were intended to support a baseball stadium, at least in Lukenbill's dream. But Major League Baseball was a closed campus. Two teams were already in Northern California, the San Francisco Giants and Oakland Athletics. Lukenbill lobbied team owners and organized bus caravans to A's games from Sacramento to demonstrate his market's strength. But he couldn't get the right people to pay attention.

He also believed the NFL would be an instant success in Sacramento. Opportunity presented itself in the image of a silver and black buccaneer with an eye-patch and football helmet. Lukenbill arranged to meet Al Davis, owner of the Oakland Raiders, who in 1982 moved to Los Angeles because he couldn't get luxury boxes built at the publicly owned stadium he shared with the A's.

The problem with buying baseball and football teams, Lukenbill learned, was that they were both very expensive with insular ownership structures. Baseball and football were the toughest parties to crash. Those sports required a personal invitation and huge amounts of money. An outsider like Lukenbill would not get a warm welcome.

Professional basketball, a smaller, cheaper, lower-profile game, made sense in 1983. The NBA's gritty glory days of Bill Russell and Wilt Chamberlain were over. Teams could be scooped up for reasonable prices. Broadcast rights were minimal, confirming the NBA's lowly status as a fringe attraction.

CBS paid the league $23 million a year to televise 32 NBA games in the early 1980s, with the ESPN and USA cable networks throwing in another $5.5 million. (Within 20 years, NBA broadcast rights would trade for billions of dollars.) Arenas could be built from boxy warehouse designs. The NBA was a carnival, a circus. Anyone with a credit line was welcomed to join.

Appropriate for a carnival, the NBA had an entrepreneurial attitude that accepted outsiders, one and all. Teams in Portland, Salt Lake City and Phoenix proved the league had learned to appreciate small and mid-sized markets, especially when basketball was the only big-league game in town. "We foresaw the reality of bringing an NBA franchise to Sacramento was a lot quicker than baseball and football," Lukenbill said. "And it would increase our credibility as far as getting football and baseball later."

The sports editor of The Sacramento Bee, Joe Hamelin, had covered pro basketball in San Diego and maintained connections around the league. He told Lukenbill several NBA teams were for sale, including the Indiana Pacers and quite possibly the Kansas City Kings, who had been languishing since the move from Cincinnati in 1972.

Soon, a lawyer named Lewis Schaffel, who would later create the Miami Heat, called Lukenbill and offered to help broker a sale for the Pacers. Lukenbill and Benvenuti spent two weeks chasing the Indianapolis team, offering $11.5 million before they decided they were being used to leverage other potential buyers.

Frustrated by the Indiana process, Lukenbill declared he would eliminate the intermediaries and negotiate future opportunities alone. He knew the Kansas City Kings were losing money. The team had declared a profit just once since moving from Cincinnati. He called team owner Leon Karosen. When he learned Karosen would soon be talking to potential buyers from St. Louis, Lukenbill booked an immediate flight to Kansas City and pushed for a fast negotiation. To Lukenbill's surprise, Karosen, the Kansas City clothing maker, was ready to talk business.

Within 72 hours after landing in Missouri, Lukenbill had an agreement to buy the Kings for $4.5 million in cash, $4.5 million in deferred payments and $1.5 million payable to Karosen and his partners if (or more realistically when) the team left Kansas City. The deal closed on June 8, 1983.

And just like that, the Sacramento developers had their trophy, a real NBA team. Crowed Lukenbill, "This marks the turning point in improving the quality of life in Sacramento."

Chapter Eight: People Have Raised Valid Concerns

Gregg Lukenbill would serve as managing partner of the Kings, but Joe Benvenuti controlled the largest single piece, a fluid number that opened at 50 percent and dwindled to 15 percent by the time he died. Soon after he bought the Kings, Benvenuti began to boast how he agreed to buy an NBA team without ever having bothered to attend an NBA game. It was a line Louie Jacobs would have enjoyed from his desk in the big casino in the sky.

Louie never let himself become a sports fan. He felt fandom might cloud his business judgment. Benvenuti followed the same logic. Between June 8, 1983, and the day Joe Benvenuti drew his final breath in 2012, it's impossible to know how many NBA games he attended, but a reasonable guess would be significantly fewer than the actor Jack Nicholson.

There were details, such as the requisite league approval for ownership changes. The NBA Board of Governors, comprised of one partner from each team, would have to agree to the sale. Another detail would be the public response to basketball fans in Kansas City, where many people suspected the sale was a precursor to a move to Sacramento. The team's general manager, Joe Axelson, made the pretense of visiting NBA headquarters to argue for an expansion team at Sacramento, which would allow Kansas City to keep the Kings. His pleas, such as they were, were ignored.

The Board of Governors swiftly approved the transfer of ownership. As for moving, Lukenbill knew the Kansas City fans were right about losing their team. Of course, he could not level with them, not at first. Kansas City would be given a fair chance to keep the Kings by showing stellar box office support,

Lukenbill promised. Besides, he noted, the Kings could not move. They had nowhere to play in Sacramento. Despite the bombast, everyone knew the long-term prospects for pro basketball in Kansas City were not good.

"We were the No. 5 sports franchise in Kansas City," Lukenbill said. "There were the Royals and Chiefs, and then there was the golfer Tom Watson, who was like a franchise all to himself. Then came the indoor soccer team. They did a great marketing job. If they couldn't sell tickets, they gave them away. People loved them. Then there was the Kings."

Lukenbill tried to squeeze more money out of the Kings' home building, Kemper Arena, but his landlord, the municipal authorities of Kansas City, were not in a generous mood. "We identified about eight revenue sources, way ahead of our time," Lukenbill said. "There's parking and novelties, food and beverage, clubs seating and suites, and signage and tickets. We knew we had to get operating control, but the city wouldn't go for it. I told them we would keep the Kings in Kansas City and go for an expansion franchise in Sacramento if they would agree with me, but they refused. They basically ran us out of town."

A dozen years after the Kings left, Gary Sage, a manager with the Economic Development Corporation of Kansas City, agreed that making the NBA team happy was not a priority for the city. "The Kings were a flicker on our economic growth chart," Sage said. "They frankly didn't mean that much from an economic standpoint. It's much harder to measure what pro sports means from a spiritual standpoint. But spiritually you can always recover by bringing in other opportunities for people."

Kansas City basketball fans could not be expected to know the details of Lukenbill's political situation in Sacramento, where, in 1984, the debate raged between real estate entitlements and major league sports. So Lukenbill and Benvenuti decided to build a temporary arena, a simple, box-like structure with prefabricated, tilt-up concrete walls that could be converted to warehouse or office space, only a few hundred feet outside the city limits in North Natomas.

The Kings' owners didn't control as much land then in unincorporated Sacramento County, but they could expect swift approval for the temporary arena by the county board of supervisors. The five board members were friendly to developers and not inclined to worry about traffic congestion, floods and pollution in an agricultural part of the county that had no residents, much less voters.

Lukenbill and his partners lined up their county support. They were careful to call the building a warehouse or office complex rather than what it was: a temporary arena for the Kings. They won immediate approval and went to work grading the site. In late 1984, days before the Kings were to start their second season in Kansas City under Sacramento ownership, news finally broke that the tilt-up warehouse in North Natomas was a temporary, $12 million basketball arena for an unnamed NBA team. Kings season ticket sales died that day in Missouri and Kansas.

THE KANSAS CITY Kings limped through their final season with a 31-51 record. Attendance hovered around 6,100 at Kemper Arena. The last game became a community farewell with 11,371 fans present on a Sunday afternoon, April 14, 1985, watching the Kings lose to their familiar nemesis, the Los Angeles Lakers, 122-116.

The audience gave the Kings' players a two-minute standing ovation. The crowd directed its anger not at Lukenbill or Benvenuti, but at Joe Axelson, the general manager who brought the Royals from Cincinnati in 1972 and would soon have the distinction of having relocated the franchise twice (or three times, counting Omaha).

An enterprising Royals fan, Mike Randall, printed 300 black and white cardstock masks with a life-sized photo of Axelson. The masks were distributed in the West end zone and quickly spread through the building. With six minutes to play, two fans in the West end zone produced a rope and a cloth dummy dressed in a black suit, its face defined by a Joe Axelson mask. The dummy was hung in effigy. Fake money was thrown into the air. If nothing else, Kansas City basketball fans had a sense of humor and a fine feel for theatrics.

Adding to the ignominy for Kansas City, the NBA Board of Governors was scheduled to meet in New York on the following Tuesday to approve the move to Sacramento. The vote would be 22-0. Axelson refined the insult he made 13 seasons earlier, when the team moved from Cincinnati. This time, speaking of Kansas City, he said, "It isn't a good basketball town. People here think it is, but they haven't proved that." And like Rochester and Cincinnati, Kansas City became a forgotten NBA market.

Since the founding in 1948 by Les Harrison and his fellow team operators, the NBA had never relocated into a city that had no basketball arena. The new commissioner, David Stern, who had been on the job only 14 months in 1985, identified the potential risks and rewards of doing business in Sacramento. "There's something about being the first major-league team in a market," he said. "It's a challenge, but I think they will live up to that. We are committed and confident that they will do us, and, more important, the people of Sacramento, proud." He wasn't joking when he used the word "committed."

To help stimulate the pride, Stern and his owners added a condition to Sacramento's entry into the fraternity of NBA cities. If Sacramento didn't christen a permanent arena, something not designed to become a warehouse or office, by 1987, the league could buy the team from Lukenbill and Benvenuti and partners and move it. The contingency clause put more pressure on Mayor Rudin and the city council.

The pressure increased for more than a year while Lukenbill and Benvenuti gained momentum. Axelson printed bumper stickers—"The Kings Are Coming"—to help drive ticket sales at the temporary arena. More than 22,000 seat requests were mailed in, even as the warehouse at 1625 North Market Drive remained a muddy construction site. By opening night, the Kings were guaranteed an unprecedented benchmark. Every home game that season was sold out before the first dribble of the first game.

The temporary arena was small, with seats for only 10,333, but the overwhelming demand for tickets eliminated marketing and sales pressures from Lukenbill's list of worries. The sold-out building provided the city council with a relentless reminder of the team's public support, a drumbeat repeated every time the Kings played at home.

Soon, council members would see reminders of the Kings on dozens of street corners across Sacramento. Borrowing a strategy from 1984 Los Angeles Olympics promoter Peter Ueberroth, Lukenbill signed a $7 million naming-rights deal with Atlantic Richfield oil company. The building became Arco Arena. Corporate stadium names were uncommon in 1985. For a few years, the Arco Arena label brought ridicule to Sacramento. "Hey, we didn't go name it Preparation H Arena," Axelson said in defense.

The Vagrant Kings began their California era with a 108-104 loss to the Los Angeles Clippers on October 25, 1985. One man dominated the Kings: Clippers guard Derek Smith, who scored 36 points that first night. As the celebrations continued into the next morning in Sacramento, the score was irrelevant. Hundreds of season ticket holders tuned out in formal attire, out-dressing even the postwar Rochester Royals' audiences.

In gowns and dinner jackets, they drank champagne. They rented limousines for the ride to the arena. This is how major league audiences were supposed to act!

The Kings won 37 games their first season, good enough to reach the playoffs. The Houston Rockets erased Sacramento in three straight playoff games, but who cared? The community loved its big-league status and loved the team that provided the energy, headlines and bright lights. Any possibility that the Sacramento City Council would deny permits for a new arena and fail to approve entitlements for the surrounding acreage grew smaller each time the Kings trotted onto the court.

The loudest boos on opening night were not for the Clippers or Derek Smith. They were for Mayor Rudin, who was introduced at courtside and jeered. Smiling at first, then realizing the booing was for her, she looked perplexed and finally sad.

SENSING THE arrival of his moment, Lukenbill pushed the Sacramento City Council to its limits. On October 28, 1986, the council was asked to approve not just permits for a new, permanent NBA arena with 17,500 seats, but also entitlements for an outdoor stadium that would expand to 73,000 seats.

And there was more. Lukenbill and Benvenuti wrapped their sports complex around the council's acceptance of an adjacent 1,620-acre, mixed-use development for the budding tech industry, supplemented with houses, retail shops and offices. The real estate game had come down to its final play. Lukenbill pushed everything into the center of the table. And he waited for the city council to fold.

The development plans were massive. North Natomas included 22 square miles, almost half the size of San Francisco. The public improvements alone, the roads, sidewalks, sewers, drainage ditches, schools, parks and fire stations, were estimated to cost between $500 million and $1 billion. "When the numbers were first put in front of me, I gulped," City Treasurer Tom Friery said. "We can't be scared of it just because the number is big. However, I have to be prepared to protect the city's interest."

Council members heard public testimony and debated for almost three hours, not particularly long considering the significance of the agenda item. Various infrastructure conditions were pressed upon the developers regarding sewage, access roads, minority hiring, parking and bus shelters.

A community activist named Heather Fargo argued that the arena and stadium would create runoff floods from poorly planned drainage systems. Fargo was a person of budding influence in 1986. She would soon run for city council and be mayor in 2000. Campaigning for a third mayoral term in 2008, she would be defeated by Kevin Johnson, ending a political career that took flight the night the city council decided the fate of the Kings, over her protests.

The vote that night was 9-0 to approve everything desired by Lukenbill and Benvenuti. Even Mayor Rudin marched into line. "I think people have raised valid concerns and deserve assurances that these things will be watched and monitored and won't be neglected or overlooked in our haste to get the projects online," the mayor said. She was right about the haste. Construction on the arena was scheduled to start almost immediately.

The city's involvement in the arena was not quite completed. Environmental groups, less impressed by Lukenbill's assurances than the city council, threatened litigation to stop the huge sports project. The Allied Bank of Texas, which was ready to loan the developers $28.5 million toward construction of the arena, held back its money, fearing legal actions against the project and possible default by the developers.

The banks worried that the Sacramento gamblers were getting in over their heads. Lukenbill quietly turned to City Manager Walter Slipe and asked to borrow $8 million for a certificate of deposit, held as good-faith collateral for Allied Bank until the litigation threats were resolved. Slipe agreed and removed $8 million from the city's employee pension fund to buy the CD.

The arrangement was kept secret from all but two city council members, Mayor Rudin and Joe Serna, another future mayor, and wasn't made public until six months later. The city official who engineered the deal was the Kings' reliable old friend, City Treasurer Friery. "This is one of the tightest, hardest business deals I have ever done," he said. "I have these fellows pretty good."

Tom Friery wasn't worried about losing the pension fund's money. He felt confident the city would be protected by the tight structure of the deal. Assuming everything went right, he even predicted the city's pension fund would earn about $180,000 in interest from the quiet little maneuver. He was right about the earnings. The fund was protected, with interest. In North Natomas, however, everything did not go right.

A new arena rose from the farm fields once called "upstream" by the Maidu people. Then came bankruptcies, broken promises and disastrous maneuvers by the NBA team whose promise had been to put Sacramento on the map of progressive, eclectic, emerging and liveable Western cities.

Chapter Nine: They Appear To Be Open To My Approach

Building permits. Concrete poured over rebar and gravel. New roads cut and paved. Land values soaring from $5,200 an acre to $26,000, or even $40,000. Those victories were not enough for Gregg Lukenbill. He owned an NBA team. He wanted his team to win. And the Kings were losers, locked in the basement of the NBA standings.

The slump that took hold when Louie Jacobs gave elephants and peanuts priority over playoff games at Cincinnati Gardens showed no willingness to subside, despite the Kings' popularity in their new hometown. Not only were the Kings losers, they were getting worse.

The team that delighted fans with the minimalist accomplishment of reaching the first round of NBA playoffs in April 1986 was dismantled by Joe Axelson four months later. Like an elephant, Axelson never forgot the Opening Night 1985 basketball clinic presented by Los Angeles Clippers guard Derek Smith.

As the Kings' president, Axelson believed he gained unique perspective from his special perch, a baseline seat high on the aisle behind the basket near the visitors' bench. "If you knew the game, that's where you'd want to watch from," Axelson said. "Any basketball man will tell you that. Up above the baseline is where you see the teams come at you and set up on defense." From that fixed position, studying the Kings and their opponents like Jabba the Hutt in suit and tie, the rotund Axelson saw revelations only he could comprehend. He grew determined to buy Smith's contract, no matter the price or consequence. Both would be large.

Axelson acquired Smith by trading two important Kings players, Larry Drew and Mike Woodson, to the Clippers. The Kings agreed to pay Smith

$4.5 million over five years. They declared the new man the centerpiece of the franchise. But there was a fatal flaw in Axelson's strategy. Jabba the Hutt bought damaged goods.

After his Opening Night triumph in Sacramento, Derek Smith missed most of the 1985-86 season with torn cartilage in his left knee. He was diagnosed with mononucleosis. Three physical exams were required before a doctor could be found to declare Smith medically fit for trade, which should have raised suspicions all around. The evidence was dismissed.

As always, Joe Axelson maintained absolute faith in Joe Axelson. His employers tagged along, nodding their heads. The financial commitment made by the Kings to Derek Smith was the largest in the team's history at the time. "The moves Joe has made have been made to win basketball games," Lukenbill said.

While Smith may have been physically sound in one doctor's opinion, his ability to play basketball was plainly diminished by the knee injury. None of this was Smith's fault. He struggled in games scheduled on consecutive nights. He complained of nagging pain. Starting their second season in Sacramento with Smith as their hero, the Kings won nine of their first 35 games. The new centerpiece spent his practice hours seated at courtside with an ice bag taped to his left knee. "The worst part is the burden of not being able to live up to my contract," Smith said. "I don't feel I've earned it yet. I'm doing the best I can, but physically, it hasn't been enough."

With Smith unable to perform at peak capacity, the Kings had no focal point. There was nothing much left for the team to do, other than lose. The coach, a weary, taciturn NBA pro named Phil Johnson, who moved with the franchise from Kansas City, was fired in February 1987 after a 36-point loss to the Lakers.

Johnson, whose habit was to never smoke or drink at home but do both with gusto while on the road, was helpless. Against the Lakers in Johnson's final game, the Kings failed to score a field goal in the first quarter. They trailed 40-4 after 12 minutes, the fewest points by an NBA team since league President Podoloff introduced the shot clock in 1954. "I have never seen anything like that before in my life," Lakers forward James Worthy said.

Kings assistant coaches Jerry Reynolds and Don Buse took over what had become a suicide mission, replacing the ashen-faced Phil Johnson, who had done his best with the team handed him by Axelson. James Worthy would need multiple lifetimes to see anything like the Kings.

The trade for Derek Smith came to represent everything wrong about the team. He was a walking (rarely running) reminder of impetuous, regal moves based on gut instinct rather than proven fact. His presence demonstrated the Kings' belief in quick, theoretical fixes, a fascination with rehabilitation projects, constant over-optimism and the myth that Joe Axelson was the cleverest man in the NBA.

The centerpiece position was unfair to Smith. He was miscast. Smith was not designed to be an NBA star, a go-to guy. In temperament and talent, he was a better second violin, a player who could supplement an all-star teammate, keep defenses honest, sneak up and take control of games in special moments, the perfect example being Opening Night in Sacramento 1985. "I can jump, but jumping in traffic is another story," Smith said. "I've got to build confidence in my ability to jump in a crowd. It's going to take time." And with his knee injury, his time as a star had passed. His promotion as the Kings' savior was a basketball tragedy.

Smith's life would end as a real tragedy in 1996. Five years after his retirement as a player, Smith worked as an assistant coach for the Washington Bullets. During the off-season, he took his family on a summer cruise to Bermuda aboard the ship MS Dreamward. It was a working holiday. The vessel's passengers included about 100 season ticket holders and staff members from the basketball team and the Washington Capitals hockey club. Smith and other players enlivened the cruise by giving basketball lessons.

After a cocktail party to celebrate the final night of a happy journey, Smith went to the observation deck for dinner with friends from the team. In the midst of conversation, he opened his eyes wide, gasped and fell over. His dinner companions thought he was joking around. Smith's family, scattered in other parts of the ship, was called. His wife and children watched as the Dreamward medical personnel pronounced Derek Smith dead, the victim of a heart attack at age 34. Smith's son Nolan, named for the baseball pitcher Nolan Ryan, was eight years old. The Portland Trail Blazers drafted Nolan Smith 15 years after his father's death. He signed with a European team in 2013.

STIMULATED BY their community and box office success in 1986, tearing apart the team and bringing in Derek Smith, the Kings were throwing money around as never before. But there were cash flow issues. Players rushed to the bank on payday to make sure the money cleared. Lukenbill and Benvenuti scrambled to piece together financing required for the new arena and outdoor stadium, which were being built next to each other on farmland south of Del Paso Road, west of the temporary arena.

The Sacramento owners asked the NBA for a one-year extension on the promise to open the permanent facility by 1987. The league agreed, understanding the complications, sensing progress and not wanting the Northern California move to dissolve into an embarrassing spectacle that would damage the NBA's restored credibility. When the Kings' second season in Sacramento ended, the team had won 29 games. Joe Axelson called it the unhappiest year of his life, which, in the professional sense, was saying something.

Redemption was found in Axelson's marketing playbook, an old trick from his Cincinnati days, when Axelson purged an aging team, created a distraction and shifted responsibility from himself by hiring an iconic coach whose golden reputation could make all troubles vanish.

This time, Axelson exceeded even himself. He did not phone up Bob Cousy again, but reached out to the greatest of them all, the legendary Celtics center Bill Russell. Thirty-one years and 11 championships after Les Harrison drafted Si Green and let Russell tumble into the arms of Boston coach Red Auerbach, Russell would officially join the franchise that let him get away in 1956.

The details of Russell's coronation were presented to the public as a uniquely linear lifetime arrangement, Sacramento Kings style. Russell would coach the team for a few years, teach the lads to stand tall and, with a little luck, position them for a championship run. He certainly knew about that! After the victory parade, Russell would slide into Axelson's job as president and general manager while the true genius, Joe Axelson, sailed off to San Diego in self-satisfied retirement. The team's sense of destiny, its eagerness to defy gravity and produce a brilliant resurrection, all in one spectacular move, was at its zenith.

The contract with Russell was for an average of $200,000 per year over seven years, incredible by contemporary standards. The money and time commitments were irrelevant, Lukenbill pointed out, because Russell would eventually own part of the Kings. This was a lifetime marriage.

The fairy tale seemed plausible enough in Sacramento, where the depth of common knowledge about Russell was limited to his 11 championship rings—"My bookends," he called them—his duties as a sports broadcaster, his worldly image as an author and Seattle newspaper columnist, his work as a TV pitchman, his public speaking appearances, his cultural sagacity and obvious genius for basketball.

The flirtation between Russell and the Kings began on February 27, 1987, two weeks after the disastrous Lakers game when Phil Johnson was fired, with a phone call from Russell to Axelson. The men had been acquainted since Axelson's Cincinnati days, and it was hard to say who was hustling whom. Both men needed something. Russell, then 53, wanted to get back into the NBA spotlight and make some money. Axelson, whose contract was running out in five months, wanted to lock down a few more years as team president by grooming a legend only he could deliver.

Soon after the phone call, Russell and Axelson met for a four-hour lunch at Aldo's restaurant in Sacramento. Lukenbill had never been a stargazer, but Russell came from another stratosphere. The young owner was smitten. Lukenbill pursued Russell to the legend's home near Seattle, and closed the deal after two weeks of negotiation, with Russell playing several masterful rounds of hard-to-get.

The partnership was announced on April 27, a week after the season ended, and allowed the Kings to quickly turn the page on the Year 2 debacle. "It's been a terrible year for me, because nothing I've planned for worked," Axelson said. "But I can make up for a 29-win season. If this guy wins, I can make up for anything."

Bill Russell did not win. He did not earn an equity stake in the team, did not even survive one full season as coach. He was kicked into the Kings' front office as vice-president for basketball operations, a dangerous place to put a man whose knowledge of contemporary players and future prospects was willfully and blissfully minimal.

But Lukenbill was drowning. He desperately grasped for a way to salvage the situation created by Axelson and squeeze some value, any value, out of Russell's contract. Maybe the legend still had an eye for talent. Maybe he could use his unparalleled status and sense of the game to build a winning team. Maybe ... well, it was worth a try. But there would be no value. No miracle recovery.

RUSSELL SPENT three years with the Kings, awful years, after which he left Sacramento, hibernated, contemplated life and emerged to re-establish his position as an American folk hero, honored at the White House by President Barack Obama, co-author of books about leadership and his special relationship with Boston coach Red Auerbach. Writers would eventually seek Russell out for biographical material, placing him at the forefront of the nation's long, hard march to Civil Rights, celebrating him for his pivotal role in helping build the NBA while shaping a culturally diverse, modern America.

The 21st Century deification of an elderly Bill Russell was no doubt appropriate. The man of the hour bore no resemblance to the Bill Russell who arrived in Sacramento on April 27, 1987, to coach the Sacramento Kings.

Among his first moves was the decision to draft Kenny Smith over Kevin Johnson. During his three years working in North Natomas, Russell seemed to have no idea what he was doing, much less how he was supposed to do it. Worse, he lacked the willingness to ask for help and fell back into a defensive posture of well-practiced indifference, detachment and boredom.

It was coincidental that when Russell was hired to coach the Kings, I was assigned by The Sacramento Bee to cover the team as the daily beat reporter. By then, I had reported on regional high schools and major college sports, plus Major League Baseball and the NFL. I didn't know much about the NBA, but that was not a shortcoming in Sacramento, where nobody knew much about the NBA. I had developed a touch for reporting on sports personalities, writing profiles on Willie Mays, Bill Walsh and the Olympic swim champion Mark Spitz, among others. Russell would be within my strike zone, the editors figured.

When I first came to know Russell, it was apparent he wanted everybody to think he was a philosopher-guru well past caring about the earthly details of his job. I sensed he cared very much and simply got himself lost in the unmapped marshland of his new responsibilities. I really wanted to like Bill Russell, to have him like me. He ended up hating me, maybe because I felt sorry for him.

There was no single, handy Wiki repository of background-source material about Russell when I began to cover him that summer of 1987. There were files full of yellowed newspaper and magazine clippings. And there was "Second Wind: The Memoirs Of An Opinionated Man," a 1979 autobiography written with Taylor Branch, the brilliant journalist who would later produce the benchmark trilogy on Martin Luther King, Jr. So in the summer of 1987, "Second Wind" became a must-read in Sacramento.

Our formal relationship began with a pathetic introduction. I stated my name, shook his hand and told him I would be reporting daily that season on the Kings. I told him I was eager to learn from him, that I admired him, and had just finished "Second Wind," which of course I found fascinating. "That's nice," Russell said before he walked away.

My feelings might have been hurt, but several players and team staff members told me not to worry about it. Russ treats everybody that way, they said. From "Second Wind," I knew Russell was interested in Vietnam. I gave him a paperback copy of Francis FitzGerald's "Fire In The Lake," a classic exploration of the differences between Vietnamese and Americans. Russell was not familiar with the book. "Thank you," he said. He never mentioned it again.

My first assignment was to write a long profile about Russell for The Bee. Newspaper profiles typically required interviews and time spent in the company of the person being profiled. But Russell had neither the time nor the interest in sitting down and answering questions. The profile would be written and published whether Russell cooperated or not. He must have known that's how newspapers worked. But I could never be sure. The story would be read and dissected by his employers and the Kings' sponsors and fans, the very same people who paid his salary and supported the team he coached and the franchise he would one day supposedly own. He didn't care.

I asked him several times for an audience. He always politely said no, thank you. Instead, he instructed me to go ahead and ask whatever questions I had, there and then. He would answer them at once. There was no need for a lengthy, formal interview. And hanging around with him after work was out of the question. We should just get it over with now, he said. He already knew what the questions would be. He had the answers down cold.

So we talked for about five minutes. The profile ran more than 2,600 words, encyclopedia-length in those days. Most of the story was sourced from "Second Wind." There was only one substantial original quote from Russell: "The players understand that everything I do is intended to make them better players. We'll never do anything to hurt them. I recognize that this is a players' league. It's my job to put the players into a position where they can do their best. They appear to be open to my approach. It will take time to see how open they really are." That was it.

Maybe I didn't ask the right question.

Chapter Ten: He Felt Relieved By The Whole Thing

The willingness of NBA players to embrace a coach's approach is easily judged by a sportswriter who loiters around the team everyday. My job required me to practically live with the Kings. Travel with them, attend practice, interview them after games, scribble endless reports from training camp to the last game of the season, seven days a week.

In the preseason, we went to Alaska and Montana together for exhibition games in college and high school gyms at Anchorage and Fairbanks and Shelby. On the team bus, Bill Russell would sit in the front seat, glancing at automobile magazines, speaking to no one. At the hotel, he would stay in his room and emerge only for meals, games and practice sessions.

When we passed through lobbies or public places, people stared at Russell and silently mouthed his name. Some people asked for his autograph. He was always polite: "I don't sign autographs, but thank you for asking."

In Anchorage, I joined several players at a strip joint called the Great Alaskan Bush Company. We joked about how one Kings player, Reggie Theus, seemed to have taken lodgings at the Bush Company, impressing everyone with his full length Russian diplomat's fur coat. "When you travel, you should always make an attempt to see what makes the place and the people unique," Theus said, thoughtfully. Russell was not spotted at the Great Alaskan Bush Company. And in any case, he would not have signed autographs there, but thank you for asking.

Back in Sacramento, Russell banned reporters from watching practice sessions. I wondered if he understood what would happen next. Russell's secret practice sessions would become a story theme.

Reporters began to interview players about practice immediately after each session. Russell had no input over what was being said. Joe Axelson explained, "Bill is a very private person and he wants to have closed practice sessions. His reasons don't have anything to do with his feelings about the media. He simply doesn't want to worry about having to watch what he says while reporters are sitting there. He doesn't want the papers to report something he might say to somebody." Plausible answer. But a dangerous communications strategy for a rusty coach with a losing team and unhappy players.

Bizarre revelations began to leak out. They made for juicy gossip. Coach talked about philosophy and let his assistants run practice. Coach tried to install plays but got confused and gave up. Coach sat in stands, read newspaper and fell asleep. The veteran Theus, a philosopher in his own right, told me, "Don't you ever wonder why he won't let you guys watch practice? It's because he doesn't want you to see him just sitting there."

Bill Jones, the Kings' gentleman trainer, whose tenure with the franchise dated to the Bob Cousy years, had a nonintrusive way of verifying stories about Russell's detachment. Jonesy was loyal to all team members, Russell included, but the trainer would never tell lies to the sportswriters who covered the team. "We needed an extra pot of coffee to keep everybody alert this morning," he would say after practice. That meant Russell had fallen asleep.

I was discreet about these behaviors and kept them out of the headlines. My stories focused on how bad the Kings were on the basketball court. There was plenty to write about. My inspiration came from a guy I called Larry the Painter. He represented the fan in the cheap seats. He bought low-priced, upper-deck Kings tickets not to entertain clients or impress new friends but because he loved the Kings. I wrote about Larry, presenting myself as a consumer watchdog for fans just like him.

Some people assumed I invented Larry the Painter as a convenient "common man" character. He was my neighbor, Larry Christ. He painted houses for a living. Larry loved the Kings always. Even when it looked like they were moving to Seattle in 2013.

Bill Russell said he was long past caring what the newspapers printed about him, but he must have been reading my stories in The Bee. Our relationship collapsed to a point where we both stopped speaking to each other. Russell was not unaccustomed to rocky relationships with the media.

In 1973, he claimed Boston sportswriters were racists, which prompted at least one Boston journalist, Larry Claflin of the Boston Herald-American, to write, "I am not a racist sports writer. I suspect Russell is the racist."

While he did not accuse me of racism, Russell eventually tried to prevent me from being present at events relevant to the Kings, even their games. He sent a letter my bosses and I at The Bee stating the Kings would no longer let me ride their team bus, and would no longer book my road accommodations. Russell inquired about pulling my press credentials and forcing me to buy a ticket if I wanted to report on a Kings game. Axelson told him that would not be appropriate.

> *"Dear Bob:*
>
> *"Historically we have extended certain courtesies to the press representatives traveling with our team. They have included making airline and hotel reservations and providing ground transportation to and from hotels, practices, and games. We intend to cease extending these courtesies to you.*
>
> *"You will be responsible for airline and hotel reservations and ground transportation immediately.*
>
> *"Regards,*
>
> *"William F. Russell"*

The letter did not have the desired effect, an outcome, again, that Russell should have anticipated. I went to the local American Express travel office and asked the booking agents to put me on whatever flights the Kings were taking. Same with hotels. (The newspaper always paid for my flights and hotel rooms, so Russell's ban was not a financial burden.) The team bus obstacle was easily circumvented. When I landed at Cleveland or Miami or Portland or wherever, I would hail a taxi and tell the driver to follow that bus.

Players made jokes about the absurdity of it all. Other reporters and editors around the country heard about the ban and laughed at Russell's audacity. My reputation, not much to start with, improved. (And it turned out Russell was ahead of his time. The cozy relationship he terminated between a ball club and a reporter would not be allowed today by pro teams or the legitimate media.)

Willis Reed, the former New York Knicks star whom Russell recruited as an assistant coach, found it difficult to reconcile his memories of the brilliant Celtics center with the man who had trouble keeping his eyes open at Kings practices. Reed did not have a relationship with Russell before getting the job in Sacramento, but he had unconditional respect for Russell's basketball legacy and accomplishments. Reed was hungry to learn from the master.

Serious and professional about his duties, Reed had been tacitly promised the Kings' head coaching job when Russell moved into Axelson's executive position. But after a few weeks in Sacramento, Reed was dismayed. The team was out of control. As an assistant, there wasn't much Reed could do.

Then Willis got lucky. He was hired to coach the New Jersey Nets. He left in February, less than six months after joining the Kings. For me, Reed was a highlight of the 1987 season. Decades later I would treasure the hours spent commiserating in hotel bars with Willis and listening to his stories, all made smooth and memorable by shots of Seagram's VO, my friend's favorite tonic that sad, cold winter.

THE KINGS' second assistant coach behind Reed was Jerry Reynolds, a former community college teacher who moved west with the team from Kansas City. Reynolds had three important characteristics. He was remarkably loyal. He was funny. And he had unusual provenance.

His loyalty was astonishing. Reynolds endured not only Bill Russell, but also every hardship suffered by the team during its first three decades in Sacramento. He was forever willing to take on whatever task the franchise demanded, from assistant coach to interim head coach, from talent scout to director of player personnel to broadcast color commentator and radio commercial voice talent. As for his humor, he favored a self-deprecating mockery that poked fun at his lack of sophistication and humble origins.

The humor served Reynolds well when he passed out from excitement while coaching a game against Portland. He was removed from the arena by ambulance and spent two days in a Sacramento hospital. "I didn't know I was lying around like a drunk," he said. "I didn't think I had a heart attack but I knew that wasn't the normal way to leave."

And there were his origins. Reynolds was from French Lick, Ind., home of Celtics legend Larry Bird. Reynolds and Bird were great friends, two basketball men who could make one another laugh by reminiscing about the lard sandwiches somebody's uncle created from stale goods left in a second cousin's pantry. Reynolds loved to study the history of basketball and was thrilled to work for Russell. The thrill was gone in a few weeks. Jerry Reynolds, like Willis Reed, had no idea how to live with the legend.

There was one person who knew Russell better than anyone, his personal assistant, Jim Hadnot, a 6-foot-10, 300-pound man who spent much of his life in the legend's shadow. Hadnot was six years younger than Russell, but their youthful paths were identical: gangly, uncertain teens reared in Oakland and educated at McClymonds High School. Russell was already a star in Boston when Hadnot finished high school. Of course, Big Jim was projected as the Next Big Bill Russell.

There was pressure on Hadnot to follow Russell to the University of San Francisco. Russell heard about the young man, took a liking to him and came up with another plan. He arranged for Hadnot to attend Providence College, near Boston, where Russell could act as mentor. The lessons helped, but Big Jim was not the Next Big Bill.

Big Jim was afflicted with mediocre speed, bad knees, inconsistent training habits, a love for people and laughter and a complete absence of killer instinct. Hadnot played one pro season with the Oakland Oaks, and retired to raise a family with income from various enterprises, including a nightclub and a liquor store. When Bill Russell arrived in Sacramento, 82 miles from Oakland, to coach the Kings, Big Jim was at his side within hours, pulling up to Arco Arena in a battered brown Mercedes.

Hadnot had various tasks, from working with the Kings' big men to scouting opponents. He would pick up sandwiches for Russell at Sam's Hof Brau downtown at 17th and J Street, ordering sliced roast beef, or turkey or pastrami and chilled salads and slaw and pickles from a wooden barrel. Russell loved the food but didn't like the commotion that followed when he walked through the swinging doors at Sam's. So he sent his friend Big Jim.

I often intercepted Hadnot on his food runs. Sam's had a long mahogany bar and ice cold beer, which we both liked. I tried to get Jim to explain Bill Russell while the pastrami aged in its paper sack. "Don't worry about it," Big Jim would say. "Russ is just different." Maybe there was no explanation, I decided. Maybe Russ was just different. When Big Jim Hadnot died in 1998 from lung cancer at age 58, we all lost a friend.

IT WAS ONE thing for Russell to confound assistant coaches and sportswriters. For a rookie accustomed to championship programs, the twilight zone existence of life with the Kings under Russell was disastrous. Kenny Smith, the point guard from North Carolina drafted over Kevin Johnson, essentially wasted the first third of his nine-year NBA career while stuck in Sacramento. Kevin Johnson made an immediate impact once he reached Phoenix, but Smith struggled to breathe in his early days as a pro. In this sense, Kevin was the lucky one on Draft Day 1987.

Kenny Smith never found his footing in a Kings uniform. He missed the start of his first training camp while his agent completed contract negotiations with Axelson. He tried to catch up and sat out 11 games with a broken finger. Those were trifles compared to the uncertainty Smith endured under Russell. One day Smith was a point guard. Next game, he ran the wing as a shooting guard. One day he was told to pass. The next day, he was told to shoot. Then he was criticized for poor shooting and bad decisions with his passes.

His biggest problem was the environment. "From high school to college, I've been in successful programs," Smith said. "But to tell the truth, this is the best team I've played on as far as talent and athletic ability are concerned. They just haven't showed it yet." Smith was traded to Atlanta halfway into his third season. He ultimately helped the Houston Rockets win two championships. After retirement, he built a successful sports broadcast career and pushed the Kings from his memory.

Ten years before he arrived in Sacramento, Bill Russell coached the Seattle SuperSonics. He was more engaged in those days, closer to the game, more active in practice and far more focused on discipline. He required players to run laps in practice, with the number of laps determined by the points the Sonics yielded in their last game. The punishment drills from the 1970s would not have played well in the NBA of 1987. Russell did not push old-fashioned discipline tactics onto his men in Sacramento.

He did talk about team-building exercises and his "horizontal game" philosophy. The horizontal game speech was Russell's way to distinguish him from the chattering classes, to make the players believe all the talk about pro basketball being played "above the rim" was nonsense shoveled by sportswriters and broadcasters and fans in sports bars.

Truly exceptional players saw the game horizontally, spread out before them, the Tao of Basketball, in harmonious, timeless patterns, not just bouncing vertically above the rim. A journey of a thousand victories begins with one long rebound.

Most Kings players did try to appreciate Russell. But each of them understood the basic truth about the NBA. It was a game for runners and jumpers, and not much else. For the players, the "horizontal game" was something to be played in hotel rooms after a meal, typically with women. By the 1980s, the teams that ran faster and jumped higher won games in the NBA. The Kings were not among those teams.

By the time he reached Sacramento, Bill Russell must have sensed that the gap between his generation, the 1950s basketball men who were chased out of gyms and denied hotel rooms and seats in restaurants because they were black, who would punch a point guard in the chest if he dribbled the ball between his legs (unless his name was Bob Cousy), and the modern players had grown too wide. There was no point in trying to fill the gap, vertically or horizontally.

TWO GAMES revealed the disconnection between Russell and his modern players, illustrating the separate worlds of the legendary coach and the Vagrant Kings. The first occurred on December 23, 1987, when the Kings played the Lakers in Inglewood. Russell refused to call timeout during a 17-1 rally by Los Angeles. Even by church league basketball standards, this was incredible.

Players looked at their coach in disbelief, convinced that his goal must be to humiliate them. The professionally indifferent referees watched Russell in bewilderment. "Sometimes, when you call time out, it helps the other team more than it helps your own," Russell mystically explained afterward. He seemed annoyed that anyone would dare ask about his timeout strategy. The Lakers won by 14 points. They needed no help from Sacramento timeouts.

The second disconnected game took place on January 15, 1988, at Boston, during the Kings' annual visit to the cathedral of Russell's glory, Boston Garden. Russell knew what would happen. The sports-crazed Boston reporters would flock around him and resurrect stories about his problems in Boston, about his attempt to move into a white neighborhood, his hatred for the racial politics and racist attitudes in Boston, his comments that he owed the public nothing, even about the little joke he made when he took the Sacramento job: "I'd rather be in jail in Sacramento than mayor of Boston."

Russell, who refused to attend the public ceremony when his No. 6 jersey was retired at Boston Garden, exchanged a few brief acknowledgements with the Boston media and politely refused to answer their questions. Boston sports fans were left to argue yet again whether Russell was a prophet, an iconoclast or a troublemaker.

The "What Is Bill Russell?" debate would not be resolved in Boston until 1999, when Russell attended a second No. 6 retirement celebration, this time at the city's new arena, the Fleet Center. He received a five-minute standing ovation the second time around, and ended the evening by telling the crowd, "I love you, too." All was finally, justly, forgiven at last. Jim Hadnot would have been proud of his mentor that night.

None of that happened in 1988, when Russell went to Boston with the Kings. After the Garden announcer introduced Russell, the crowd stood and cheered. A minute passed. Two minutes. The audience was on its feet, yelling and whistling, showing admiration and love for the greatest player to wear a Celtics uniform. Russell ignored the applause.

At last, Kings center LaSalle Thompson said, "Come on, coach." Shamed by a player half his age and with none of his stature, Russell finally looked up into the crowd and waved his left hand. The gesture was the highlight of the game, which was decided very quickly. The Celtics won 122-86. "It proves the Celtics are a very good team and we're a very bad one," Russell said. Ten weeks later, with the Kings' record 17-42, he was fired as coach and promoted to vice-president for basketball operations.

THE CHANGE in scenery, hours and responsibilities did not improve things. Russell lived at Rancho Murieta, a gated golf course community in rural southeastern Sacramento County. He spent many hours on the golf course. More juicy leaks made their way to reporters:

He missed trade opportunities because he didn't return phone calls. He allowed center Ralph Sampson to put himself on the injured list. He let Ralph hire a private coach. He gave center Purvis Ellison a two-week Christmas vacation when the rest of the team had to plod through a tough schedule. He received a phone call from his replacement coach, the faithful standby interim skipper Jerry Reynolds, who was preparing for a game in Texas that night against the Dallas Mavericks. Russell's first question: What are you doing in Texas, Jerry?

His greatest sin from the Kings' standpoint had nothing to do with the daily details of basketball operations. Russell was having a negative impact upon the balance sheet and box office. The Kings moved into their new building in 1988, with a relieved Commissioner Stern present for the ceremony, waving and smiling. The new arena was a basic structure but serviceable, a modern version of Rochester's Edgerton Park Arena, minus the youth prison history.

For the next year, the Kings continued to claim sell outs of 17,014 each game, but the numbers were fast becoming fictional. Hundreds of empty seats were visible in the upper deck for many games at Arco Arena. The Kings insisted the empty seats were sold. Not everybody used the tickets, the team explained. But the idea of hundreds of Sacramento consumers buying Kings' tickets and throwing them away was hard to believe. I knew Larry the Painter would never throw away tickets bought with his hard-earned dollars.

Finally, Axelson admitted the team held back about 150 tickets each game to sell to walk-up customers. He counted those tickets as sold, whether they were or not. The answer was classic Joe Axelson: Somewhat reasonable, highly convenient, completely beyond reach for verification. From that moment, I never trusted Kings attendance figures.

More likely, people in Sacramento were sending a message by not buying tickets. Why? Bill Russell was a good place to start. He was at least part of the explanation, along with the team's awful record. Russell had become the lightning rod for public frustration with the Kings, blamed because he took the city's favorite commodity out for a spin around the block and crashed.

In the 1960s, Russell's personality hurt attendance at Boston Garden. Now he was doing it again, without the poison of bigots in a racially charged city. Sacramento was not Boston. But Russell was still Russell. He had to go. Gregg Lukenbill told him to clear out his office on December 18, 1989. A public announcement would be made the next day.

When the news broke, Jerry Reynolds said, "I talked to Bill last night. He felt relieved by the whole thing." The legend went home to Rancho Murieta, turned on his television and barely stirred for two weeks. His favorite program was "Jeopardy!" and he had plenty of time to watch his game show.

Soon afterward, Bill Russell put his house on the golf course up for sale and drove back to Seattle.

Chapter Eleven: They Have To Learn To Pay Their Dues

Danny Ainge was on the phone, his voice urgent. "Can you come over to my room?" he asked. Now this was something different.

While I was friendly with most of the Kings' players, they didn't invite me to their hotel rooms on road trips. Fraternization was a reporter's friend, good for gossip and tips, but there were limits. It was healthy to maintain an objective distance, or at least the ability to claim one, if only to avoid the chore of having to write about something I wished I hadn't seen.

Ainge was the most thoughtful and strategic player on the Kings, a religious family man who didn't spend his free time in nightclubs or bars. He was brash and could joke in the locker room and invent sick nicknames for his teammates, but I didn't expect to smell marijuana or find cocaine packets and two strippers waiting when he opened the hotel door that afternoon in Phoenix.

Sure enough, there was only Danny. He had a proposition. "You see what's going on," he said. "There's no way I can stay here. You've got to help me get out."

Players on bad teams commonly tried to get themselves traded by making unadvised comments to reporters, criticizing the coach or style of play or ownership or even the fans, then halfheartedly apologizing as they waited for a deal to form. Ainge, who in 2008 would become president of the Boston Celtics, was too smart to blurt out insults and demand a trade in 1990.

He was already considered a prima donna among the Kings, reminding teammates of his two championship rings with the Celtics, sitting out practice because his knees ached and he was 31 years old and Robert Parish and Kevin McHale and Larry Bird didn't practice in Boston. So why should Ainge practice with the Kings? And why should he waste another day of his valuable but finite career in Sacramento?

He had a point. Danny Ainge didn't belong in a Kings uniform. He was exiled to Sacramento thanks to his advancing age and because the Celtics wanted Kings center Joe Kleine, whom they believed could clog the lanes beneath the basket with his immobile 300-pound frame.

Ainge arrived late in the 1989 season and tried to make the best of it, showing the younger players what a real champion looked and acted like. He arrived near the end of Bill Russell's tenure as vice-president for basketball operations. It was one of those days when Russell stayed away from the golf course, went to the office and answered his phone when the Celtics called. Too bad for Danny.

Ainge played hard and hustled for Dick Motta, the compact, cerebral coach with a perfectly sprayed 1970s Ken and Barbie hairstyle and a lengthy NBA track record running through Chicago, Washington and Dallas. Gregg Lukenbill hired Motta as an antidote to Bill Russell. Motta saw himself as a coach who coached coaches and shaped young talent. One of his students was Jerry Sloan of the Utah Jazz, who played for Motta in Chicago.

Motta never stopped talking about basketball. He had a remarkable ability to appear relaxed, almost serene, in moments of high tension. Motta knew when to call timeout and loved being credited with the phrase, "The opera isn't over until the fat lady sings," which entered the sports lexicon as a warning against premature celebrations. He enjoyed the fact that he stole the line from a Texas sportswriter, Dan Cook, who borrowed it from a Texas sports publicist, Ralph Carpenter, who heard it as a child while growing up in the South. Motta happily took the credit.

Ainge knew the whole routine with Motta was a waste of time. Danny knew the Kings could not win with (or without) the new coach and his Ken doll hair. And Danny suspected something worse: that the team was cursed, ordained to misery and chased by a dark, ominous shadow thrown down by the basketball gods. The Kings, Ainge believed, would destroy what was left of his playing career.

He had to get out. The image of Danny Ainge in a Kings uniform could make the fat lady scream.

NO NEWSPAPER stories appeared about Ainge demanding to be traded. But there were stories about his value to the Kings and, more important, the value he could bring to a real playoff contender. That was the kind of stuff he wanted me to write. I found the request reasonable, because I believed it was true. A sportswriter could make decisions like that, unilaterally.

The latitudes granted sports reporters were wide in comparison to other categories of journalistic scribblers. Sportswriters were special because we reported on events that tended not to matter much. The final score of a basketball game hardly qualified for discussion in the same pantheon as a gas main explosion or a tight mayoral election. And we were eyewitnesses to the stories we covered.

Crime and courthouse reporters weren't standing in the alley or jury room when the trigger was pulled or the verdict decided. Sports reporters sat there and watched and listened and wrote what we saw and heard, then usually went to a bar to argue about it, after our stories were filed with the sports desk.

Most sports teams realized that having journalists around was good for business. Sports reporters could be cynical and whiney, but we generally told laudatory, inspirational stories about courage and hard work. And we helped sell tickets. Only the most self-absorbed team executive would try to hinder the sports media, overreacting to the rare negative headline.

Sports journalists didn't like to admit it, but most of us were extensions of fans, wearing a mask of critical and objective observance while wrapping our self-images around the locker room access credentials and free parking placards.

By the early 2000s, teams and leagues would hire sportswriters and pay them to write for company websites, eliminating the middleman (the newspaper) while controlling the message. Reading the reports on team and league-owned websites was frequently similar to reading newspaper reports, proving the pliant nature of most sports journalism. Smart athletes knew sportswriters wanted to be liked by players, just like I wanted to be liked by Bill Russell and Danny Ainge. Sportswriters were like traffic cops. When dealing with us, attitude was everything.

Ainge was a smart athlete with a good attitude. He knew he could move toward his goal of escaping the Kings and securing a trade by working the sportswriters. He provided insight and candor, even a hint of friendship to the guys who covered the team. Ainge knew if he worked the relationships right, the stories would be positive and aligned with the desired outcome, which would arrive the moment Dick Motta walked up to Ainge before practice one morning and said, "OK, Danny, you've got your wish. We just traded you to Portland."

Danny worked me and pushed and goaded Motta, never to the point where they would openly clash, but enough to make the coach believe Ainge was more burden than benefit, a challenge to Motta's basketball vision, a royal pain. Ainge worked hard to force a trade without being too obvious. He called upon his gifts of manipulation, gifts that in future decades would exploit the weaknesses and pick the pockets of fellow NBA executives.

Pushing Motta could be tricky. When another player, Antoine Carr, asked me to print that he was seeking a trade, I rushed to Motta with the scoop, requesting a response. The coach laughed. "Tell him if he doesn't like it here he can quit basketball," Motta said. "There's no law that says he has to work here in the NBA. Tell him to go drive a bus or take some job where he doesn't get paid hundreds of thousands of dollars for working three or four hours a day eight months a year."

I told Carr precisely what Motta said. Carr did not get angry. He was perplexed. He wondered why his coach would discuss jobs that were irrelevant to someone who played in the NBA.

PLAYERS OFTEN misunderstood Motta. His first speech to the team featured a monologue about how the players would not be able to exploit his job security (or lack of it) and control him. Many NBA coaches believed they had to get along with key players to prevent the squad from organizing a mutiny against the coach and getting him fired. Coaches always knew it was easier to fire one man than trade three or four key players.

Motta told the players he didn't care if they conspired to get him fired. He had $1 million stashed in an Idaho bank for retirement and could happily leave tomorrow. The coach's message sailed past the players. "We felt sorry for Coach after he told us that," veteran forward Wayman Tisdale said. "He's been in the league forever but he's down to his last million."

Motta's legacy with the Kings was his squad's spectacular ability to lose games on the road. Stretched over the 1990 and 1991 seasons, the Kings lost 43 consecutive games away from home under Motta, an unprecedented feat that became a national joke. Fans around the country came to cheer the Kings (they were never a huge road attraction) as the team discovered new ways to lose.

Inevitably, the Kings were compared to the Washington Generals, the theatrically hapless straight men for the Harlem Globetrotters and losers of 2,495 consecutive games. The Generals broke their streak in Martin, Tenn., in 1971, when the Globetrotters lost track of the game clock, fooled around too much and ran out of time to catch up. Without being reduced to playing with confetti buckets, eye charts, umbrellas and weighted basketballs, the Kings finally ended their streak in Orlando on November 23, 1991, defeating the Magic 95-93.

After the victory, Motta stripped off his clothes and lathered up in the visiting locker room shower, alongside his players. The squad was relieved to win but found the coach's sudsy celebration somewhat bizarre. Maybe it was an Idaho thing, they suspected. Tisdale requisitioned the game ball. He stuffed the basketball into his travel bag after the victory. "This is going up in my trophy case," he said.

Tisdale would become his own sad story in 2009. He built a successful music career after retirement from basketball but died at age 44 from cancer. Part of his right leg was amputated nine months before his death.

A CURIOUS companion to the losing streak was Airball One, a private jet acquired by Gregg Lukenbill in 1990 to haul the Kings around the country. Private jets became an NBA accessory in the late 1980s, after the Detroit Pistons obtained a plane and flew onto the NBA championship. The Kings' Airball One was a 1960s vintage British Aerospace 1-11 twin-engine gas-guzzler retrofitted with off-white leather seats and gold-painted trim. Unlike the Pistons, the Kings were tormented by the convenience of private luxury travel.

They compiled a 1-40 road record during their first season aboard Airball One. Motta banned beer on the plane and threatened to make rookie Kings fly commercial airlines. "They have to learn to pay their dues, and this is spoiling them," he said. Lukenbill hoped to help pay for the $4 million jet by selling package deals of Kings road trips to fans. A few rich sponsors caught short hops to road games in Los Angeles, Phoenix, Portland and Seattle. The seats for paying customers went mostly unsold.

Motta was fired on Christmas Eve 1991, not quite two years after his inaugural speech about his $1 million retirement savings. It wasn't a player mutiny that sent him away. It wasn't his technical knowledge of the game or work ethic, all of which were excellent. And it certainly wasn't his perfect haircut. He was fired because he could not get his players to perform in a manner expected of a pro basketball team when they were away from home.

One Kings player who dodged the losing streak was Danny Ainge. Motta traded Danny to Portland in 1990 before the road losses began. The transaction proved how luck would favor the future president of the Boston Celtics.

In a reminder of the interconnected world that is professional sports, Ainge, who endured the lowest point of his playing career with a team formerly owned by Louie Jacobs, ended up going to work for the Celtics in a new Boston arena owned by Delaware North, the hugely successfully company started by Louie and his brothers in 1915.

Another coincidence: Between his trade to Portland and move into the front office at Boston, Ainge played for the Phoenix Suns, where he backed up Kevin Johnson in the 1993 NBA Finals against the Chicago Bulls. The NBA presents itself as a global octopus, but the league is really a small, cloistered Land of Oz. Everybody knows everybody, and everybody's brother-in-law.

One last connection to the Jacobs era in Cincinnati was Kings president Joe Axelson, who twice directed the relocation of the franchise, first from Cincinnati Gardens to Kansas City and Omaha, then westward to Sacramento and Arco Arena. Axelson made his final move, out the door, in the months after Russell was sent home to Seattle. Russell was the weight that finally sank Axelson, marking the first time in a 22-year NBA career that Axelson was unable to dodge responsibility for blunders that ruined the Royals and wrecked the Kings.

Axelson was led gently out to pasture, reduced in title and authority as punishment for his leadership in the decision to hire Russell. Axelson was given nominal control over team marketing and began to spend more time in Coronado, near San Diego, at his long-planned retirement home. Few people in Sacramento noticed when he finally declared himself out of the game for good. The Sacramento Bee ran a brief, six-paragraph story about Axelson's exit. The story was printed on page D4, back among the shotgun and tire ads, a place reserved for a guy nobody had ever heard of.

For all his bluster and sway and belief that he knew more about basketball than anyone west of the NBA Hall of Fame in Springfield, Mass., Axelson faded away quietly, leaving his baseline seat empty on the aisle. He died in 2008 at age 80, a sports executive who managed to consistently and unapologetically diminish the franchise's quality until there was almost nothing left to cheer about.

At the same time, he watched the team's financial value climb and its significance as an incubator of civic pride increase. That was a credit to his stewardship, it could be argued. Axelson didn't know a basketball from a pumpkin, as Oscar Robertson said, but he knew how to make pumpkin pie from basketballs.

Axelson represented himself as a marketing genius, and by the time he retired, the Kings were expertly practiced in the classic distraction routine that marketing pros embrace in crisis: change the subject. The Kings constantly changed the subject with trades and staff purges. They were particularly good at getting fans excited about rookies. They directed the public's attention toward a promising young player from a strong college program and implied, without exactly saying it, that the new kid could be the next Magic Johnson or Larry Bird.

I found it interesting that a young black player would never be tagged as the next Larry Bird or a white player identified as a future Magic Johnson, even if their playing styles were vaguely similar. By the 1990s, the NBA was justifiably proud of its racial harmony and color-blindness, but there were subtle reminders that race counted when teams communicated with fans. The first rule was: be racially consistent when making comparative predictions about rookies for marketing purposes, no matter how absurd.

NO ONE compared Ricky Berry to Magic Johnson, but Berry had potential. He was a 6-foot-8 forward who could run and pass. He had a gift for the game. The Kings were convinced they made an inspired choice when they drafted Berry in 1988. They even agreed to hire his father as an assistant coach and scout. The senior Berry coached his son at San Jose State University.

Ricky Berry's Northern California heritage was appreciated in Sacramento. He made quick friends and investments in his new community. He bought a $360,000 home on Keane Drive in suburban Carmichael with his young bride Valerie. They began to anticipate a successful life all the way into NBA retirement, when Ricky and Valerie would buy a car dealership and indulge Ricky's passion for automobiles. At least that was the plan.

Then something happened on the night of August 19, 1989, at the house on Keane Drive. Valerie and Ricky argued. Valerie packed an overnight bag and left to spend the night with friends. When she returned the next morning at 9:30, she found her husband lying dead in a pool of blood.

Hours earlier, Berry had pressed the barrel of a 9mm semiautomatic pistol against his right temple and pulled the trigger. He was 24. He bought the gun a year earlier for personal protection.

Among the friends who gathered on Keane Drive that morning was Kevin Johnson, by then a star with the Phoenix Suns. Johnson arrived on Keane Drive in his Porsche and sat in the car outside Berry's house. He sat and talked to friends and several times covered his face with his hands.

Like all of Berry's friends, Johnson was mystified by the suicide, which was never explained beyond some whispers of domestic discord. "I know his wife," Johnson said later. "She's a very nice lady, and if they had some marital problems or a spat, it wouldn't be anything that any other husband and wife had. From what I saw, there was nothing extreme. It was a just a good, normal marriage."

Jerry Reynolds, who would be pressed into duty whenever the Kings fired somebody in the front office, tried to read a statement to the media but broke down in tears. Kevin Johnson told a reporter, "If you look at his life, he had everything that you'd think would make someone happy. He made a lot of money, had a beautiful wife, had a nice car, a nice home, a very promising career ahead of him, he was drug-and-alcohol free and in the prime of his life at 24 years old. What could he want?"

There were many questions and no real answers. Eventually, Ricky Berry's suicide faded from memories in Sacramento. But the tragedy fortified the belief that there was something deeply wrong with the Kings, something that caused the franchise to suffer far more than its share of misfortune.

Chapter Twelve: Am I Going To Die?

Bobby Hurley, an acclaimed two-time NCAA champion guard from Duke University drafted in 1993, was two months into his NBA career when his universe shifted in a very bad way.

Leaving Arco Arena after a 112-102 loss to the Clippers on December 12, Hurley drove west on Del Paso Road, crossed the bridge over Interstate 5, and made a left turn at El Centro Road, a rural four-way intersection framed by farm fields and irrigation ditches. It was the route he followed home every day after games and practice sessions.

As Hurley began the left turn, he was rammed by a 1970 Buick station wagon driven by Daniel Wieland, a 37-year-old house painter who was traveling without lights on the black winter's night. Wieland, whose driver's license was expired, was going about 55 miles per hour. Bobby Hurley didn't see the other car until it was upon him.

Hurley's new Toyota SUV was pushed 125 feet. Driving without seatbelts, the basketball player was thrown 20 feet from his car. He landed in an irrigation ditch. Another motorist, Mike Batham, witnessed the collision, stopped and discovered Hurley lying in 18 inches of water. Batham pulled the 22-year-old from the water and prevented him from drowning. Kings teammate Mike Peplowski was soon at the scene, heading home behind Hurley. Peplowski carried Hurley from the ditch and gently draped a hunting jacket around his friend's shoulders to keep him warm. Hurley was in shock but awake. "Am I going to die?" he asked.

Hurley was alive but just barely. He had terrible injuries. Two collapsed lungs and the windpipe trachea severed from the left lung, broken back, five broken left ribs, shattered left shoulder, torn anterior cruciate ligament in right knee, broken right fibula, sprained left wrist, many lacerations. He was taken to the UC Davis Medical Center, the city's trauma hospital, in critical condition.

Word of the accident quickly spread. I was settling in at Paragary's bar on 28th Street when the call came. I rushed 14 blocks to the hospital lobby, where I spotted Dr. Richard Marder, the Kings' team physician. He beckoned me away from the other reporters. He opened a "no entry" door and soon we were in a hallway near the surgery.

Marder presented a positive prognosis. He said Hurley's three essential components, head, heart and spine, were not damaged, which was a miracle. Almost everything else was broken. The other driver, Wieland, was in much better shape. His leg was broken and he had minor injuries.

There was some luck that night. A renowned trauma physician, Dr. William Blaisdell, just happened to land at Sacramento airport from Washington minutes after the crash. Blaisdell picked up his messages, heard about the emergency, went to the hospital and coordinated Hurley's treatment. The right man was in the room.

As Marder explained all this, I began to think, insensitively, of Hurley's chances of playing pro basketball again. Readers will want to know, I said. Marder hesitated before answering, then said anything was possible but it was too soon to predict.

Being a sports orthopedics specialist, Marder understood the challenges Hurley would face. "Think of it this way," the doctor said. "Only a very small percentage of people are able to compete at the level required for an NBA player. And that very small percentage, they do not have these kinds of injuries. If he had a normal job, we might be able to say he could be 100 percent again, maybe. But he doesn't have a normal job. As an NBA player..." The doctor did not finish the sentence.

The question of legal responsibility required two criminal trials at the Sacramento County Courthouse, Department O. Michael Brady, attorney for Wieland, blamed Hurley, claiming the basketball player rolled the stop, his Toyota's door was defective, he wasn't wearing seat belts. For good measure, Brady said the police conspired with Hurley in a cover-up and destroyed evidence, purposely breaking the headlights, which would have proved Wieland's innocence.

The defense of Dan Wieland touched on everything but Dan Wieland, whose lights were on, Brady claimed, despite the testimony of three independent witnesses who swore they saw a blacked-out old station wagon moving fast northbound on El Centro near the Del Paso intersection a minute or so before the crash.

The first jury was deadlocked. The second jury walked back into the courtroom after 4 hours and 45 minutes of deliberation and said Daniel Wieland drove without headlights and recklessly crashed into Bobby Hurley, nearly killing him. Wieland was fined $300 and placed on three years informal probation. His license was suspended for six months, not for the crash, but for driving with an expired license. Hurley had no comment. The legal process never explained why the station wagon's lights were off.

A painful, courageous training regimen pulled Hurley back onto the Kings' roster for the next season. He played five years altogether, including two seasons where he logged more than 1,000 playing minutes. His production was modest, but considering his physical condition while lying in the irrigation ditch, the fact that Hurley resumed his NBA career at all was to my thinking an accomplishment equally as impressive as Bill Russell's 11 championship rings, only different.

Russell's accomplishments required luck, brains, talent, teamwork, fortitude and longevity. Hurley's return was something more eternal. Start with a miracle. Add top-level medical care and determination. And pray. After retirement, he bought racehorses. And he returned to basketball as head coach of the University of Buffalo in 2013.

A suicide and senseless car crash. A hopelessly inept team, setting records for road losses. The Vagrant Kings pin-wheeled into an existence of darkness. They thudded to earth in the early 1990s, falling faster and more decisively than at any time in their history. The tragic events that befell the team's youngest, most promising players were reflective of an era when big promises and half-truths from the past caught and devoured the Kings, destroying the basketball team's ability to drive land values, zoning entitlements and profit margins.

WRITING NEWSPAPER stories about the Kings during that period had its challenges. Conflict, tragedy and mistakes made by famous, rich and important people were always the mother's milk of daily journalism. I was gorged while covering the Kings.

There was always conflict to write about. The team made mistakes on a daily basis. The downside was that as the key messenger who described the Kings' problems to the community, I began to catch some of the community's frustration.

Readers called my editors and demanded I be fired for bad attitude. At one game, a man walked up behind me and dumped a box of popcorn over my head. I thought, at least it wasn't a Coke or beer. Players reacted negatively to some stories. After I wrote about the sorry state of Ralph Sampson's knees, pointing out that his lamed status wasn't his fault, Ralph stopped me in the locker room, all 7-foot-4 of him, and said he would beat me up in the parking lot at Arco Arena.

Wayman Tisdale intervened and gently pushed Sampson away. "Don't worry," Tisdale winked to me, "if he comes after you in the parking lot, even you can outrun him." It was an accurate, sad comment about us both.

I was not able to run away from another center, 6-foot-11 Olden Polynice, who attacked me one night in 1995 in the locker room after I wrote several columns suggesting he was a coward. I noted how Polynice got into fights with teammates, Coach Garry St. Jean, and players from opposing team. He never fought another center, but rather found smaller victims he could intimidate. Once, he was fined for swearing at an 11-year-old boy. I wrote in the newspaper that Polynice never seemed to pick on anyone his own size.

Eager to prove the point with a 5-foot-11, flabby sportswriter, Polynice called me into the shower area of the Kings' dressing room. He was nice enough at first, but escalated to shouts and profanity. He said he knew people who could hurt me. I told him we could discuss his complaints, but not in the showers with him threatening me. I turned to walk away. His left hand reached over my shoulder and he spun me around. I was now looking up at his right fist, which was cocked about a foot from my face. "It's assault and battery," I said.

Before Polynice could hit me, players Mitch Richmond, Duane Causwell and Walt Williams grabbed their teammate and rescued me from harm's way. My shirt was torn open and my chest was bloody, scratched by Polynice's fingernails. Geoff Petrie, the Kings vice-president for basketball, brought me to another room and asked what I had done to provoke his player.

Provoke? I asked Petrie. I'd been a sportswriter for many years and knew better than to pick fights with 6-foot-11 professional athletes. "OK," Petrie said. "I'll have him call you and apologize."

Polynice phoned me at home the next day and apologized. And he told the media I had baited him. At that point, an apology wasn't enough.

I called Rod Thorn, who was in charge of player discipline for the NBA. He knew about the incident, but considered it closed with the apology. I protested to both Petrie and Thorn, pointing out that if I were an NBA referee, Polynice would be fined and suspended without pay for the rest of the season. And if I were a woman sportswriter, Polynice would be in jail. "You're not a referee or a woman," Petrie said. Fair enough, but the disparity of consequence, from telephone apology to lengthy, expensive suspension to criminal prosecution, stuck with me.

My bosses at the newspaper told me to forget about it. I wasn't seriously hurt, and the paper didn't want trouble with the Kings. Determined to extract some sort of accountability, I spoke to an attorney friend, Eric Hintz, who advised me to file a police report.

Hintz doubted anything would happen. And he was right. But I had grounds for a civil suit based on the assault and battery and the terroristic threat, which Hintz considered most serious. We filed the suit several weeks later. Polynice settled for a small dollar amount. I calculated it was less than one day's pay for him. But at least it was something, modest accountability for a pro basketball player who seemed to live without consequences.

The Kings released Polynice from his contract in 1998 after he was arrested for hitting his girlfriend, Rachel Taylor. At Taylor's request, he was not prosecuted. She later married him.

IN SACRAMENTO, basketball was never just about basketball. When the Kings weren't dealing with tragic or stupid events involving players, the team's owners were dealing with economic problems. That was the consequence of buying an NBA team for secondary motives, of mixing basketball with the real estate game.

The blend of economics and free throws produced a toxic brew. Despite vast land holdings, the Lukenbill and Benvenuti partnership was unable to make payments on money the developers had borrowed to support the North Natomas infrastructure. Asset seizures and land auctions were the next steps.

The Black Monday stock market crash of October 19, 1987, triggered a recession that still slowed the economy in 1992. A thick frost formed over Lukenbill's plans to plow up the North Natomas fields for homes and office buildings. The City of Sacramento foreclosed on a 114-acre parcel south of Arco Arena when the sports developers missed payments of $381,968 for streets and sewers.

City Treasurer Tom Friery was pressed into duty as a repo man for Sacramento. Friery didn't enjoy foreclosing on the Sacramento Sports Association property, where one parcel included a tiny airport just south of Arco Arena considered historically significant by aviation people. The land was sold at auction to satisfy bondholders.

Lukenbill and Benvenuti, the business partners who bought the Kings to show Sacramento they meant business, were now in the business of defending themselves against business creditors. When they weren't dodging bill collectors, they were suing each other. Partner Bob Cook sued Lukenbill for fraud. Benvenuti sued Lukenbill for withholding profits from the Sacramento Sports Association. Kings-related lawsuits ricocheted off the walls at Sacramento County Superior Court like desperate three-point shots.

Work stopped on the baseball stadium next to Arco Arena after about $14 million went into the ground for engineering, architectural, site preparation and construction. The concrete pillars and half-built baseball dugouts were soon covered with dust and entangled by weeds. They became home to jackrabbits. Seafirst, the Seattle bank that became prime lending agent for the stadium and temporary arena, repossessed both properties, claiming the Sacramento Sports Association stopped making payments on $45 million worth of projects, with $33 million outstanding.

The bank took a severe haircut, accepting just $1.25 million for the stadium and surrounding 100 acres, and $3 million for the first, temporary arena on North Market, along with two nearby office buildings. The buyers were Sacramento real estate developers Marvin "Buzz" Oates, Fred Anderson and Bill Cummings. They talked about finishing the baseball stadium, but only if they could negotiate a partnership with the city. In this sense, they were 15 years ahead of their time.

The real estate men wanted public dollars to help build out the sports complex. They hoped to expand on a theme begun by Lukenbill when he tried to talk Al Davis into moving the Raiders to Sacramento.

The Al Davis story was either a heartbreaking near miss for Sacramento or a lucky break for the city, depending on your views about public financing for pro sports. At Lukenbill's urging, the city borrowed $40 million to cover the Raiders' potential relocation costs in 1989. But civic leaders in Sacramento had an escape route. They publicly promised to spend the bond dollars on libraries, sewer improvements, parks, community centers and the local animal shelter if Davis ultimately refused to move to Sacramento.

And of course Davis refused. He returned to Oakland after giving up his new stadium dreams in Los Angeles. The Raiders' owner, who embraced the tough guy image with greased-back hair and silk jackets and silver-rimmed glasses, was afraid of the shaky partnership between Lukenbill and Benvenuti. Al was afraid that the volatile Sacramento situation would devour the Raiders.

Sacramento was too risky, Davis believed. So the city's $40 million in bond dollars flowed into the community projects. Lukenbill switched the stadium's design from football back to baseball. He vowed to build a Major League ballpark on spec. He ran out of money in 1991, with his stadium about 20 percent finished. In 2013, it was still sitting there, about 20 percent finished, next to the tired old arena.

Some residents cheered Lukenbill's failure. They claimed libraries and animal shelters were a better use of public funds than football or baseball. City Treasurer Tom Friery had another opinion. He wanted the Raiders in Sacramento. "I sincerely and honestly feel bad that that transaction did not come through," he said. "It was the kind of shot in the arm this community needed. It was a great disappointment."

The fractured dealings with the Raiders created mistrust about public-private partnerships for sports in Sacramento. Many residents figured Davis played the city against Los Angeles and Oakland. After Al Davis, there would be no public money for Oates, Anderson and Cummings to finish the stadium at Arco Park. The trio gave up and finally donated the unfinished baseball stadium and 100 acres to the city in 1995. The land would sit untouched for the next two decades.

But even in abandonment, the stadium and land still had value. The real estate that served as the core of Lukenbill's dreamy sports complex would eventually become an equity sweetener in the downtown arena plans pushed by Mayor Kevin Johnson and the city of Sacramento in 2012 and 2013. Decades passed. Investors died. Dreams faded. The land endured.

THE FINANCIAL turmoil of the early 1990s brought ownership changes to the Kings. In came Jim Thomas, a successful Los Angeles developer with rich friends. Out went Lukenbill as the Kings' managing general partner. Hungry for cash, under attack in multiple lawsuits, weary after a decade of fighting, battered by the economy and the dramatics created by Joe Axelson, Bill Russell and Dick Motta and personal mistakes and recklessness, the young, chain-smoking visionary cut his equity holdings in the Kings to 5.25 percent. Within months, Lukenbill owned zero stock in the team that was made possible by his vision, the Sacramento Kings.

He cashed out to a San Francisco Bay Area property developer named John Kehriotis in October 1994, and was promptly sued by Benvenuti, who demanded the proceeds. One day among many spent at the Sacramento County Courthouse, Lukenbill mused about his old partner, the man whose tolerance for risk and easy access to money allowed the $10.5 million purchase of the Kings when the vagrant team was going nowhere in Kansas City.

"You know, we never really got along," Gregg Lukenbill said of Joe Benvenuti. "We tolerated each other."

Chapter Thirteen: No Reason To Doubt Their Sincerity

Jim Thomas bought the Kings because he liked basketball. It was that simple. There was irony in that fact, but it was lost on the community when Sacramento welcomed its new Kings owner after the transfer papers were signed in April 1992.

Nobody ever bought the Kings just because they liked basketball, not since Les Harrison created the club from the taproot of his Rochester Pros in 1945. Les Harrison loved basketball, same as Oscar Robertson and Kevin Johnson loved it. Subsequent Royals and Kings owners dabbled in the game for side benefits, not love.

The Kings were traded and transferred for many reasons over the decades, including real estate leverage, a splash of ego and peanut sales. A perennial motive was convenience. The team was usually available for a relatively low price. And the franchise was portable.

Before Sacramento, the Kings did business in cities ambivalent about pro basketball. There was always a fast route out of town when the time came to move. Now they had a strange new species, an owner with eyes as bright as a child's on Christmas morning, a guy who wanted nothing more than to lean over the brass rail of his luxury suite at Arco Arena and scream, "Deeeeeeeefense!"

There was not much else to Jim Thomas, no hidden agenda, ulterior motive or strategy to alter the planning and zoning priorities of the city and promote his real estate interests. Of course, Jim Thomas wanted to sell peanuts. He owned Arco Arena and its concession operations. But peanuts were not why he bought the team. He bought the Kings because he loved basketball.

It would be Sacramento's fate that Thomas, compared to the other men who had run the Kings, was the first proprietor who possessed the true legitimacy to leverage the franchise for economic development purposes, to be an owner who created smart new real estate developments and rehabilitated old neighborhoods and built office towers. Those were the investments Sacramento could have used.

Thomas and his partner, Rob Maguire, ran one of the largest commercial property development companies in the U.S., with holdings valued at $7 billion in Southern California, Dallas and Philadelphia. Maguire Thomas Partners was among the early believers in the revival of downtown Los Angeles. They built four high-rise towers in downtown L.A., including the 73-story Library Tower, when the blocks around L.A. City Hall were unsafe to walk after dark.

Being real estate men, Thomas and Maguire paid tribute to the potential of the Sacramento market when they bought the Kings. They adopted Gregg Lukenbill's chant about a sports stadium and entertainment district in North Natomas. They marveled at the walkability of the downtown grid. They noted the city's intoxicating proximity to San Francisco. "We'd be interested in having involvement downtown," Maguire said.

They said those things, but the real motive was fun: Jim's fun. Maguire indulged his partner, as did colleagues Ned Fox, Richard Gilchrist and even Eli Broad, who had long been active in suburban Sacramento real estate. They posed for pictures at the arena, visited players after games, shelled out money for scoreboard upgrades and new dressing quarters.

They enjoyed the celebrity of big league sports ownership, for a while at least, and were comfortable with the knowledge that they had paid relatively little: $20 million in cash and the assumption of $60 million in debt-service obligations, for 53 percent of a franchise and arena valued at $145 million.

The investment seemed sound. And it was enjoyable. The new group's controlling interest pieces were collected from Lukenbill, who reduced his Kings stock from 28 percent to 4 percent before liquidating in 1994, and Benvenuti, who shrank from 48 percent ownership to 24 percent. The final 5 percent came from taking out an original minority partner, Steve Cippa.

This being the Kings, there were problems. Minority partners argued over how many of their shares should be included in the Thomas deal. Bob Cook filed a lawsuit to stop the sale. The biggest problem from a public relations standpoint was a rumor that Thomas planned to move the

Kings to Anaheim. The new owners issued multiple denials and pointed out, logically, that Maguire and Thomas also bought Arco Arena and the parking lots surrounding it, fixed assets that would be worth far fewer dollars if the Kings relocated to Orange County.

The Anaheim rumor was a rude Sacramento greeting for Thomas, whose reputation for playing his cards on the table, face up, was solid. The partners met with Mayor Rudin and convinced her of their honorable intentions. "They have verbally given us assurance they will keep the Kings here no less than seven years," Rudin said. "The new owners seem like very straightforward people and I have no reason to doubt their sincerity." Seven years would prove a stretch, as Thomas demonstrated five years later when he asked the city for $73 million or else.

THOMAS EARNED his NBA indulgence. In the tradition of Les Harrison, Thomas was a solid high school basketball player. He stood just 5-foot-11, but swore he could dunk the ball as a teenager and was the best free-throw shooter in the city of Cleveland. He was 55 years old when he bought the Kings, but enjoyed ownership so much that he would fly up from Los Angeles for home games, often accompanied by his wife Sally, who was her husband's match in passion for basketball. (They flew commercial, not private, Sally reminded me on several occasions.)

They could have been a quintessential Sacramento couple, plainspoken and almost boring, no flashy haircuts, clothes or jewelry, flying commercial, and crazy about their Kings, if not for their star-studded Bel Air address and weekend place on the private 17-Mile Drive in Pebble Beach. They owned Bing Crosby's old house at Pebble.

In many ways, Thomas was the perfect owner for the Kings. He appreciated and understood basketball, had money to fuel his interest and wasn't counting on the team to launch other investments. The positive energy rubbed off. The Kings began to improve under Thomas. They enjoyed consecutive wins of 58 and 56 points over Dallas and Philadelphia, victories that the Kings' beloved broadcaster, Gary Gerould, would describe as among his best memories in three decades.

The Kings won 39 games in 1993-94, hardly an awesome number in an 82-game season, but the team's best season since the Kansas City days. They had a true star on the roster, still in his prime, Mitch Richmond, acquired months before Thomas took over. They reached the playoffs in 1996, their first postseason appearance in 10 years.

But it wasn't enough. Thomas was victimized by the economics of the game and the realization that a mediocre NBA team was a money pit, far worse than a yacht, a deep, dark hole into which suitcases stuffed with cash were thrown around the clock and never seen again, until the team was sold. Fun and indulgence were acceptable for a while. But Thomas was a businessman. And the businessman was losing $5 million per year on the Kings.

Thomas could not abide a subsidiary whose balance sheet was habitually rocky, if not fundamentally unhinged. His Southern California partners learned the lesson and began to divest themselves of the Kings rather than answer Thomas's cash calls. Humiliatingly for a man who owned Bing Crosby's house, Thomas went begging before the Sacramento City Council in 1997, seeking the $73 million loan to maintain operations.

He got the money, thanks to the city council, Treasurer Tom Friery and City Attorney Sam Jackson, but the thrill was gone. Everything Thomas did was publicly mocked. It became impossible for him to attend Kings games for fun. He went looking for new partners in 1998, like Les Harrison in 1957, hoping to find somebody who wanted to buy a basketball team. Harrison met his match in Cincinnati. Thomas found his marks in a place Louie Jacobs would have appreciated: Las Vegas.

The Maloof family members were Las Vegas originals, but not the Las Vegas most people think about. They came from Las Vegas, New Mexico, where a Lebanese immigrant named George Maloof arrived in 1892 and opened a general store. Old George had a talent for numbers and an appreciation for hard work and money. He started a trucking business based on the delivery of dry goods. In 1937, he expanded to the delivery of wet goods: wine, spirits and a negligible Colorado beer called Coors.

His son, who would be called George Sr. after his father's death in 1944, expanded the family holdings. George built on the old man's principle of always being available when a neighbor needed something. Often, what the neighbor needed was another keg or case of Coors, frequently at hours not convenient to traditional business practices.

The Maloof family is famous for stories about George Sr. loading beer kegs and bottles onto his truck at 1 a.m. to make emergency deliveries. The family's primary business, George Sr. knew from his father, wasn't beer but service.

He hammered that lesson into his four sons, Gavin, Joe, George Jr. and Phil, and daughter Adrienne. The boys would boast about their beer warehouse blisters, about their simple, down home New Mexico ways, about the fundamental rules of the Maloof family: give people what they want, make them happy and get rich. "We don't try to outsmart anyone. We're service people," Joe said, memorably.

Two things people wanted were a place to stash their money and a place to blow it, so the Maloofs progressed to banking and gambling. The banking opportunity came when George Sr. was invited to become chairman of a New Mexico bank that was slipping toward insolvency. He was honored by the opportunity, but his wife Colleen had a better idea: just buy the darned bank. He did, and when the bank was sold 17 years later, in 1993, the stock was worth $140 million.

The family reinvested its windfall in small casinos in Central City, Colorado, and North Las Vegas, Nevada. The Nevada investment would prove most fortunate. They built a modest, locals-only style casino and hotel called the Fiesta, which would become one of the most profitable casinos in Vegas, measured by square footage. Maintaining their probity, they acquired stock in another bank, Wells Fargo, when the New Mexico bank, First National of Albuquerque, was taken over in mergers.

THERE WAS ONE more base to cover: sports, the perfect extension of the Maloof universe. Sports were a place to sell beer and provide entertainment and promote an ambitious new casino and hotel the family was planning, a $265 million hipster haven with 470 rooms called Palms, west of the Strip. Palms would have spectacular nightclubs, cool shows and hot tubs. It would be a sinner's paradise for the outrageous swagger set that didn't want what happened in Vegas to stay in Vegas.

The Maloof brothers, all bachelors, were born with perpetual grins and close-set eyes that seemed to squint with the constant uncertainty of college freshmen. Earning an independent living was not among their skill sets, but they were gamblers. They lived large and were ready to make their mark on the real Vegas, not the New Mexico namesake. The family sold the Fiesta for $185 million and set to work on Palms.

This was far more ambitious than a West Coast variation of Louie Jacobs' strategy in Cincinnati, where Jacobs bought the Royals to sell peanuts and fill dates on the arena calendar and slipped money to Moe

Dalitz for Vegas hotels and casinos. The Maloofs were service people and basketball people, with a haunted NBA pedigree.

George Sr. enjoyed basketball. He bought the Houston Rockets in 1979 for $9 million, but did not live to enjoy the team's success. Barely two years after George Sr. took control of the Rockets, the patriarch was dead from a heart attack at age 57, leaving son Gavin to run the franchise at the tender age of 24. When the Kansas City Kings were knocked out of the conference finals in 1981, the victor was the Houston club owned by the Maloofs.

Family warfare followed George Sr.'s death, led by his two sisters, Mary Jean Koury and Helen Sei. The sisters demanded liquidation of various chunks of the empire, including the Rockets. The women claimed George Sr.'s surviving issues were not competent to run a complex operation. They were eventually silenced with cash. Their argument would prove to have merit.

The Rockets were sold in 1982. The loss of the NBA team became an obsessive regret among the Maloof children, described by Gavin and Joe as the worst decision the family ever made. Gavin and Joe desperately wanted back into sports. They spoke to the NBA and NHL about available franchises. They almost bought an NHL team, the Tampa Bay Lightning. They invested in second-tier pro football.

It was during this period that Gavin and Joe became accustomed to receiving mentoring telephone calls from NBA Commissioner David Stern, who was originally charmed by the Maloofs when the family owned the Rockets and Stern was legal counsel for the NBA. Stern was trying to navigate the family's return to the league, but he frequently had to pull Gavin and Joe away from a casino card game or craps tables for a conversation.

Gambling was a conflict of interest that did not please the commissioner. Years later, Stern would still refer to Gavin and Joe (and sometimes George and Phil, all collectively) as "The Boys." He would yell and swear like a frustrated father exhausted by his habitually delinquent sons.

Stern would watch The Boys lurch through life for almost four decades. He grew old and wise and gray while The Boys lounged in place, perennial fraternity brothers on double-secret probation. When The Boys ignored Stern's admonitions to embrace Mayor Kevin Johnson's arena plan 2012, an action that crushed Johnson and turned him into a mayor without a portfolio, Stern filled the air with swear words and told Johnson there was nothing else to be done with the family. The intransigence of The Boys was ancient news to the commissioner.

In a sense, Stern had only himself to blame. He knew Jim Thomas was ready to exit the NBA in early 1998, and knew the rough-edged but charming Maloof family wanted back in the game. With a matchmaker's touch, the commissioner helped guide The Boys into position to buy 24 percent of the Kings for $37.5 million. Controlling interest of 53 percent would follow within a year. With partner Bob Hernreich, they eventually controlled 65 percent.

With control came the obligation of paying the $73 million loan from the city of Sacramento. "The transaction follows the team," Treasurer Tom Friery said. "The new owners are responsible for it. And if they try to move the team, the loan must be paid off immediately." The loan was a minor detail to The Boys. They were in the game again. That's what really mattered.

Suddenly, the Maloofs had everything. The beer, wine and spirits distributorship was a cash machine. Tower cranes lifted iron for a hip new Vegas casino. There was an NBA team to promote an aura of cool. Palms opened two months after September 11, 2001, which, as luck would have it, would be an unlucky time to open a hotel and casino in Las Vegas.

The family pressed ahead, focused on the long play. George Jr. ran the show in Vegas. Gavin and Joe concentrated on the Kings. The Boys positioned Palms as a reflection of their fantasies. And fantasies could not be interrupted.

Chapter Fourteen: People In Sacramento Have A Sense Of Humor

There was a strategy of synergy. Palms ads sprouted where NBA fans would see them. The casino was cast as the place to visit if you wanted to watch NBA players unwind. George Maloof Jr. arranged for the hotel to become a staging area for rap music productions, skateboard events and the MTV reality show "The Real World." Palms hot tubs became sets for soft-core orgies captured by the MTV cameras.

And so the fantasy unfolded, with drunken laughter and too much mascara. The Maloofs made space for a Playboy Club, a cobwebbed relic that was attempting a comeback from its 1960s heyday. "We've resurrected the brand for the 21st Century," George Jr. said, his dream firmly stuck in an earlier century.

Full of big hair, spiked heels and parties hosted by Kim Kardashian and her friends, Palms found a trashy niche in Las Vegas, but never presented a serious challenge to the mega hotels on the Strip. Apart from a few novelty suites, Palms was more Holiday Inn than Caesars Palace. Midweek $69 packages were easy to find at the Maloof fantasy island.

The Boys weren't interested in bargains themselves. They could blow thousands of dollars in marathon poker sessions and crap games. They were determined to enjoy life, knowing that their father dropped dead from heart attack at age 57. They existed outrageously and generously, bouncing among Vegas and Sacramento and hideaway lairs in Los Angeles. Everyone was welcomed at the party, which never ended.

After a Kings game one night at Arco Arena, Joe Maloof was desperate for a cigarette. He went outside the employee entrance where staffers enjoyed their smoke breaks. He asked janitor Patricia Villegas for a cigarette, which she supplied. He made her accept a $100 bill in thanks. Every janitor at the arena began to carry cigarettes, just in case.

Like her brothers, the lone daughter in the family, Adrienne, was willing to share her large lifestyle and personal travails with the world. She appeared in a reality TV show, "Real Housewives of Beverly Hills." One storyline featured Adrienne navigating reality after a divorce from Los Angeles plastic surgeon Dr. Paul Nassif. She found new romance with Sean Stewart, whose claim to fame was an apparent genetic link to his father, rock music legend Rod Stewart.

While the family lived out its fantasy, Palms devoured Maloof money at an astonishing rate, even by Las Vegas standards. The nation's worst financial calamity since the Great Depression was underway, but the family was stubborn, still holding its dreamy course despite the economic meltdown.

Vegas was on its back economically, among the hardest hit cities in the U.S. And the Maloofs doubled down on the recession. They borrowed to finance a condominium tower. Never mind that nobody was buying condos. The value of Palms collapsed from $386 million to an estimated $20 million. The math was not sustainable. A decade after its debut, Palms and its hot tubs had new, no-nonsense owners, TPG Capital and Leonard Green and Partners, who gained 98 percent control of the property by taking $400 million in debt the Maloofs were not able to service.

The family was left with 2 percent of its fantasy. TPG was part of Caesars Entertainment, the world's largest gambling company. From its vantage point on the Strip, TPG anticipated the Maloof implosion and stood ready to sweep up the pieces. The Maloof's empire came apart.

Before it lost Palms, the family sold its legacy business, the beer distributorship begun by Grandfather George in 1937. Colleen and Joe unloaded mansions in Los Angeles. Joe Maloof tried to make liquidation seem strategic. "We want to concentrate on our other businesses in Sacramento, L.A. and Las Vegas," he said.

More indignities made headlines. George Jr. was arrested near Spanish Trail Country Club in Las Vegas for drunk driving, texting while driving and driving with an expired license. The fact that a local casino operator could be taken into custody for vehicle misdemeanors in Las Vegas, rather than receive an escort home (or to the Playboy Club), underscored not just the professionalism of Clark County law enforcement, but the Maloof's tattered status in their adopted home town.

Another blow came in 2012, when TPG confirmed it would remove a marquee on the road outside Palms that read, "A Maloof Family Resort." Joe Magliarditi, the TPG president of Palms, explained, "That's only because we're trying to change the brand and brand image of the property." The Maloof brand was next to worthless in Las Vegas, making prophets of Mary Jean Koury and Helen Sei, the elder Maloof sisters who feared the children would ruin everything.

A FINAL public piece of the empire stood apart and seemingly immune from the financial cataclysm, the Sacramento Kings. The Boys insisted they would never sell the team, which they saw as the spirit of their father.

The Kings had been the source of the family's proudest hour, the near victory over the Lakers in the 2002 Western Conference finals. That team featured players and staff set in motion by Jim Thomas and led by Chris Webber, who was traded for Mitch Richmond. Two other key players, center Vlade Divac and forward Peja Stojakovic, joined the Kings with Webber, and the group progressed under an experienced winning coach, Rick Adelman.

The Boys stood back and let the basketball guys, Adelman and his boss, vice-president for basketball Geoff Petrie, run the team. The Kings became NBA darlings, a club with flair and personality and a winning record. The Kings would never be a dynasty, but in 2002 they finally proved it was possible to build a solid, competitive team in Sacramento.

The NBA is a place where success can happen quickly with the addition of one or two players. They must be the right players and the circumstances must be serendipitous, with the ideal coach and supporting cast. With just five players on the floor and 12 on the roster, it doesn't take years to spin the silk of success.

Even snake-bitten teams like the Kings have their moments. The allure of breakthrough, sensing that a team is this close to a championship run, is the NBA's sweetest elixir, the bright hope that keeps fans coming back in two dozen cities every season.

The 2001-2002 season was that moment for the Kings and their fans. Credit was owed to Petrie, who joined the Kings after resigning as vice-president of the Portland Trail Blazers in 1994. His first management move in Sacramento was to hire his friend Rick Adelman. Like Petrie, Adelman was an original member of the Trail Blazers in 1970. As vice-president and coach of the Trail Blazers, Petrie and Adelman engineered two appearances in the NBA Finals, losing both.

Rick was a poetic choice to become Sacramento's eighth coach in 13 years. He ended his playing career with the Kings at Kansas City-Omaha in 1975.

He was difficult to categorize. Adelman could be tough and disciplined. He could be nice. He was a student of the game. He was a player's coach. He focused on defense. He ignored defense. In fairness, Adelman was all those things, with two main characteristics: he treated people with consistency, and knew how to build a squad around its parts, making the most from the available talent. "I like what's here," he said when he arrived at Sacramento. "I think there's room to grow."

Success soon arrived, with the team reaching the playoffs but losing to the Utah Jazz while Adelman settled into the job. The Kings continued to grow, winning 44 games the next season, their best performance since 1973 in Kansas City-Omaha. They were coming together. Webber and Divac were forces around the basket. In the backcourt, Jason Williams and Stojakovic brought quickness and outside shooting.

There was one incontrovertible bit of proof that the Kings were getting better. The Los Angeles Lakers began to insult Sacramento. For years, the Lakers barely took notice of the Kings. They brushed Sacramento aside. But something changed in the 2000 playoffs. The Lakers beat the Kings in the first round, but had to work at it. Los Angeles needed five games to win three.

The highlight came after two victories by the Kings at North Natomas. Lakers Coach Phil Jackson described the Sacramento audience by saying, "You're talking about semi-civilized Sacramentans. Those people up there may be rednecks in some form or fashion." In context, he was favorably comparing the Northern California fans to wild crowds he had seen in Puerto Rico, but the nuance was missed. Next, Lakers center Shaquille O'Neal said, "I'm not worried about the Sacramento Queens." The Kings had arrived.

By 2001, Doug Christie established a defensive presence in the backcourt to supplement Williams and Stojakovic. Now the Kings had a top-tier rotation. They finished with 55 wins and reached the second round of playoffs, but were sent home in four straight games by Lakers. It was a team Les Harrison would have enjoyed, reliant on guards, tough, fun to watch.

The Kings were effective from long range and around the basket. Mike Bibby replaced Williams, bringing more backcourt defense, and the Kings won 61 games in 2001-2002, a franchise record that included 25 road victories. (Adelman did not shower with the squad after those wins as Dick Motta might have.)

Bibby made the difference. No nonsense, serene and forever working, he pushed the Kings past Utah and Dallas in the playoffs. And he was steady as the Kings built a 3-2 game lead over the Lakers in the Western Conference Championship.

In the pivotal and controversial Game 6 at Staples Center in Los Angeles, Bibby personified the outcome for the Kings. Blood and tears spread across his face late in the game after he caught an elbow in the nose from Kobe Bryant. No foul was called. Bibby missed a shot that would have tied it. The Lakers won 106-102 and ended the series two days later with a 112-106 overtime victory in Sacramento.

Next season, Chris Webber fell and tore the meniscus in his left knee. Micro-fracture surgery was declared a success, but Webber's stretch as one of the best running and jumping big men in the NBA was finished. So were the Kings, who suddenly couldn't advance past the second round of playoffs.

Adelman was fired in 2006. The Maloofs decided the Kings' defense wasn't adequately prepared. "That was the Titanic," Gavin Maloof said about Webber's injury. "We never recovered. We went down with him. We didn't want to face the fact that maybe we should start over."

OPPORTUNITY had come and gone. As Sacramento's attentions were focused on the Kings in 2002, the Maloof family should have been making moves to replace Arco Arena, which was deep into middle age more than a decade after its debut.

NBA owners can have fleeting love affairs with their arenas, especially when a rival NBA owner opens a new building. Arena envy and trophy buildings are communicable diseases in the NBA.

The have-nots quickly calculate the financial advantages brought by new suites and more club-level seats and sponsorship opportunities missed by teams with older facilities. Arco Arena was on borrowed time the day it opened, with every aspect of its budget, from framing nails to caulk, squeezed by Joe Benvenuti. By 2002, the building was ready for retirement planning. A replacement strategy should have been a priority. It wasn't.

The psychic boost provided by a hugely successful season did not automatically create a political environment friendly to a new arena. Elected officials in Sacramento and the surrounding counties affirmed their love for the Kings in 2002, but nobody called a press conference to demand the construction of a new arena with tax dollars. For that to happen, Sacramento would have needed secure, respected leaders who were able to devise a long-range plan with a high tolerance for risk. And those leaders would have needed a competent, professional team ownership willing to share the burden.

Sacramento had neither. The local politicians had not forgotten Al Davis and the aborted public-private partnership with the Raiders. "This isn't the kind of project that you can shove down anybody's throat," Sacramento County Supervisor Roger Dickinson said. "You can't come in the back door, you can't sneak in under cover of darkness. You have to be very upfront with the public and say, 'Are you interested?'"

Dickenson wanted a new tax-supported arena but recognized a fundamental problem. The public didn't want to pay for it. Kings fans enjoyed their Arco Arena experience. They loved stamping their feet on the wooden steps, which had been hauled over from the temporary arena on North Market. The acoustics were awful at Arco Arena, but people appreciated the sight lines and easy access to restrooms, parking lots and freeways.

They had nothing else to compare against. Sacramento was a one-horse town for major league sports. The only people who understood that Arco Arena was a slender bargain at $40 million were people who visited other NBA arenas built at twice the price. Sacramento had few such people. In the 1990s, 16 NBA teams built new arenas. In Sacramento, nobody noticed or cared.

The $40 million spent by Lukenbill and Benvenuti on Arco Arena was by far the lowest price of the three NBA buildings christened in 1988. That year, The Palace of Auburn Hills opened as a rare $70 million monument to private development. Bradley Center in Milwaukee debuted as a celebration of Wisconsin opulence with a $90 million price tag. In Sacramento, fans were left with unfinished drywall and broken ceiling tiles that resulted from tight budget limitations and no direct public subsidies.

A few days before Arco's grand opening in 1988, the owners treated me to a tour. Lukenbill pointed out locations where marble would be installed. "No, it's finished," Benvenuti interrupted. Lukenbill persisted. Benvenuti kept saying, "No, it's finished." And it was finished. There would be no marble.

One rainy night the roof leaked. Play was suspended while Lukenbill climbed onto the steel rafters 80 feet above the floor and positioned the Sacramento Sports Association banner to catch the water. When the Maloof family first toured the building in 1998, George Jr. expressed concern about the cramped, outdated kitchen and inadequate bar facilities. He recommended against buying the arena, but was outvoted by his brothers, sister and mother.

The Maloofs never produced a coherent replacement strategy for the North Natomas arena. They had annual opportunities, but let them pass. Or worse, they wrecked them, including a 2004 proposal to build an arena at the Downtown Plaza.

The Sacramento Metropolitan Chamber of Commerce issued a report concluding Arco Arena was outdated and should be replaced within five years. The city council voted to explore a March 2005 ballot measure for a $350 million arena downtown. Local business leaders rallied under the Chamber of Commerce flag and suggested the downtown mall as the site. Rather than steer the city council to a prospective partnership, Joe Maloof pushed hard on the breaks. "We're not in favor of this. We were never consulted," he said.

If there was a reason why the Maloofs tried to undermine every arena idea, it was never explained to the public or city officials. I hoped to unwrap the riddle and talked to various Kings limited partners, team sponsors, politicians, bureaucrats and The Boys themselves. I came away with nothing but theories and deflections. Clearly, The Boys were not sold on the financial models of downtown arenas, which were very much in fashion in the NBA.

The Maloofs feared the loss of parking dollars and encroachment on their concession profits by nearby restaurants. And they thought NBA teams should pay nothing for arenas beyond a minimal rent. A limited partner told me the Maloofs felt they could not field a competitive team if they were shoveling equity dollars into an arena. And after the economic collapse of Palms, the question of direct cash participation by the Maloofs became moot. By then, they didn't have the money.

Heather Fargo, the former North Natomas neighborhood activist who opposed the original arena because she believed it would cause flooding, was an arena advocate by 2000. She ran for mayor of Sacramento and won. A replacement facility for Arco Arena was prominent on her agenda.

Fargo liked the downtown rail yards location, 240 acres made available when the historic locomotive repair shops closed in 1999. One of her chief advisers was involved in the rail yards' development. "It is about more than an arena," she said, inventing a phrase Kevin Johnson would borrow as his trademark a decade later. "I want people to focus on the magnitude of this part of the city." Fargo sought a November 2002 arena vote, with the city using redevelopment funds to supplement an equity investment by the Maloofs. The plan went nowhere.

A year later, Fargo tried to broker another arena deal with the Maloofs and the private developers who controlled the rail yards. The plan would include surcharges on food and drinks sold near the facility. The discussions became public when The Boys accused City Manager Bob Thomas and the rail yards developer of conspiring against the family. "They lied to us. We will never do business with them. We're going to walk away," Joe Maloof said.

Fargo sought a diplomatic resolution, but finally pointed out the obvious. "I don't think they have done a very good job of explaining why they would even want a new arena," she said.

A group of Natomas property owners, led by prominent local developer Angelo Tsakopoulos, revived the Lukenbill game plan and proposed financing a new arena with profits generated by rezoned farmland. The idea died when several property owners refused to participate.

THE DOWNTOWN rail yards were a bewitching site, the largest urban infill opportunity in the United States. They were the place where the Transcontinental Railroad's western-approach equipment was built.

The site, near the confluence of the Sacramento and American rivers, was a swamp and small lake when the California Gold Rush began in 1849. It was useless for agriculture and too unstable for homes and storefronts, even by the minimal standards of young Sacramento.

When engineer Theodore Judah surveyed a route for the first rail tracks west of the Mississippi in 1854, he mapped his course along R Street, about 10 blocks south of the swamp. Eight years later, when the Central Pacific began to build the Transcontinental Railroad, the Goss and Lambard Iron

Works at Front and I streets won the job to assemble the company's first locomotive, a machine brought in pieces by ship from Philadelphia. The engine was named the "Gov. Stanford."

The Central Pacific opened its own shops in 1863, next to the lake, four blocks east of the Goss and Lambard factory, after the city deeded the swampland to the railroad. The Central Pacific drained the lake and filled in the swamp and built eight large shops where workers constructed trains from scratch.

By World War II, Southern Pacific owned the yards and employed about 7,000 people there. They were blacksmiths, mechanics, boilermakers, carpenters, painters, electricians and upholsterers. "Sacramento was a railroad town," said Victor Ruiz, a car man at the shops for 44 years.

From steam to diesel, they built and repaired trains until Union Pacific bought Southern Pacific in 1996 and began to close the shops. The plan was to develop the property with condos and retail stores, preserving several of the historic buildings as a rail museum and mall.

But the railroad left another legacy. For 133 years, workers poured paints and varnishes and cleaning fluids and fuel into the landfill above the ancient swamp, creating a toxic plume underground. By 2013, state and city officials, the Union Pacific and private developers still argued about what to do next. The plume had spread from the rail yards into the earth beneath downtown Sacramento.

An arena for the Kings seemed like a good fit for the rail yards. It would attract public dollars and promote retail development, housing and jobs. A pattern was established. Local politicians worked to conjure an arena replacement scheme based upon a public-private partnership. And The Boys found ways to sabotage the plans.

The Maloofs, who from their earliest days claimed they were simple people who would never try to outsmart anyone, seemed determined to prove that point. Their capacity for unforced errors compounded, and in 2006, The Boys placed themselves in a remarkable position. They worked against a ballot measure that would have built an arena at no real cost to the Maloof family.

The ballot measure, written and placed before voters by the Sacramento County Board of Supervisors, asked citizens to approve a $1.2 billion sales tax that included an arena valued at between $470 million and $542 million in the downtown rail yards. After a short period of enthusiasm,

The Boys called a press conference. They claimed the county, the city and the rail yard developer, Thomas Enterprises of Atlanta, misled the family. City and county officials who backed the initiative were accustomed to outbursts from The Boys. This was ridiculous.

The Maloof family's only obligations at the new arena would be a $20 million fund for capital repairs and $4 million per year in rent for 30 years. The Maloofs had another perspective. When they learned they would not receive income from 8,000 parking slots near the arena and that independent restaurants would be permitted to operate within yards of Maloof hospitality facilities, The Boys withdrew support.

A plan to build a practice gym over a nearby seven-story parking garage was another insult, the Maloofs implied. They never explained why, but they didn't believe practice gyms belonged on garages.

THE BOYS didn't disappear during the sales-tax campaign, though many people in Sacramento wished they had. Instead, the Maloof brothers found a unique way to draw attention. They agreed to appear in a Carl's Jr. television commercial, portraying the brothers as billionaire casino-owning playboys who enjoy $6,000 bottles of wine with their hamburgers at Palms.

The billionaire routine was the only part that required acting. They weren't that rich. The Boys were renowned for big appetites. They often shocked lunch guests by ordering double entree platters of meat and potatoes. They munched their way through business meetings with bowls of Cheetos. They argued deal points waving crusty orange fingers in the air.

The Vegas lifestyle made The Boys a great catch for the marketing team that created the Carl's Jr. $6,000 burger campaign. While the Carl's Jr. creative executives might not necessarily have been sensitive to the political climate in Sacramento or the need for a new arena, the hamburger people did try to steer The Boys away from political trouble.

The ad execs asked whether the Maloofs might want the commercial to skip its broadcast rotations in the Sacramento market. After all, the billionaire glutton message could make Sacramento County voters a little less likely to support a $1.2 billion tax initiative largely to benefit the Maloof family.

The Boys dismissed the concerns. They approved the commercial for all to see. "I said, 'People in Sacramento have a sense of humor. They'll understand,'" Joe Maloof said. Three weeks later, the votes were counted. The 2006 arena initiative, called Sacramento County Measures Q and R, lost by margins of approximately 80 to 20 percent. The Boys misjudged Sacramento's sense of humor in such stunning fashion that even people who disliked the Maloofs figured the family must have been acting strategically. They could not be so absurdly self-destructive.

Or could they be? After the election disaster, a man who knew the Maloofs well, David Stern, announced he was coming to Sacramento to take control of the recovery process. "Although I have a full-time job, it dawned on me that there's really nothing more important than this," the NBA commissioner said.

And with that, David Stern headed west to pick up the pieces of Les Harrison's cursed, battered and beaten old franchise.

Chapter Fifteen: Had To Go Oak Park On Him

The crisis that brought David Stern to Sacramento in November 2006 did not impress Kevin Johnson. The retired basketball star understood the need for a replacement arena. But he had no love for the franchise that refused to draft him 19 years earlier. When he drove out to Arco Arena for NBA games, it was to watch the visiting teams, not the Kings.

He found Kings games boring to sit through. He preferred to watch the NBA on TV. Johnson was the restless type, a person who needed to be in constant motion, who boasted about how little sleep he required, who always had to be doing something, leaning forward, making progress. "You've got to keep your foot on the pedal," he said. "Otherwise, you become just like the rest of them."

In 2006, when Sacramento politicians were talking about arena ballot measures and the Maloof brothers were filming a commercial with expensive wine and cheap hamburgers, Johnson's pedal was pushed toward something more important than the Kings.

Kevin was focused on education. In his opinion, the public schools of Sacramento, of California, of the entire nation, had failed to educate their most vulnerable children, kids from challenged neighborhoods in large cities, especially the daughters and sons of African Americans, Latinos and Southeast Asians.

The educational system was broken, he believed, co-opted by teacher unions and school boards more responsive to protecting an educator's tenure, seniority, academic freedom, vacations and pension than to ensuring that a third-grader, being raised by a single parent working a janitorial job, could read.

Johnson memorized data showing that in Sacramento, a majority of third-graders in the city's public school district could not read at expected levels. He studied the numbers and decided it would be statistically impossible for these kids to catch up. Many of them would end up in jail, he predicted.

Johnson did not have children himself, but the idea of thousands of youngsters in Sacramento, millions across America, being ordained at age 8 to lives of functional illiteracy, academic failure, poverty and incarceration was not acceptable. He was determined to do something about it.

The solution, Johnson believed, was charter schools. Charters, in his view, were entrepreneurial, market-driven sites run by enthusiastic educators and experienced administrators who wouldn't hide behind collective bargaining agreements and Byzantine grievance procedures to protect burned out, incompetent teachers and diffuse adult accountability.

In the three years before 2006, Johnson opened two charter school campuses in Sacramento, including an elementary school he named Public School 7, in honor of his draft pick by the Cleveland Cavaliers and favorite number. Fixing a broken education system was a Herculean task. But Johnson convinced himself he was the man for the job.

Now he was ready to take his crusade national. A camera crew from the Oprah Winfrey show was in Sacramento in March 2006, filming Kevin as he declared, "Education is the 21st Century civil rights issue." It was a dramatic statement from a man born in 1966 as the original Civil Rights movement marched across America. And it was more than a slogan. Johnson truly believed it.

The TV crew interviewed parents from the secondary school run by Johnson, Sacramento Charter High, the reconstituted Sac High campus from which Kevin graduated. Oprah would interview Johnson for her program broadcast on April 12, 2006, where the basketball star was placed next to education reformers Bill and Melinda Gates. A community viewing party and discussion was staged by Kevin at the Guild Theater in Sacramento, a renovated movie hall where the writer Joan Didion viewed French and Swedish movies as a young woman.

The theater was more than a movie hall in 2006. It was a two-story brown brick gathering space and triumph of Johnson's determination, the apex of a redevelopment project the basketball star created at 35th Street and Broadway in Oak Park, his old neighborhood. It was a street corner considered dangerous when Didion wandered there to find rapture in the cinematic shadows of Ingmar Bergman and Francois Truffaut.

For Johnson, the appearance with Oprah would be one piece of a strategy to bring attention to the crisis he saw in public education. He created Stand Up, an organization to promote parent involvement and accountability in neighborhood schools, helped by a $500,000 grant from a foundation run by Eli Broad, the real estate developer and former Kings limited partner. Johnson joined the boards of the Charter Schools Association and California Business for Educational Excellence Foundation in 2006.

He knew reform required mountains of money. Teacher unions spent millions of dollars on school board and legislative elections in California alone. Kevin became skilled at tapping business leaders and reform minded millionaires (or billionaires, such as the Gates family and Broad) in support of charter schools, reform and accountability. "Accountability" became his favorite word.

He disliked asking for money, but was very good at it. Raising dollars for personal pet projects would become one of Kevin's exceptional talents. There was a positive side to the retired NBA all-star collecting money. With his name and sports legacy, he could go straight to the top of various organizations to ask for support. He loved the view from the top.

Johnson took pride in mingling with the leadership and entrepreneurial class of American CEOs at high-dollar fundraising events, executive retreats and luxury resorts. He convinced himself he belonged there, that he was one of them, a natural born CEO, smart, tough, able to think on his feet and make quick decisions. He was not interested in the small, insignificant problems that bothered average people, only the big issues that shaped America. He wanted to lead, not follow. To influence the lives of hundreds, thousands, even millions of people.

Armed with his mission to fix the schools, Kevin didn't mind asking his high net-worth CEO friends for financial help to solve the problems that damaged his community and nation, problems made worse by the broken system of public education. In this environment, the Kings and their aged arena hardly qualified for discussion. Kevin Johnson had higher mountains to climb.

After Johnson was elected as mayor, people would ask me about his political ambitions, the next job on his ladder. Publicly, he always said he wasn't thinking past mayor. But in private he would make a point of saying he had no interest in serving as a state legislator or a member of Congress.

Those were jobs for the common herd, jobs for politicians who followed orders. At the Mayor's Office, staffers knew there were only two political jobs that interested our boss. Both were chief executive positions. One was down the street at the State Capitol. The other was on Pennsylvania Avenue in Washington, D.C. For Kevin Johnson, it was the top spot or nothing.

IN A MANNER common to many people born on the margins of society, Kevin Johnson hungered to be inside, where the big decisions were made. His mother, Georgia West, an audacious beauty who loved to sing and dance, was 16 when she became pregnant with Kevin.

He barely knew his father, Lawrence Johnson, who drowned in the Sacramento River near the Tower Bridge downtown, when Kevin was 3 years old. The drowning was an accident prompted by Lawrence's decision to swim to shore from a fishing boat filled with friends. The Sacramento River is muddy and treacherous no matter the season. A whirlpool pulled him under and he was gone.

Kevin Johnson was raised by his maternal grandparents, George and Georgia Peat, who instilled a blue-collar work ethic and the Christian values of humility and service amid the tough environment of Oak Park. The community has gentrified somewhat in four decades, but in 2013 it still looked much as it did when Kevin was a boy. It was a weary place of small homes with wood sidings and asphalt shingle roofs and small shops with red brick facades and many chain link fences and pit bulls lounging in the sun. The residues of poverty, the street gangs and the drug dealers, have lingered in Oak Park for generations.

Oak Park was home to the city's Black Panther Party and civil unrest when Kevin was a child. Police wore helmets while patrolling the community in the 1960s. George and Georgia were white (Kevin's mother was born from a relationship between her mother and an African American man), but the Peats had no apparent problem making the decision to live in a largely black neighborhood. People were people, Grampy Peat believed. Kevin Johnson never displayed the collateral scars of racism.

The young man was able to navigate among all groups. As an adult, Johnson proudly told stories about his grandfather's experiences as a humble sheet metal worker, followed by tales from his own history as a University of California, Berkeley graduate who managed to make a fortune in the NBA.

As mayor, he enjoyed Town Hall meetings with the city's essential work staff: the garbage truck drivers and utility department ditch diggers. He escaped their world decades ago, but wanted to remind them that, yes, the mayor too had been born an outsider, on the fringes. He was one of them! If he could succeed with hard work and brains, so could they. Or so the message went.

Sometimes, a garbage truck driver or ditch digger would challenge Kevin at a Town Hall event. The skeptic would point out that Johnson was a millionaire, that he wore fancy clothes and had a police driver. How could a millionaire be counted on to look after real working people? At these criticisms, Kevin would not walk away.

He would puff up his chest and stick out his chin. He would argue, giving as good or better than he received. His voice would rise and he would slip into street dialect. After these sessions, in a back room eating pizza and drinking from a plastic water bottle, he would grin and say, "Did you see me get after that one dude? I had to go Oak Park on him. Oh, yeah, Oak Park came out. That dude saw Oak Park for real!"

For Johnson, the "going Oak Park" moments were controlled and theatrical. He never swore (and never touched alcohol or drugs). And of course, Kevin never went Oak Park around the CEO crowd. But he enjoyed reviving the routine when appropriate, showing he could still handle the old neighborhood corner crew, like a stroll down memory lane.

George and Georgia Peat were comfortable on the Oak Park fringes, but Kevin, or Frog as he was known as a youngster, began to see another side of life, the side where the insiders lived, worked and played. School integration balances required young Frog to be bused from Oak Park to Land Park for junior high. It was a distance of only about two miles, separated by a freeway and a solar system.

Black Panthers, drug addicts and prostitutes lived in Oak Park. Judges, doctors and city council members lived in Land Park. "The bus would take me to California Middle School, and all of a sudden, we'd come around a corner and I'd see these big houses with sidewalks and nice green lawns, and wonder why we didn't have any sidewalks in Oak Park," Johnson said. He hoped to attend C.K. McClatchy High School in Land Park. Joan Didion and U.S. Supreme Court Justice Anthony Kennedy graduated from McClatchy. But Oak Park called him home.

Sacramento High School, the pride of Oak Park, needed his athletic talent, especially his basketball skill. The principal of Sac High refused to approve Kevin's transfer to McClatchy. After a rough start on Sac High's junior varsity team, Johnson became one of the best high school basketball players in California, averaging 34.2 points per game.

Success in basketball earned Johnson a scholarship to UC Berkeley. Cal was an elite public school, one of the leading universities in America, a place where the children of insiders, along with the highest-achieving kids from other households, were educated and sent into the worlds of academic research, leadership and money.

Kevin was quickly reminded of his marginal status at Cal. He could dominate kids in the gym, but he was an outsider in the classroom, lacking the academic skills to compete at the highest levels. One day, a freshman English class discussed the word "euphemism." Kevin recalled, "I was the only one in the room who had no idea what the word meant. Up until then, I thought I'd gotten a pretty good education at Sac High. At the moment, I knew I'd been fooled because of where I'd grown up and where I'd gone to school. I looked around that class and didn't see anybody from Oak Park but me." The humiliation over the word "euphemism" tossed Johnson back to the fringes. He promised himself he would not be a fringe player again.

THE PERPETUAL battle against being an outsider, against living on the margins and playing on the fringes, would continue in the NBA and at Sacramento City Hall when Johnson was elected mayor. The battle was joined in 1987, when the Kings bypassed Kevin and drafted Kenny Smith, whose college, North Carolina, was hallowed ground for basketball. It continued when Johnson began working for the Cleveland Cavaliers and realized he was little more than an insurance policy in case something happened to the real point guard, Mark Price.

Kevin worked hard to find a place on the Cavaliers. He was making good money and moved Georgia West and her young son Ronnie West, Kevin's half brother, to posh Shaker Heights. Kevin was ready to sweat and strive and create a career for himself in the NBA. But he soon realized he was a fringe player.

Nine months after drafting Johnson, Cleveland traded him to Phoenix, an awful team where six present and former players had been under indictment for cocaine and marijuana possession and drug trafficking. Compared to the Kings, who were loveable losers and for the moment stable in their new home of Sacramento, the Suns were a disaster. Phoenix was the end of the line in the NBA.

The Cavaliers didn't explain the trade to Johnson that day, January 25, 1988. They barely acknowledged him at all. The team's trainer simply told Johnson he could not get on the Cavaliers' bus because he now belonged to the Suns. Good luck, kid, the trainer said. Johnson's brief career in Cleveland was over.

The move to Phoenix might have buried Johnson and ended any hopes of leaving the sidelines. Instead, the trade marked the end of his fringe status. No more would he be the outsider, thanks to a serendipitous combination of talent and faith among the Suns and their new owner, Jerry Colangelo.

An experienced NBA scout and front office marketing man, Colangelo had been the Suns' general manager since 1968, when the franchise began life as an NBA expansion team. By 1987, Colangelo was respected enough within the Phoenix business community to organize local investors, led by executives with the Greyhound bus company, to buy the Suns for $44.5 million.

The purchase coincided with the drug scandal involving six current and former Suns players. There were days when Colangelo feared he might have the franchise taken from his control by the NBA. It soon became clear that Maricopa County authorities exaggerated the drug accusations. All charges would be either dropped or reduced. But the damage was done. Colangelo and his investors were deeply embarrassed.

The Suns had to be rebuilt, and fast. Searching the vulnerable rosters of other NBA teams with his personnel director Cotton Fitzsimmons, who previously coached the Kings in Kansas City, Colangelo unloaded one-third of his roster in a 48-hour stretch in 1988. The Suns looked for stable, mature players with clean backgrounds.

The youngest among the new men was Kevin Johnson, 21 years old. He was swapped for Phoenix forwards Larry Nance and Mike Sanders. The Cavaliers threw in two big men who didn't play much, Tyrone Corbin and Mark West. "I think most people in Phoenix thought the Suns had hit rock bottom when they traded Nance for three guys they'd never heard of," Johnson said. "Cotton and Jerry may have felt they had no choice, but they took an unbelievable risk."

As much as the Phoenix community disapproved of the drug controversy, some fans were even more upset by the team's dismantling. They saw the trade as an overreaction. "There's a train leaving at midnight. Be under it," Phoenix Gazette sports columnist Joe Gilmartin wrote about Fitzsimmons.

Neither Colangelo nor Johnson realized it at the time, but the trade was something more substantial than what it appeared to be, which was just another desperate transaction by a bad team. Within a year, Kevin would become the catalyst around whom the Suns were reborn.

And Colangelo would gain an additional family member. He already had four children, but overnight he discovered a second son whom he could mentor in the ways of executive-style leadership. A son named Kevin Johnson. Colangelo gave Kevin a private graduate business school tutorial, inviting the point guard to see how life worked in the big corner office.

Colangelo showed Johnson how to identify people by their leadership skills and social levels. The team owner taught the young man how business was done among CEOs. "If he needed to raise money for a community project, he would say, 'Watch this,' and dial up four or five guys and say, 'I need this much,' and they would say, 'OK,'" Johnson said. "When the state of Arizona decided not to observe the birthday of Martin Luther King, he knew how much money the state would lose and how harmful it would be, so he got on the phone and raised enough money for the campaign to defeat it. He let me sit there and watch. It didn't take him longer than 45 minutes of calling and he had all the money he needed."

The Phoenix Suns made one of the grandest recoveries in NBA history, winning 55 games in 1988-89 after only 28 victories the prior year. In one season, Johnson's first full year with the Suns, the victory-defeat ratio was flipped.

On April 17, 1989, Phoenix defeated the Kings 140-85. The game was a 55-point statement about two teams headed in opposite directions. By 1993, the Suns were playing the in the NBA Finals against the Chicago Bulls. Kevin Johnson was no longer a fringe player. He was a star. A sprawling home at Camelback Mountain became his retreat away from basketball.

And the retreat became a refuge of poor judgment and scandal.

Chapter Sixteen: Bring It On. I'm Running

In 1989, Kevin Johnson started an after school program called St. HOPE (Help Our People Excel) for Oak Park youngsters in Sacramento. Now he began to mentor teens in Phoenix. He wanted to share the ethics and values drilled into him by Grampy Peat, Jerry Colangelo and other role-models, including a new friend he met during his NBA travels, the iconic UCLA basketball coach John Wooden.

Johnson, who rarely locked his home and disliked carrying keys, allowed his mentored teens and friends to hang around the Phoenix house. The open-door policy was a demonstration of extraordinarily sloppy behavior by a professional athlete who otherwise took pride in being highly disciplined in his professional and personal life.

The presence of one troubled teen, a 16-year-old girl later identified as "Amanda," almost destroyed Johnson's future. They met when Johnson, 29 years old at the time, taped a TV public-service announcement warning teens to avoid guns. Before long, Amanda and Kevin were talking on the telephone. Soon he was sending her flowers.

They spent time together in the summer of 1995. Amanda would later claim they had intimate contact that stopped short of sexual intercourse. They showered together, she said. When she received psychological care after being admitted to a mental health facility for depression and anorexia, Amanda told her story to a counselor.

The counselor was Kristan Larson. She followed up with a phone call to Johnson. In the call, he acknowledged "an incident," and said the couple did not have sex. As a counselor, Larson was legally mandated to contact police with information involving minors and adults and sex. She phoned the Phoenix police and told them the story. Authorities orchestrated a "confrontation" phone call between Amanda and Johnson, hoping to draw an incriminating statement from the basketball star. Kevin was a word or two away from being arrested and prosecuted for allegedly molesting an underage woman.

In the phone call taped by police, Johnson deflected the teen's efforts to implicate him. At one point, he said Amanda was "looking at it different" than he did. The Maricopa County District Attorney's office in Phoenix chose not to prosecute Johnson, citing lack of evidence and the inconclusive taped phone conversation. Amanda hired a lawyer, Kent Turley, who threatened a civil lawsuit against Johnson. Embarrassing testimony was guaranteed. Turley suggested a settlement figure of $750,000. He accepted $230,000.

The question of whether Kevin Johnson molested Amanda faded away. But in May of 1997, New Times, an alternative weekly newspaper in Phoenix, published a lengthy article by Paul Rubin based on the police investigation. Major daily newspapers rarely followed up investigations by alternative weeklies. It was a conceit of the big papers. The absence of an indictment gave the traditional media a reason to mostly ignore the story about the basketball star and the 16-year-old girl.

Editors at The Sacramento Bee saw Rubin's story. They sent a reporter to Phoenix to gather information from police and check the New Times material, but declined to publish a lengthy report. The Bee's editors believed Johnson was guilty of monumentally poor judgment, but felt he deserved the same benefit of doubt from his hometown newspaper as he received from the Maricopa County District Attorney's Office. Whatever happened between Amanda and Johnson might have ended there, at least from the public's standpoint.

But a decade later, Johnson began to contemplate a run for mayor of Sacramento against Heather Fargo, by then a two-term incumbent. Once Kevin placed himself on center stage by seeking the city's highest elected office, The Bee would reach a different conclusion about examining his activities with Amanda and several other young women. The story would transcend gossip. It would become part of the campaign for mayor.

IF THERE is one category of skilled worker who can be said to have unlimited opportunities to indulge in every possible twist of sexual intimacy as often and with as many adult partners as they wish, that category would certainly be the professional athlete. As a sexual dilettante, the pro athlete is limited only by time (the team bus won't wait) and stamina (playing four games per week takes its toll).

So why, with so many eager options legally available, would a pro athlete pursue an underage, emotionally unstable girl? In Johnson's case, while the activities from all accounts did not include sex, they raised serious questions about judgment.

A second allegation became public in 2007. A teenaged girl who worked with Johnson's St. HOPE organization claimed she was groped while Johnson gave her a massage during a field trip at Yosemite. The three problematic words in that sentence—teenaged, massage, groped—raised more questions. The St. HOPE organization investigated the allegation before police were notified.

The girl, 17, recanted her accusation when interviewed by law enforcement. Police dropped the matter. Sacramento Police spokesman Sgt. Matt Young said, "I really don't know how many different ways we can convey the fact that there's nothing there." A third allegation of inappropriate touching surfaced, this one involving another St. HOPE volunteer. The young woman was over 18 years old, and police determined the alleged contact was not criminal.

The coincidence of accusations, of young women, massages, uninvited hands, made their way into a formal inquiry by a federal government watchdog, AmeriCorps Inspector General Gerald Walpin, who was investigating allegations that St. HOPE misused $847,673 in AmeriCorps program dollars. The money was intended for tutoring, theater arts programs and real estate redevelopment, under a federal grant. Instead, Walpin's investigators said, it went to salaries, political campaigns and personal staff for Johnson. Some of the AmeriCorps money was paid to young people who washed Johnson's car.

The Walpin investigation was serious, but it was awash in politics. There was a mayoral election underway in Sacramento, with Kevin Johnson as the high-profile candidate. And there was inspector general himself, who seemed determined to deploy the Johnson controversies as a tool to embarrass Barack Obama.

Walpin tried to portray himself as above politics, but he had been appointed by President George W. Bush and was mired in politics. The AmeriCorps Inspector General position was a patronage job handed to political loyalists, a routine Washington reward. When Walpin turned Johnson into a target and was then fired by President Obama in 2009, the dismissal gave Obama's critics the conspiratorial crumbs to claim the new president sacked the bulldog to cover up for an Obama friend, Kevin Johnson.

To describe Obama and Kevin as friends would be a long stretch. The president was obviously aware of Johnson, and Kevin received invitations to various White House events as mayor, but the men were not friends. Kevin campaigned on behalf of the president in 2008 and 2012. He said he almost didn't vote for himself as mayor in 2008 because he wanted to save the ballot sheet with his name printed below the words "Barack Obama."

Johnson was not on a first-name basis with the president. If anything, Kevin was more of a surrogate and acolyte than a buddy. Obama was one person Kevin admired without qualification. And they never played basketball together.

Johnson loved to tell the story about the first time he visited the Obama White House with a group of mayors. He stole an embossed napkin from a White House restroom to prove to his mother he had really been there. At a Kennedy Center event in Washington, he saw Obama seated in the Presidential Box and waved to the Commander In Chief. "That was really a rookie mistake," Johnson said. "Totally uncool." The President nodded at Kevin and quickly looked away. "He was totally cool," Kevin noted. The Obama White House was one place where Kevin happily volunteered for a fringe role.

With Obama's critics still expressing outrage over a friendship that didn't exist, the U.S. Attorney in Sacramento, Lawrence Brown, made a deal with Johnson and St. HOPE to settle the financial irregularities uncovered by Walpin. The former basketball star and his nonprofit organization agreed to repay half the federal money taken from AmeriCorps, $423,836, and improve their bookkeeping procedures.

JOHNSON HAD other problems. Evidence suggested he was a slumlord. Since his days in Phoenix, Johnson had been buying property in Oak Park. By 2007, Kevin or his organizations owned 37 parcels in a two-mile radius around his old neighborhood.

Some of those parcels had been turned into praiseworthy redevelopment projects, such as the bookstore, apartment house, barber shop and art gallery attached to the Guild Theater, and a beautifully restored bank building across the street. Others were not so beautiful, such as the circa 1910 bakery next door to Johnson's private office at 3408 Third Avenue.

A brick wall collapsed at the empty old bakery and Johnson did nothing about it. There was a derelict bar, Don Ju's Swiss Club, which the city's code enforcement department declared uninhabitable. And there was a vacant lot on 33rd Street, where somebody made a habit of dumping the remains of butchered sheep and goats.

City officials in Sacramento generally admired Johnson before he ran for mayor. He was a famous athlete who returned home to his community to help young people. And he was the only serious investor willing to sink money into Oak Park real estate (other than the University of Pacific, which had its law school there). But the city drew the line at collapsing walls, uninhabitable buildings and dead animals.

In the decade before he ran for mayor, Johnson's properties amassed 73 code violations and 42 fines totaling $32,080. The city was patient, understanding that matters such as illegally dumped dead animals were not the fault of Johnson or his real estate organizations, Kynship Development and St. HOPE Development. The city was working with Johnson. The local redevelopment agency gave him about $3 million to help with projects such as the Guild Theater complex.

But Johnson had enemies downtown and in Oak Park, people who thought he was too rich and powerful, even narcissistic, people furious at him for gaining control at Sacramento High School, where he fired union teachers and replaced them with nonunion staff. Those enemies found a place that would listen to their whispers: The Sacramento Bee, which in 2007 decided its readers should get a closer look at Kevin Johnson's development activities, charter school business and relationships with young women.

The Bee focused first on the collapsing walls and voluminous code violations, publishing three stories on Johnson's property troubles in October 2007. The stories included more than 7,000 words and multiple photos and maps. The package took weeks to produce.

Buried deep within the stories were three statements that went largely unappreciated amid the outrage of the goat and sheep parts, three statements that addressed fundamental problems within every organization Kevin Johnson touched, from St. HOPE to City Hall.

The first statement involved money. St. HOPE Development, according to 2006 tax statements, was broke, carrying $6.2 million of debt and running an annual deficit of about $900,000. Despite Johnson's skill as a fund-raiser, his appetite was bigger than his balance sheet.

The second statement noted that Johnson's enterprises had no employees with professional experience in real estate development or property management, and that the employees who worked for Johnson were afraid to make decisions. Kevin was a habitual micro-manager who hired friends and friends of friends for their loyalty and servitude, not their expertise. He especially didn't like experts who told him he was wrong when he knew he was right.

The third statement was a comment by Randy Stratton, Code Enforcement Manager for the city and the official responsible for getting Johnson to maintain his properties. Speaking about the bakery with the collapsed wall and Don Ju's derelict Swiss Club, Stratton said of Kevin's staff, "I didn't get a sense that they had any direction, any idea what to do with those two buildings. I told them to think holistically. They've got a lot of properties to deal with." In other words, Johnson was a visionary who had big, worthy goals but he lacked the ability to bring perspective and focus to the small things, the details that really mattered.

In my years with Johnson at Sacramento City Hall, those three observations would describe with remarkable precision how life worked in the Mayor's Office. Those sentences would explain why Johnson got next to nothing done once his high-octane, 5 a.m. bursts of enthusiasm wore off, why he clashed with bureaucratic professionals who plodded through projects and were proud of incremental success, why he had problems reporting his fund-raising activities to state authorities, why his staff members came and went like breezes through the delta.

Once Kevin grabbed hold of something, he knew exactly what he wanted, but rarely knew how to get there.

AS WORD spread through Sacramento political circles that prominent business owners were pressing Johnson to run for mayor against Fargo, The Bee followed up with its code violation stories and began to plunge into the financial irregularities at St. HOPE. Along the way, the newspaper dredged up the sexual misconduct allegations that dated from 1995.

A Sacramento bounty hunter, gadfly and perennial mayoral candidate, Leonard Padilla, who sucked on toothpicks and wandered around town dressed in a black hat and cowboy costume, made sure the local media received copies of police reports concerning Kevin and Amanda. The Bee obtained a draft copy of the $230,000 settlement with Amanda's lawyer, noting the agreement included an apology and denial of guilt by Johnson. By 2008, Johnson, who refused to speak to the media about the code-enforcement problems, could not stay silent about suggestions that he molested young women.

He was now a candidate for mayor, running against a woman incumbent in a crowded field (which included the drugstore cowboy Padilla). Johnson went on the attack. He called the collection of stories "part of the ugly and dirty politics of Sacramento." He said the rumors against him proved Fargo didn't want to confront the real problems facing the community. "Sacramento needs to have a healthy discussion about the issues, about ideas and the vision of this city," he said.

Voters agreed with Johnson. Enough of them didn't care about Amanda or the collapsed brick wall on Third Avenue. They laughed off news reports about an unauthorized, after-hours tour of City Hall that Johnson was given by a star-struck security guard three days before the election, when Kevin was caught on closed-circuit security cameras testing out Fargo's chair. Fargo wanted Johnson arrested for trespassing after his tour. Chief of Police Rick Braziel refused to let his department get entangled in the political clothesline of mayoral ambitions.

And on Election Day in November 2008, voters gave the former basketball star 57 percent of the vote. Kevin Maurice Johnson became the 55th mayor of Sacramento.

The election was one of the most acrimonious political campaigns in modern Sacramento history, but it accomplished the task of bringing Frog, the kid from the fringes of Oak Park, into the heart of municipal authority. Johnson was the first African American to win the mayor's title in his hometown and the first Sacramento mayor to have been born in the city he led.

He privately said his motivation for running was a challenge presented by The Bee. He learned several reporters from the paper bragged they would wreck his candidacy by threatening to write about Johnson's transgressions, real, imagined and alleged. "I heard they were saying I wouldn't run because I was afraid of the stuff they would dig up," Johnson said. "That's when I decided, OK, you want to play that game?

Bring it on. I'm running." Oak Park came out when Kevin Johnson decided to run for mayor.

His first-year agenda included special initiatives on arts and culture, homelessness, volunteer service and education, a whirlwind of activity for a mayor whose legally defined role was, essentially, to run city council meetings and represent the city at ribbon-cuttings and funerals. The new mayor wanted to make a difference. His slogan was, "The City That Works for Everyone." He was not worried about the Kings or their arena. He hardly mentioned the basketball team during his first 11 months in office.

Two years earlier, after the lopsided defeat of the Sacramento County Measures Q and R, which would have built a new arena with taxpayer dollars, Commissioner David Stern had come to Sacramento to lead the community's fight to stay in the NBA. Behaving like the take-charge type of CEO Kevin Johnson admired so much, Stern devised a plan to create a winning environment for a new arena without interference from the local politicians who, Stern believed, helped to make a mess of things. Live from New York, it was Commissioner Stern to the rescue.

The commissioner's Sacramento recovery plan had taken shape by 2008. The timing was perfect. In the California Governor's Office, there was a former world champion bodybuilder and movie actor, a man who would surely understand the importance of sports and culture and support the NBA in the nation's largest state. In the Mayor's Office, there would soon be a retired NBA all-star surely eager to help Commissioner Stern build a new arena for Sacramento and give the Vagrant Kings a permanent home.

The pieces were in place. Everything was set. The trouble was, the movie actor and the basketball star were sitting out the game.

Chapter Seventeen: There Is No Plan B On The Table

David Stern spent 30 minutes talking to Gov. Arnold Schwarzenegger about the future of sports in California. The NBA commissioner came away with a cigar. "Well, I didn't smoke it yet, but I got it," Stern said.

The meeting between the famous sports executive and the action-hero governor took place in a shelter designed not to inspire, but to relax. They talked inside the governor's smoking tent, a temporary dirty-white canvas structure with rattan furniture and potted palms in a courtyard outside the windows of the Governor's Office at the State Capitol in Sacramento. Green plastic grass covered the concrete floor. To call the setup "cheesy" would be polite.

The governor's formal offices, with threadbare carpets, wood paneling and cubbyholes where staff worked, looked not much better than the tent. Outdated by decades, the governor's suite honored the rugged Western tastes of Gov. Ronald Reagan, circa 1972, rather than the political heart of the world's sixth largest economy in 2006.

Schwarzenegger used his smoking tent as a place to talk, muse and reflect with special guests in an informal atmosphere, all of which, to Schwarzenegger's way of thinking, demanded cigars. When he became governor in 2003, Schwarzenegger would light cigars inside his State Capitol office. He filled the room with the aroma of custom-rolled tobacco, as if the rules against smoking in California public buildings didn't apply to him. Visitors complained. His staff looked at their shoes. The idea of a smoking tent was born. "My negotiating tent," the governor called it.

Schwarzenegger and Stern should have been natural allies: two famous, confident, powerful men, who enjoyed the spotlight, had wry senses of humor and loved to win. They were both politicians, a necessary component of their success. Both loved sports. But more than anything they were businessmen. Three words ruled their thoughts: return on investment.

David Stern had come to Sacramento to stamp out a crisis, the embarrassing defeat of two Sacramento County ballot measures that would have raised $1.2 billion in sales taxes and constructed a $450 million arena for the local NBA team about 10 blocks from the governor's negotiating tent.

The NBA commissioner knew Schwarzenegger was a sportsman and open to discussions about arenas. And Stern knew that local issues such as the arena vote in Sacramento County were not topics worthy of the governor's time. So Stern broadened the agenda and introduced the idea of a statewide authority to support the construction of stadiums and arenas across California. Now this might appeal to the sportsman governor.

There were challenges in Los Angeles over competing efforts to build a new stadium and bring the National Football League back to the nation's second-largest city. Oakland, San Jose and Santa Clara were thinking about ways to build football and baseball stadiums. Then there were the Sacramento Kings, the capital city's only major league sports franchise. The Kings needed a new arena.

For several years, civic leaders had tried and failed to orchestrate a replacement plan for the Kings' old rural arena, which was rapidly being surrounded by suburbs. Sacramento was growing fast in the new century. Four local communities were experiencing astonishing suburban expansion, with streets, strip malls and production homes being erected as fast as the framing crews could drive nails.

Three of the growth areas were in nearby towns, Folsom, Roseville and Elk Grove. The fourth was North Natomas, Gregg Lukenbill's field of dreams, the place the Maidu called "upstream."

Other states used governmental entities to help build stadiums and arenas. The results had been positive, Stern said, giving cities and counties the extra leverage needed to pull together the hundreds of millions in construction dollars that would otherwise be beyond a community's reach. The real issue was California's untapped potential, the state's economy of scale.

California political leaders, working for large constituencies that sprawled across hundreds of miles, could craft a mechanism to deliver huge buying power and financial protections to the sports and entertainment industry. They would create thousands of jobs and economic and cultural benefits worth billions of dollars.

The pitch was nothing new. Smaller, less progressive states had already demonstrated how sports promoters could partner with the State House. And Stern was a remarkable salesman. But as he puffed on his cigar, stoking the red ash with each draw, the governor of California wasn't interested.

For all his bluster about the importance of athletics and his legacy as the world's greatest bodybuilder, Schwarzenegger was not willing to spend political currency on people who owned professional sports teams. He would sign legislation to kill an environmental lawsuit designed to block an NFL stadium in Southern California, but his motive had nothing to do with football. Rather, he believed California environmentalists had gone too far in cooking up nuisance lawsuits to frustrate business interests. He wanted to send a message, not build an arena.

THE DAY BEFORE he met the governor, David Stern visited Sacramento City Hall, where he rode the elevator to the fifth floor, turned left and walked into the mayor's conference room. No cigars there. No lofty discussions about statewide authorities and economies of scale. Stern met with Mayor Heather Fargo (Kevin Johnson would not arrive at City Hall for another two years) and five of the eight city council members, plus executive staff from the City Manager's office.

The commissioner's message was polite and simple. For the next several months, you must stand down and do nothing about the Kings. The time had come, Stern said, for local elected officials to remove themselves from the seven-year soap opera involving the Kings, Arco Arena and the family that owned them, the Maloof clan.

Stern understood the good intentions of the mayor and her colleagues. And better than anyone, he knew the challenges of trying to negotiate with the Maloof family. The commissioner repeated his position on Sacramento. He didn't like franchise relocations. And he absolutely did not want to see the Kings move. He had a new strategy to keep the team in Northern California.

His plan had two elements. First, the Commissioner's Office would represent the Maloofs in all future discussions about a new arena. This time The Boys were on triple-secret probation. Second, a consultant named John

Moag would serve as point for Stern while the league searched for a critical path to finance a new arena for the Kings. Moag would need a free hand and political support. Time was running out for Sacramento. Arco Arena must be replaced. John Moag was the community's best hope to build a new arena and keep its NBA team.

Relocations were a scourge to Stern. They signaled instability. Carnivals moved, circuses moved, and the NBA was well past those days. Major League Baseball went 50 years—the first half of the 20th Century—without moving a team. Deep roots and credibility! That was the sort of stability Stern wanted for his league. The Kings stood for everything but stability. David Stern was determined to fix the Kings, or retire trying.

Under Stern's leadership, the NBA grew roots for 16 years after the Kings left Kansas City. Nobody moved. A sense of permanence formed over the league while many franchise values grew to 10 times their worth from the drugged-out early 1980s. Three teams relocated between 2001 and 2008. The Charlotte Hornets went to New Orleans. The Vancouver Grizzlies left for Memphis. And the Seattle SuperSonics bolted to Oklahoma City.

There were unique reasons for the relocations, but they represented failures for Commissioner Stern, the failure of the NBA to function in medium-sized markets.

Now John Moag would be the appointed savior of another smaller market, Sacramento. He had the raw materials to build a compelling case. By 2007, new NBA arenas were planned in Orlando and Brooklyn. The buildings in Auburn Hills and Milwaukee, which opened in 1988 with Arco Arena, were in far better shape than the Sacramento facility, which was erected at about half the price.

Soon, only the Golden State Warriors and New York Knicks would play in arenas older than Sacramento. And that comparison was false, because the auditoriums in Oakland and Manhattan had received expensive, extensive upgrades. Arco Arena was not just old by NBA standards. It was exhausted.

JOHN MOAG was an interesting choice for the job of saving Sacramento. For almost 30 years, he maintained a career by placing himself at the crossroads of politics and professional sports. He started as a runner for the State Senate President of Maryland, but eventually learned the dynamics of public stadium financing, which involved the art of extracting huge dollars from municipal or state governments in trade for shiny stadiums and arenas that could be hailed as economic catalysts and job generators.

Moag knew sports team owners hated to spend their own money on facilities. This was not because they feared big construction projects or lacked the capacity for complex financial deals. No, it was because sports facilities almost never turned a profit and rival owners were getting arenas built practically for free by taxpayers. Owners believed they put themselves at financial and competitive disadvantages when they paid for arenas and stadiums.

At the same time, Moag recognized a significant problem with pro sports: people loved their teams and would sleep overnight outside the box office to buy playoff tickets, but they didn't want to pay for stadiums. He worked to resolve the problem, finding ways to present the construction bill in a less stressful way, letting it masquerade as a hotel or car rental tax, a sales or parcel tax, a lottery benefit, a redevelopment project, all supplemented by seat licenses, user fees and taxes on food, drinks and tickets.

The tricks behind financing sports facilities were not secret. The moves were commonly shared, repeated by everybody in the trade, like the checklist protocols in an airplane cockpit. But Moag, like most consultants, needed to make his work seem mysterious and elusive, which promoted the need for more consultants and longer, richer contracts.

The beating heart of Moag's work was the relationships he had worked hard to establish with people who mattered in pro sports. Sometimes he helped those people buy and sell teams. Other times, he watched their backs. One of his best friends was David Stern.

For all his gravitas, Moag could claim just one truly big deal. He helped move the Cleveland Browns to Baltimore in 1996, when he was the volunteer head of the Maryland Stadium Authority. The Browns' relocation was a heroic deed in Maryland, revenge for the theft of the Baltimore Colts by Indianapolis.

The Maryland Stadium Authority, which used lottery money and state bonding capacity to build baseball and football stadiums in Baltimore, had no comparable organization in California. In Maryland, the Authority had authority. It could condemn private property and negotiate stadium lease terms. The Maryland agency and similar governmental sports authorities in other states were the sort of examples David Stern talked about when he sat down on the rattan chair in Gov. Schwarzenegger's negotiating tent.

THE COMMISSIONER returned to New York after his visit to the Capitol. John Moag was instructed by Stern to stay in Sacramento for a couple of weeks. Moag would meet the right people, learn the local customs, drill down into the problems and apply his experience toward finding a solution to the arena problem.

The Maloof boys had been ordered by Stern to provide Moag with whatever assistance he needed and to stay out of his way. There would be no more talking to the media, no more Carl's Jr. commercials. And one more thing: they would have to pay Moag. Cashing checks from the Maloof family and having The Boys silenced were important benefits for Moag, but they didn't solve another issue. The consultant knew nothing about Sacramento.

The NBA commissioner and his consultant were operating under the principle that one NBA city was essentially like another, that all communities shared common goals and suspicions when it came to pro sports, but that a steady, experienced hand could navigate through those turbulent seas. This was optimistic, considering that Moag's most recent big assignment in California ended in disaster.

Four years before coming to Sacramento, Moag was hired by the organization that managed the Rose Bowl in Pasadena. His job was to bring an NFL team to that iconic football stadium. Riding on the accolades of his Baltimore Ravens triumph, he promised a quick and exclusive deal with a happy ending for the Rose Bowl.

That is not what happened. Instead, Pasadena was guided into a bidding war against three nearby cities, Los Angeles, Anaheim and Carson. A bidding war was the last thing Pasadena wanted or needed. Moag had a temper and it surfaced at the end of his Southern California assignment. He told a reporter the NFL had "purposefully and intentionally blindsided us."

In spring 2007, Moag made several trips to Sacramento. He was getting to know the community. He was intrigued by one particular expanse of land, 350 acres in the center of the urban infrastructure that comprised the greater metropolitan area, a piece of property called the California Exposition and State Fair, or Cal Expo.

The fairgrounds, Moag believed, were better than the rail yards. At the downtown site, tons of dirt made toxic by decades of lead and paint and fuels were still being removed. A toxic underground plume was spreading. And the private developer with site control, Stan Thomas of Atlanta, seemed more interested in retail stores and condos than sports facilities.

Cal Expo had the benefit of being state owned and outside the jurisdiction of both the city and county of Sacramento. A board of directors, whose majority was appointed by the governor, made decisions at Cal Expo. The local politicians could be cut out from an arena project at Cal Expo.

Best of all, Cal Expo was hungry for love. Like Arco Arena, the facility was collapsing beneath the weight of neglected repairs. The fairgrounds had fallen upon tough budgetary circumstances created by declining attendance at the State Fair. The facility had run up $40 million in deferred maintenance. The site's major buildings and attractions hadn't been upgraded since the 1960s, when Gov. Ronald Reagan opened Cal Expo and characterized it as a potential Disneyland North, a year-round playground to celebrate the sunny California lifestyle.

The rhetoric from Reagan was positive but not realistic. Under state law, Cal Expo was not even eligible for taxpayer support from the state's general fund. The fairgrounds were required to earn and reinvest every dollar and behave like a business, not a bureaucracy or charity. The dream of Disneyland North became a stigma for Cal Expo. While Disneyland was called the "Happiest Place on Earth," Cal Expo was "Where Funds Are Tight." Amid the asphalt midways and concrete moats of California's crumbling state fairgrounds, John Moag saw the promise of a new arena.

Moag was not the first consultant who saw opportunity at Cal Expo. In 1975 and 1979, consultant studies indicated Cal Expo was the best location for a new stadium or arena in Sacramento. Questions about site control and money complications, such as who would pay for the land and stadium, could not be resolved. There were debates over traffic mitigation. But Moag, armed with the NBA's proxy, believed all those troubles could be overcome.

He publicly identified Cal Expo as the new arena site in September 2007, highlighting the announcement with his trademarks of speed and certainty. "There's a lot of discussion that has to go on, but I think we're very quickly getting to the point where we can roll up our sleeves and see if we can work something out," Moag said. "The Commissioner has kind of set the first part of November as a target date for having something wrapped up. I think that's realistic."

HUDDLED IN a cramped meeting room at the Cal Expo administration building as an audience of about 50 people sat on folding chairs, the Cal Expo board voted unanimously to negotiate with John Moag and the NBA on an arena plan. Consultants would be hired to study environmental and traffic considerations.

The fairgrounds were next to the worst freeway bottleneck in the Sacramento region. The freeway would have to be fixed. And a pact was made to avoid proposing a tax hike to pay for the project. The lessons of the failed 2006 ballot initiative had not been forgotten. Moag would get creative. He would conjure a plan that would revitalize Cal Expo and save the Kings without raising taxes. The secret ingredient would be an old standby: real estate.

The emerging plan was a complex recipe of urban renewal. The Maloof family would sell the 86 acres around Arco Arena in North Natomas. The City of Sacramento would sell the adjoining 100 acres that were donated to the city by three local developers after SeaFirst Bank repossessed and dumped the property. Profits from those combined 186 acres would serve as the contributions from the city and the Kings. Cal Expo would lease a large portion of its 350 acres for retail shops, housing and office parks. The number $650 million was mentioned as a potential value.

The California State Fair would be reborn as a smaller, more human scale and modern attraction, anchored by the Kings and their new arena. In less than one year since the Carl's Jr. commercial and the crushing defeat of the county sales tax arena plan, John Moag, the consultant from Baltimore, had magically chased away Sacramento's dark clouds. "There is no Plan B on the table," Moag said. "This is something we're totally focused on, and I think it's realistic."

Audacious, maybe even insane, that was the plan. The moving parts would have to work like a Rolex. And almost immediately, springs began to pop.

Even with the Maloofs muzzled, the Kings did nothing to help John Moag. While the consultant was focused on his arena plan at Cal Expo, the basketball team made headlines with scandals. Star player Ron Artest was arrested for domestic violence and cited for cruelty to animals.

Suggestive photos of the team's dance squad were circulated on the Internet. Moag was doing his best to stay focused on the arena, but the Kings were still the Kings.

Moag should have seen the warning signs. Five months before the Baltimore consultant arrived, new Kings coach Eric Musselman was arrested for drunk driving hours after his first game. He was fired in April 2007, at the end of his first season. Reggie Theus, the philosopher who survived the Bill Russell era in Sacramento, replaced Musselman as coach. Theus was fired two months into his second season.

Typical of the Kings, the troubles involving coaches, players and dancers were petty, but they demonstrated the team's ability to have no control over the events that shaped its image. The Kings, who had not played in a championship game since 1951, were champions at letting little failures blow up into big embarrassments.

And the embarrassments kept coming.

Chapter Eighteen: And I Apologize To Hustlers And Scam Artists Around The World

There could be no surprise when Ron Artest found trouble. Trouble was his faithful companion. Playing for the Indiana Pacers in 2004, he was the centerpiece of a brawl that carried into the stands at The Palace of Auburn Hills. Struck by a Diet Coke thrown by a spectator named John Green, Artest ran up the stairs into the audience and began punching fans, followed by teammate Stephen Jackson.

The incident stunned the sports world. David Stern called it "shocking, repulsive and inexcusable." The NBA had come a long way since the days when Celtics Coach Red Auerbach punched gas station attendant Eddie Finke in Cincinnati and when somebody threw a knife into the floor at Edgerton Park while aiming for Lakers center George Mikan.

Traded to the Kings after the Indiana mess, Artest was arrested at home in rural Placer County in March 2007. He was charged with four counts of misdemeanor domestic violence against his wife, Kimsha.

The sheriff's report said Artest slapped his wife, pushed her down and prevented her from calling 911. When she finally phoned authorities, it was the fifth time deputies had been summoned to the Artest residence in 13 months. "I can be reckless at times, and things and stuff can happen," the basketball player said. "I'm always going to make mistakes, and maybe there's people out there that understand and maybe there's people that don't."

Artest pleaded no contest to domestic violence. He was sentenced to 100 hours of community service, which included picking up garbage. The NBA imposed relatively severe sanctions, suspending him for seven games without pay. A month before, Artest was cited by Placer County animal control officers for failing to feed his black Great Dane, Socks. The citation was dropped when a veterinarian determined Socks had an unrelated leg injury that prompted her to lose appetite. "I love Socks and have always tried to make sure she was being well cared for," Artest said. His tendency toward violence found its boundaries with a dog.

Kings vice president for basketball Geoff Petrie tried to provide public relations support for his troublesome player. Petrie changed the subject from domestic abuse and dog food and emphasized Artest's new path to self-improvement. "I know he's working on other things in his life that he has to deal with now: his probation, counseling and this upcoming suspension, but I think his focus will be on basketball and trying to have a good year," Petrie said.

Of course, Petrie was motivated by self-interest rather than public interest. Artest was a talented player. Petrie needed Artest and people like him to win basketball games. When the Kings traded Artest to Houston in 2008, the team regressed into the NBA cellar, winning 17 games and losing 65.

The Internet photo scandal involving the Kings' Royal Court Dancers created theatrics of the absurd. One picture showed several women bending over, their backsides pointed at the camera. In another shot, two women were about to kiss. No one associated with the basketball team claimed knowledge of the photos.

The Kings released a statement that dripped with sanctimony. "The photos of the Sacramento Kings Dance Team members circulating on the internet were published without the knowledge or permission of the Sacramento Kings, and they do not adhere to the principles and values of the Sacramento Kings organization," the statement said. Perhaps the Maloofs would have been more understanding if the photos featured Playboy bunnies, cheeseburgers, expensive wine and poker tables.

WHILE THE Kings embarrassed themselves, John Moag worked with Gensler Architects to produce a vision for the new Cal Expo. The overhaul left nothing untouched. Gone were the iconic structures that defined the State Fair: the sprawling livestock barns, the fountains, the buildings that held tacky celebrations of California's 58 counties, the dusty race track with its mile oval for thoroughbreds and harness horses. In place of those attractions were 3.5 million feet of residential properties, 2.5 million feet of office space and 1.6 million feet of retail shops.

The new arena and reimagined State Fair were the smallest components, tucked into the eastern edge of the property, just 1.5 million feet. The architect included garage space for 15,309 cars, a number that corresponded with NBA needs. The overall project was so huge that the plans didn't bother with a price tag. If Cal Expo had to ask, it couldn't afford it. Moag talked about a quarter-century build out. Nobody would estimate how many billions of dollars might be needed, or where the money would be sourced.

The drawings were oblivious to the gathering economic storms that would soon turn Moag's sunny blue skies into a hurricane of Biblical proportions. Much of the visionary design work took place between October 2008 and February 2009. The world's economy was collapsing. But Cal Expo and the NBA anticipated only a brief squall. "The whole country is cutting back," Moag said. "But that doesn't mean development is stopping. It just alters the schedule, if anything." He was wrong about that. Development stopped dead.

As the severity of the global economic recession settled over Sacramento, it became apparent why Moag's drawings did not include a financing plan. The presence of so much housing, office and retail space at the new Cal Expo meant Moag believed the majority of dollars would come from private developers capitalizing on the build out.

But in February 2009, no such developers existed. Four months after the rollout of the new Cal Expo vision, State Fair management and Moag met privately with several of the Sacramento region's major real estate developers. After the meeting, the real estate people got into their cars and quickly drove away. Brian May, assistant general manager at the State Fair, said, "It comes as no surprise, we learned a project of this size is not financeable in today's market."

In times of crisis, there on occasion appears one person with vision and confidence to find solutions overlooked by the rest of the crowd. In the Sacramento real estate development world of 2009, that person was a man named Gerry Kamilos. The son of a Sacramento grocery store owner, Kamilos did not present a dynamic figure. He was portly, with a choirboy haircut and a round face. He drove an old Volvo and carried a calculator, on which he would tap out numbers to help prove his points.

When Kamilos spoke, his sentences sometimes made no literal sense, but he strung them together with such artful dexterity that his listeners could be lulled into a suspension of skeptical disbelief, nodding and somehow understanding whatever message Kamilos was trying to transmit.

He was a real estate developer. He built offices, warehouses and modest housing subdivisions with varied success in small towns around Northern California. His accomplishments were limited. But his goals were massive. No project frightened Kamilos. If he were to walk into a room and talk about developing one trillion acres on Jupiter, out would fly the artful, passionate words and the people in the room would soon be nodding and understanding just how he planned to do it.

When major developers from the region, including executives from the Alex G. Spanos company in Stockton, which built apartments across the country, and Mark Friedman, whose family owned the biggest shopping mall in Sacramento, were telling Cal Expo that the dream of a new State Fair and an NBA arena could not be financed, Gerry Kamilos was plotting to make the project work. Kamilos had come up with a plan of such audacity that it defied description.

To me, the perfect name would have been "Operation Grand Slam," borrowed from the James Bond book "Goldfinger." In Ian Fleming's story, a portly evil genius robs the U.S. gold reserves at Fort Knox, Ky., by using crop dusters to spray knockout gas on thousands of troops guarding the vaults. Kamilos, being not Ian Fleming or James Bond but rather the kind of person who drives a Volvo and knows how to work a graphing calculator, called his plan "Convergence."

This is how Convergence worked. Kamilos would take control of three key sites in Sacramento, 350 acres at Cal Expo, 186 acres where Arco Arena was located in North Natomas, and 240 acres at the downtown rail yards. He would use the revenue generated by each chunk to fund developments at the others. The Cal Expo site would become a traditional mixed-use project, with homes, retail shops and offices. The North Natomas site would become a new State Fair. The rail yards would become the new arena, plus whatever else Kamilos could fit there.

The trio of properties would be a self-perpetuating economic turbo, not unlike a giant Rube Goldberg machine where the marble falls and starts the windmill, which pulls the string and opens the door and lets the hamster run. Kamilos even had people who would drop the marble. He insisted that Australian financier Macquarie Capital and the Pacific Coast Capital Partners investment firm were ready to climb on board, once

Kamilos could gain site control at the three locations. Gerry Kamilos didn't need crop dusters and knockout gas to get the gold.

LOCAL REAL ESTATE experts were skeptical. They knew how difficult it was to transform one large site, much less three. And several immediate problems were obvious. There was still toxic dirt at the rail yards, plus an active Union Pacific main line track looping through the southern portion of the property. There were severe building restrictions in North Natomas, imposed by the Federal Emergency Management Agency, which was worried about the aged condition of river levees in the area.

And there was the Cal Expo board, which knew nothing about plans to pack up and move the State Fair to another part of Sacramento, and which lacked legal authority to take profits from the sale of its own property.

Those were negotiable issues to Kamilos. The bigger hurdles were how to introduce Convergence to the public and secure political support. For those answers, Kamilos turned to the newly elected mayor of Sacramento, Kevin Johnson.

Johnson didn't like Kamilos. The mayor found him pushy and not deferential. And Johnson was not interested in taking on a new arena project, variations of which had frustrated four previous mayors. Johnson obviously wanted the Kings and NBA to stay in Sacramento, but he didn't believe the Kings or Cal Expo were his chief problems. And he maintained his Kenny Smith grudge against the Kings from Draft Day 1987.

Johnson barely mentioned the arena in the 2008 mayoral campaign. He ran on a theme of good government and accountability at City Hall. He believed the City Charter, a 1921 document that required Sacramento to be led by a professional manager hired by the city council, was outdated for a modern emerging city. Most residents couldn't identify the city manager, Johnson argued. And with nine city council members sharing responsibility for policy decisions, the public could not hold any one person accountable for anything.

He was right. City council members developed great skill at deflecting blame and pointing fingers at each other, or blaming the city manager and staff. In many City Hall debates, it was difficult to guess who was in charge and who was at fault. Individual council members benefitted from the smokescreen provided by the City Charter. Johnson wanted to be in charge, a strong mayor, the CEO making decisions and accepting accountability, with the city council serving as his legislative branch. That's how many other emerging cities operated. Why not Sacramento?

The Council-Manager system could only be changed by public ballot initiative, with language approved by the city council. Johnson wanted charter reform placed before the electorate immediately. The city council didn't see any reason to break up a system that suited incumbents just fine. For most council members, Johnson's proposals felt like a prima donna's power grab.

PRIORITIES CHANGED for Johnson in September 2009, when the National Collegiate Athletic Association said it was removing Arco Arena from its rotation as a host site for the regional "March Madness" men's basketball tournament. That was a blow to Sacramento's pride that transcended old grudges carried by Kevin. Calling his staff together, Johnson declared that the threat of losing the Kings was real. If the NCAA refused to use Arco Arena, the NBA would surely follow.

Johnson loved being a man of action, a first responder to the fire bell. The NCAA rebuke was an emergency that required guts, brains and leadership, qualities Johnson was always eager to demonstrate. He began making telephone calls to Commissioner Stern and to San Francisco political consultant Chris Lehane, who helped manage the successful campaign to build AT&T Park for the San Francisco Giants.

The mayor decided to give a major speech, where he would lay out the arena problem and call the community to action. That's what a real leader would do! This wasn't a sports crisis, but an economic crisis, Johnson said. Sacramento had been kicked onto its backside by the recession. The last thing the city needed was the loss of its major league franchise, one of the few recognized businesses that carried the name "Sacramento" to the world.

I joined the Mayor's Office two months earlier and helped write the big speech. Lehane provided the most memorable language, the "Rules of the Game," which would assure the public that the taxpayers would come first, that Sacramento would not be used as leverage by any sports team, that the city would not be outgunned by sharp lawyers and consultants working for someone else, and that solutions "inside and outside the box" would be studied. The "Rules" were brilliant.

Lehane knew there was danger in the mayor going it alone. But alone was Johnson's favorite way to travel. The consultant came up with a "blue ribbon" task force of ecumenical, respected community leaders. The task force would solicit and review multiple arena proposals and recommend the best ideas to the city council. The goal was to engage the public in a transparent, community-wide effort, to purge the 2006 ballot defeat, and to shift the arena from Cal Expo to downtown Sacramento.

The task force, called "Sacramento First," was another clever touch, bringing credibility and authority to the process and making it difficult for special interest groups, including city council members, who disliked Johnson, to interfere. Chris Lehane certainly knew what he was doing.

The task force was built with 12 members. Retired City Treasurer Tom Friery would serve as finance expert. There was a cultural guru, restaurateur Lina Fat, two businesswomen, Dea Spanos Berberian and Dorene Dominguez. There was Mark Harris, a public finance professor and attorney. Architect Dan Meis came aboard. A local political insider and expert, Ron Tom, was added. A real estate developer, Larry Kelley, came aboard. As did a land use attorney, Mike Kvarme. There was a labor leader, Matt Kelly, and public relations consultant, Adam Mendelsohn. Chris Lehane would be chair.

As for the publicly generated arena proposals, anyone could submit a plan for review. The process would be public and transparent. At the Mayor's Office, we presumed Gerry Kamilos and Convergence would win. But we couldn't dare rig the Sacramento First competition. The committee members were all respectable citizens. They would not have stood for us cooking the outcome.

Kamilos was the favorite because he fulfilled the mayor's ambition to move the arena from Cal Expo to downtown, a neighborhood desperate for redevelopment and tower cranes. Kamilos was much farther along than anyone else. He had been working for months on Convergence, spending money on schedules, design and lobbying. He could present a mature proposal, plus financing. Surely he would win.

The contest was open for two months. Seven groups made proposals, including Stan Thomas, who was running out of money for his purchase of the downtown rail yards. There were two competing restaurant owners, Matt Haines and Ali Mackani, a real estate agent named Rick Tripp, the Natomas Chamber of Commerce, and a Kings fan, Doug Tatara, who hoped to revive the Disneyland North dream at Cal Expo. Tatara charmingly said his plan was "just an idea." Gerry Kamilos also entered.

The seven groups came to City Hall and publicly unveiled their proposals in the grand lobby, democracy in action. Cameras from local TV stations photographed the displays while more than 100 people wandered through the hall and studied the proposals. But the camera crews didn't linger. They took their pictures and rushed one block south to the Citizen Hotel, where a second media event was underway, this one conducted by NBA consultant John Moag.

As the cameras focused and whirred, Moag declared that the NBA didn't need a public design competition or Blue Ribbon Task Force. The league had its winner: Gerry Kamilos and his partners Macquarie and Pacific Coast Capital. "The Convergence plan has the guys who are going to show me the money," Moag told the media.

Back at City Hall, Kevin Johnson was furious. Moag was trying to wreck Kevin's strategy, which was designed by Lehane to prepare and soften up the community for a public-private arena deal. Kamilos would probably have won the Sacramento First contest anyway. But the grocer's son had taken out insurance. He secretly aligned with Moag as an informal partner. "I knew I shouldn't have trusted them," Johnson said.

Days of recrimination followed. Lehane published a blog poking fun at the NBA for "shooting air balls" over the Sacramento First process. David Stern sided with his friend Moag. The commissioner called Johnson and cussed him out, saying, "Your friend Lehane isn't helping matters." Two city council members, Robert King Fong and Sandy Sheedy, always eager to embarrass Kevin Johnson, said there was no point in having Sacramento First review the seven entries. The city was going with Kamilos, they said.

Johnson stalled the city council and let Sacramento First finish its review process. Not surprisingly, Convergence won. Kamilos received exclusive right to negotiate a public-private arena deal with the city, which owned 33 acres in the rail yards, including the prospective arena site.

All along, Kamilos assured the Mayor's Office that the Cal Expo board and Gov. Schwarzenegger supported Convergence. Now I began to wonder. To make sure Kamilos was telling the truth, I walked to the Capitol in a rainstorm to see David Crane, the governor's finance expert. When I arrived, soaked through three layers, Crane had a copy of Kamilos' top-secret finance plan open on the desk. "Is this what you're asking about?" he said. Then he laughed. "This is a nonstarter. It's going nowhere."

In Crane's interpretation, the investment partners Macquarie and Pacific Coast took no risk. The general fund of the state of California would backstop any losses generated by Convergence. "This thing is not going to happen, no way," Crane said. He tossed the secret finance plan aside and sent me back into the rain. No need to worry about crop dusters and knockout gas in that weather.

OVER THE NEXT several months, the prophecy of David Crane was acted out at City Hall and Cal Expo. The realities of Convergence—a speculative series of real estate swaps backstopped by state and local general funds—rendered the plan unworkable. The Cal Expo board did not even bother to discuss who might cover any losses caused by Convergence. Instead, the board members conducted a public execution of Convergence at their September 2010 meeting.

Cal Expo rejected the idea of moving the State Fair to North Natomas. The Expo board believed the Natomas site was too small for the State Fair. And the board was insulted by the presumption that Cal Expo would go along with whatever was convenient for the city of Sacramento and the NBA. The board could not believe its friend John Moag had begun a side relationship with Kamilos. Embarrassed and insulted, Cal Expo treated Moag and Kamilos like a wife treats a philandering husband and his girlfriend. The board dumped Convergence on the sidewalk and cut off negotiations.

At the September Cal Expo board meeting, several news reporters asked me if the Mayor's Office still believed Convergence had a shot. I told them the Gerry Kamilos plan was a three-legged stool with one leg cut off. Trying to be positive, I said, "It still has a chance, but not in this format. Without Cal Expo, there is no Convergence, at least as we know it." A member of the Sacramento First task force, Mark Harris, was more straightforward. He publicly compared Convergence to a hustle and a scam. Harris concluded by saying, "And I apologize to hustlers and scam artists around the world for the comparison."

If there were going to be a three-legged strategy for an arena in Sacramento, Kevin Johnson would need a new chair.

Chapter Nineteen: Trying To Cut A Deal To Leave

Kevin Johnson surrounded himself with books, but I never saw him read one, other than the family Bible on his desk and "Good to Great," the corporate leadership primer by Jim Collins. Johnson required his staff to read and discuss "Good to Great." We carried copies around City Hall. Our red book jackets were tattered from use.

The discussions focused on how the Mayor's Office measured up to the strategies laid out by Collins. Many days, we were average to good. When it came to creating something that would survive beyond Johnson's time at City Hall, we were bad. Nothing we did seemed to stick.

While Johnson did not devour books, he made time for TV. He believed no room was complete without a TV monitor. As mayor, he was assigned an armed police driver and black SUV. There were police lights and siren on the vehicle, but no satellite TV. So Johnson paid for a mobile satellite device, a four-foot circular Starship Enterprise contraption bolted to the top of the SUV, making the mayoral vehicle instantly identifiable as it rolled around town. With his satellite, Kevin enjoyed sports events, news broadcasts and movies about strong, decisive people. Among his favorite were "The Godfather" pictures.

Sometimes Johnson made comparisons between dramatic characters and real humans. One example was David Stern, in whom Kevin saw the reflection of the mob boss created by the author Mario Puzo, the director Francis Ford Coppola and the actor Al Pacino. "No joke, this dude is not normal," Johnson said about Stern. "Normal people, they get mad, they get over it. Not this guy. You do not want to make this guy mad. You see him sitting there all cool and calm, but underneath, he's thinking, he's plotting.

I'm telling you, it's not normal. He's like Michael from 'The Godfather.' You do not want to mess with this guy."

Johnson told me this as I sat in his office after listening to a telephone conversation between Johnson and Stern. I heard many such discussions while working for Johnson. Stern's voice would boom over the conference phone speaker on the mayor's desk. The commissioner was always precise and under control but sarcastic and profane in ways he did not reveal in public.

Stern spent almost five decades crafting a public image as an unflappable corporate attorney and sports CEO, a professional who spoke in brilliantly constructed sentences. He displayed those qualities in phone calls with Johnson, but with far more intensity. On rare occasions, he sounded worn out by the process of getting a new arena built in Sacramento. Who could blame him? Stern worked a decade on the Sacramento arena. He was the city of Sacramento's biggest booster in pro sports. He had a right to be exhausted.

In 2011 and 2012, Stern was juggling many important issues. There was collective bargaining, the suspension of games over a labor dispute and even the possible contraction of the league, where money-losing franchises might be jettisoned. Those were his daily tasks. It was remarkable that Stern had time for the endless arena saga of a vagrant franchise 3,000 miles from his office in New York City.

But Stern believed in the Sacramento market. And he loved Kevin Johnson. In phone calls between the two, the commissioner shifted among various attitudes. Sometimes he was proud. Sometimes frustrated. Stern was role-playing. Like Johnson, Stern usually had an assistant or two in his New York office listening to the conversation. And he often tried to coach Johnson, to show the inexperienced mayor exactly how the NBA and its commissioner operated.

When he was in a good mood, Stern opened with small talk and a joke, usually tinged with sarcasm. When he was frustrated, which was often, he got right down to business. Always, Stern's tone was parental. He praised, scolded or guided the mayor like a responsible father leads an eager but uncertain son.

Impressively, Stern's comments revealed detailed knowledge of the minutiae of Sacramento's arena situation. He knew more about Sacramento than some city council members. There was a July 2011 phone call to

Johnson, when Stern was organizing a visit to Sacramento by Oklahoma City Thunder owner Clay Bennett.

The commissioner made references to Bennett, the Maloof brothers, the arena operating company AEG and the real estate trust Inland American, which had taken ownership of the downtown rail yards after Atlanta developer Stan Thomas stopped making payments. Stern talked about Sacramento economics and politics with a local savant's knowledge.

By the summer of 2011, it appeared Sacramento's new arena would be built on city property in the rail yards. Several neighboring acres controlled by Inland American might also be required. The city would own the building and contribute about 65 percent of the construction cost. The public would be told its investment would return $7 billion in economic activity over 30 years. AEG would operate the facility. Stern knew all of this and more as he spoke with Johnson.

David Stern: "You need to create a memo on economic development to prep Clay and the relocation committee. You will need an update on the money part. You should include stats with respect to the 70-30 regional participation and the $7 billion economic study. You'll need the AEG piece, the Inland piece, The Boys as tenants, and your understanding that if you can identify a way to produce $25 million, it allows you to bond for $250 million."

Kevin Johnson: "We self-imposed 100 days for our study. We don't want to wait for 2012."

Stern: "You will have to get moving if you want to have the ability to get plans and drawings."

While Stern's loyalty to Sacramento was proved over three decades (the Kings moved to California 14 months after Stern was promoted to the Commissioner's Office), the presence of a former NBA player in the Mayor's Office deepened the love. It was tempting to wonder whether Stern would have devoted so much time and energy to the troubled small market franchise after 2008 if not for the presence of Kevin Johnson. That love certainly would not have happened under a different NBA commissioner.

No matter who was mayor or how big the city was, David Stern disliked franchise relocations. He felt the musical chairs played by team owners and cities hurt the league's credibility, recalling the 1950s, when the NBA shrank to eight teams and the nomadic Harlem Globetrotters, with their confetti buckets and slapstick routines, were the most highly regarded organization in pro basketball.

As much as he hated relocations, the commissioner knew dollars drove his business. Dollars came from premium seats and sponsorships and advertising and broadcast rights. Stern knew it was generally a bad business practice to own your own arena. It was better to let taxpayers carry that load. And he knew that if Sacramento didn't build a new arena and a city such as Seattle did, the Kings would have to move again, even if it broke Stern's heart.

Except that it would not be quite so simple. Kevin Johnson represented a special case. NBA owners were accustomed to mayors presenting arguments on behalf of cities, showing up at the Board of Governors meeting in New York each April to explain why a team should (or should not) be blessed to move. When Johnson personally began to lobby the NBA, an effort that turned into annual visits to the Board of Governors meetings in 2011, 2012 and 2013, the owners weren't just hearing from another smiling, ambitious politician.

This mayor was family, a son of the league, an NBA success story. The owners didn't refer him to as "Mr. Mayor," but as "Kevin." After his first visit to the Board of Governors, Johnson said, "The big thing that came through is that they were really proud of me. And I was proud to stand before them as a mayor."

Stern wasn't an NBA owner. He wasn't allowed to vote on questions of relocation. But he took tremendous pride in Johnson. The commissioner wanted to make sure the mayor was well prepared for his encounters with NBA owners. Stern tipped off Johnson about potential traps and loaded questions, directing the former all-star through the minefield of forthcoming cross-examinations.

THE COMMISSIONER had seen NBA players fall to drug and gambling addictions. He steered the league around dilemmas of moral turpitude, violence and cultural disconnections between his athletes and the fans that supported them. Bad things happened to plenty of NBA players.

Good things happened too, but beyond Dave Bing and Bill Bradley, two outstanding athletes from the 1960s and 1970s who would become, respectively, mayor of Detroit and a U.S. Senator from New Jersey, the NBA wasn't accustomed to having players reach elected office. Johnson was special. Not a generational peer of Stern's like Bing or Bradley, but a younger, modern man who set a solid example for all NBA players.

Johnson reciprocated. He wasn't a friend of Stern's. But his NBA career taught him to fear, respect and love the commissioner. The Sacramento arena situation would pull them closer together. It was a unique and counterintuitive pull. Stern, the old man still vital to the NBA, needed help from Kevin, the younger student retired from basketball and pursuing other interests. Stern used Johnson to help anchor a vagrant and perpetually underfunded franchise in a city that loved its Kings. Johnson used Stern to help bring definition and legacy to a budding political career.

Stern wanted to fight for Sacramento, to prove that the league would protect small markets and loyal fans and sponsors. Johnson, who had no interest in reliving his NBA glory days, wanted to move away from basketball and prove his worth as a CEO and civic reform leader.

He refused to touch a basketball, other than to autograph one. He played the game for a few minutes on his 40th and 45th birthdays, alone at midnight in the Sacramento High School gym, just to see what it felt like. It didn't feel good. His hamstring muscles and knees hurt and the erosion of his skills embarrassed him. Basketball was yesterday.

But with Stern's guidance and persistence, basketball would find renewed relevance for Kevin. The game would become a way to show leadership and bring purpose to Johnson's days in the Mayor's Office. Johnson ran for mayor to prove he wasn't afraid of a newspaper digging up unpleasant reports from his past. And he wanted to demonstrate his vision beyond the basketball court, to make people understand he was blessed with executive talent, like Jerry Colangelo in Phoenix.

Kevin Johnson's ultimate political goal was to change the Sacramento City Charter and give the mayor CEO-style authority, like Michael Bloomberg in New York or Gavin Newsom in San Francisco or three dozen other big city mayors across the U.S. "I'm an executive, not a legislator," Kevin said. "It's how I'm wired."

Now his plans to rewrite the City Charter were stalled by the city council and going nowhere. He needed something new to keep from being smothered by the ceremonial emptiness of his job. He had far more passion for education reform and retooling the City Charter than for saving the Kings. If anything, Kevin was ambivalent about a new arena. And of course he secretly despised the Kings. But when the NCAA rebuked

Sacramento in 2009, Johnson realized the Kings and their future could fill a void in his mission, especially from an economic development perspective.

The arena needed a local champion, someone who could help David Stern bring closure to his decade of work to keep the Kings in Sacramento. Paradoxically, Kevin felt he could survive losing the Kings, but he could not forgive himself if he failed to help Commissioner Stern build a new arena in Sacramento. "As long as we can say we did everything possible to keep the team, we'll be OK, no matter what happens," Kevin said, reconciling himself and his staff to the team's possible departure.

At the same time, if Stern wanted something, Kevin would do everything possible to see that Stern got it. What Stern wanted was a permanent home for the Kings in a new Sacramento arena. The mayor did not want to mess with that guy.

Before phone conversations with Stern, Kevin was nervous. He wrote detailed notes on a yellow legal pad. He ran through mock conversations, trying to anticipate questions from the commissioner and memorize credible answers. He was anxious about getting every nuance right to impress the mentor.

The conversations were always about how much money the city of Sacramento would contribute to the arena, either through bonds, taxes or a legislative process. Johnson knew practically nothing about bond capacities and tax schemes, but he could not display ignorance to the commissioner. That's why Kevin had his friend, retired City Treasurer Tom Friery, on board.

> *David Stern: "I want a document in Clay's (Bennett) hand that lays out the funding status this week."*
>
> *Kevin Johnson: "We will have specific explanations to maintain transparency about the funding."*
>
> *Stern: "We want the memo to be from us to Clay. When he signs off, we get it to the rest of the (NBA Finance) committee. We want the Maloofs to be a happy tenant. And this is important. We want to know what we can get from the California House of Representatives (Assembly) and state legislature other than b.s. What about the JPA (Joint Powers Authority)?"*
>
> *Johnson: "That would be the city and county or city and region possibly for the JPA. They are also looking at billboard revenue from billboards on state property. It would be enabling legislation."*

THE COLLAPSE of the Convergence proposal, with the retreat of Gerry Kamilos and John Moag, liberated Johnson, allowing him to move more aggressively on the arena front. Now the mayor had the chance to do things his way, with Stern's guidance. Cal Expo and the State Fair were out of the frame. Johnson could turn the arena into a city project with the mayor in control. Nothing was more important to Kevin Johnson than control. If he couldn't control the City Charter, he began to realize that maybe he could control the future of the Kings and their arena. It was time to bury the demons of Draft Day 1987.

He got on the phone to his strategic advisor, Chris Lehane, and explored ways to adapt the work already completed by the Sacramento First task force, Kamilos and the other developers. Lehane wanted to simplify the message and boil down the confusion into a clear narrative. A real project with a budget, schedule and funding. The project needed a label, a catch phrase.

Johnson settled on the idea of creating the "Dream Team," a name from the 1992 Barcelona Olympics, when the NBA filled the U.S. team's roster. He would match the top local developer and nationally respected arena builder (David Taylor and Turner Construction, both previously associated with Convergence), a first-rate project manager (ICON Venue of Colorado, which had been interested in the Sacramento arena since 2009) and engage an internationally experienced arena architect (Dan Meis, who served as a Sacramento First committee member).

These weren't the kind of people who typically worked for free. But they all liked Johnson, appreciated his enthusiasm and figured they could cash in once the project was funded. The mayor had a persuasive way about him. Johnson promised his Dream Team an exclusive path to a $400 million arena, without the traditional bureaucratic hurdles of "Request for Proposal" document packages and competitive bids.

The mayor had no authority to make such promises, but he convinced the Dream Team and a majority of city council members to play along. The city would serve as master developer and landlord under a fast track design-build arena program. None of these shortcuts would have been possible, politically or legally, for any project less important to the city's ego than saving the Kings.

The Dream Team agreed to begin its work without upfront retainers on the presumption that dollars would flow once the project was approved.

Tim Romani, president and CEO of ICON Venue, was the most nervous Dream Team member. Romani knew the predevelopment phase was the most speculative (thus risky) part of the project.

Until the arena was funded, nobody could get paid. The plug could be pulled at any point. Yet ICON was responsible for significant predevelopment work, including the creation of budget documents and schedules, which required an investment of staff hours and trips to Sacramento from Colorado. ICON's staff time and plane tickets were expensive for Romani, yet the arena was still an unfunded abstraction. This meant ICON was throwing money at a project that might never happen.

While Romani sweated, the Urban Land Institute studied the rail yards. Independent and credible, the ULI team said the location would be tight, but would work alongside a transit hub already under construction with state and federal money. Two big questions remained. Where would the arena dollars come from? And how much would the Maloof family contribute?

The Maloof's loyalty to Sacramento was highly debatable by 2010. The family had made just one significant demonstration of permanence and stability, hiring Matina Kolokotronis as team president. Kolokotronis, a respected local attorney with deep roots in the community, had credibility across the spectrums of sponsors and fans. She had done legal work with European basketball players. The NBA and David Stern treated her with high regard. Her adopted home was Sacramento. Her husband, Sotiris Kolokotronis, was a formidable local developer.

It was remarkably (and uncharacteristically) smart of the Maloofs to hire Matina. Now she would be the highest-ranking woman in the league-wide NBA hierarchy. Surely, optimistic Kings fans thought, the Maloofs would not place a Sacramento person of Ms. Kolokotronis' reputation, caliber and pedigree in an executive position, simply to move the team.

OR WOULD THEY? The Maloof strategy was revealed on Saturday, February 19, 2011, at a press conference held by Stern to celebrate the NBA All-Star Game at Los Angeles. Without dramatics, the commissioner said the Maloofs were talking to the city of Anaheim and Honda Center operator Henry Samueli, who owned the NHL Anaheim Ducks. They were talking about moving the Kings to Southern California.

Stern gave no details, but the Maloof objective was clear. The Boys were ready to relocate to Anaheim. They would contribute nothing to Sacramento's new arena. Five days later, the Kings asked the NBA to extend the official deadline to declare their intent to relocate. They needed a little more time to close the deal with Samueli.

Unable to gain insight from a mystified Matina Kolokotronis, Kevin Johnson called a press conference and delivered a blunt message. "This means one thing," he said. "They are trying to cut a deal to leave."

The Kings, who lost $9.8 million in 2010-2011, had been secretly negotiating with Anaheim for weeks. The deal was down to the fine points, including percentage splits between Samueli and the Maloofs over luxury suites, general admission tickets, signage, food and beverage, souvenirs and parking. Samueli would loan the Maloofs $75 million and would take over the team if The Boys defaulted. Samueli's lawyers wrote the default section in bold, capitalized letters. Nobody could be surprised if (or when) Samueli had to call in his loan and seize control of the Kings.

The Kings would be secondary tenants at Honda Center behind the Ducks, a backup position for an NBA team after 26 years of owning and operating its own arena in Sacramento. The Boys had wandered into the lion's den. Indicative of the Maloof's naive position, the family seemed to expect a windfall from Honda, which was contractually obligated to increase its Honda Center naming rights dollars if an NBA team moved to Anaheim.

One problem. No dollar amount was specified in the contract, allowing Honda to increase its sponsorship by whatever number it deemed reasonable. Presumably, that number would be small, since Honda's name was already on the building. When AEG chief executive Tim Leiweke talked about how the Maloofs failed to specify the dollars they would get from Honda Center naming rights, he laughed out loud. Leiweke did not want the Kings in Anaheim, competing against the Lakers and Clippers at AEG's Staples Center. One word he used to describe the Maloof brothers was "idiots."

In April 2011, the NBA Board of Governors would hear from two California mayors, Tom Tait of Anaheim and Kevin Johnson of Sacramento. Tait would bring the man whose private company operated the publicly owned Honda Center, Henry Samueli, a UCLA electrical engineering professor who became a billionaire through the creation of Broadcom Corporation, a semiconductor company that ran wireless networks.

Johnson would bring his own billionaire, or at least a representative of one, Ron Burkle, whose proxy was carried by his friend and former staff member, Sacramento lobbyist Darius Anderson. Burkle made his money in groceries and real estate. He was ready to buy the Kings and keep them in Sacramento, if only the Maloofs would sell, Anderson told the NBA.

The Anaheim group would craft its message around three points. Our city is ready for the NBA. The Kings want to come to our city. Our market is close but separate from Los Angeles and won't impact the sales strategies of the Lakers and Clippers. There's plenty of money to go around in Southern California.

The Sacramento message was being drawn up to emphasize fan loyalty and 100 percent market share. The Kings were immensely popular and suffered no competition from other major league teams. And Sacramento was a Top 20 TV market. The community could support an NBA team despite the failures of the Maloof family to fully exploit the market. Johnson believed those were his strongest cards. David Stern picked up the phone and suggested a slightly different approach.

Chapter Twenty: OK, Keep Dicking Us Around

As they prepared for the NBA Board of Governors meeting, Commissioner David Stern suggested that Mayor Kevin Johnson not carry on too long about the Kings' popularity with everyday fans in Sacramento.

NBA owners loved and cherished the average fan, but the Board of Governors didn't really care all that much about general admission ticket sales. This was not a conceit by the NBA. It was not cynical. And it was not something that the league would ever publicly admit. It was business. General admission fan support had almost never been a major consideration in debates over franchise relocations in pro sports.

The Brooklyn Dodgers and New York Giants were successful and popular before they moved to California in 1957. But both played in derelict stadiums as new markets beckoned. Brooklyn fans picketed Ebbets Field and team headquarters when news broke about the pending move. Fans circulated petitions and held pep rallies at Borough Hall. No matter. The promise of fresh West Coast territories carried the day.

Decades later in Oakland, the NFL Raiders had one of the most loyal blue-collar fan bases in pro football when they moved to Los Angeles in 1982. Owner Al Davis was interested in luxury boxes, not general admission sellouts.

The NBA was not much different. The league was dependent on corporate support and premium level sponsorships. Stern knew the Maloofs had told other NBA owners that Sacramento lacked the corporate horsepower to support an NBA team. Sponsorships were a major issue in Sacramento.

With no Fortune 500 companies based in Sacramento, the Maloofs could go to New York and make a believable argument that dismal economic conditions were driving them to Anaheim. Johnson told Stern that many regional Sacramento corporations were eager support the NBA. The mayor insisted the Maloofs had quit trying to sell sponsorships in Sacramento. They had abandoned the market and driven the business community against the Kings. "You will have to prove that," Stern said.

Then Johnson told Stern about Burkle. After an introduction by Darius Anderson, Johnson and Burkle held secret talks to put the tycoon in position to buy the Kings. Johnson insisted on secrecy. We couldn't even mention Burkle's name around the Mayor's Office. We referred to him only as "Ralph," from the grocery chain that began his fortune.

Ralph would be a perfect NBA owner. Ralph had billions. Ralph owned the NHL Pittsburgh Penguins and had overcome many hurdles to build a new arena for his hockey team. "You have Burkle?" Stern asked. "I have Burkle," Johnson said. For once, the commissioner was silent.

The first challenge was to prove the existence of corporate sponsors in Sacramento. Johnson sent me over to the Metropolitan Chamber of Commerce office in Old Sacramento to work with Chamber CEO Matt Mahood and the city's Convention and Visitors Bureau management team. We created a list of companies to cold-call about sponsoring the Kings with new dollars.

Now this was something different. I was a city employee, earning a city salary and pension, but was acting as a Kings corporate sales executive without the Kings knowing about it. In about 10 days, we found 29 businesses willing to pay $9.2 million in fresh, new sponsorships for the next NBA season, assuming the Kings stayed in Sacramento.

Kevin Johnson was our closer. Local CEOs could not resist his pitch. The dollars we raised showed the depth of community corporate support. And it demonstrated the weakness of the Maloof sales force, which, intentionally or not, ignored dozens of potential corporate customers.

We found major companies—AT&T and Wells Fargo—and local franchise operators from McDonald's, Anheuser-Busch and Jiffy Lube. There were tribal casinos and insurance companies such as VSP Global and Western Health. There were local companies, such as Sac Jet and Zoom Copiers. Many of the CEOs told the same story. They wanted to support the Kings but had been ignored or insulted by the Maloofs.

When the Mayor's Office and Chamber of Commerce came asking for money to save the Kings, several CEOs said they didn't trust the

Maloof family, but were willing to pledge dollars to preserve a team they considered a civic asset. "The one thing I don't want to do is rent the team for one year," said Gary Johnson, whose Zoom Copiers committed $125,000. "I want a long-term commitment by them."

On April 14, 2011, at the NBA meetings in New York, Mayor Tait, Samueli and the Maloofs went first, presenting their story to the Board of Governors at the St. Regis Hotel, the Edwardian palace on East 55th Street in Manhattan favored by NBA executives. The Anaheim group spoke and answered questions for more than two hours. Johnson went second and spoke for about 20 minutes. He was intentionally brief, sensing that the Anaheim team had been long-winded and disorganized.

Johnson was accompanied by Darius Anderson, who spoke about Burkle's interest in buying the Kings, and Tim Romani, who described the plans to build an arena in Sacramento.

Many NBA owners knew Romani and ICON, his arena development company. He brought credibility. Anderson aroused the owners' interest the moment he spoke the words "Ron Burkle." Johnson focused on the pride he felt as he represented his city. He breezed over the Kings' fan support and market exclusivity. Then he discussed the sponsorship pledges. "That got their attention," Johnson said.

Before the meeting, the media and public were not aware of Ralph. Nor did they know the Maloofs had already rebuffed Ralph's first offer to discuss the sale of the Kings. The Sacramento Bee wrote, "Burkle's dramatic emergence turned the saga of the Kings completely upside down." The description was accurate. And would remain so for the next two years.

The NBA owners were impressed by Burkle's name. Even more, they were fascinated by Johnson's claim that he could collect more than $7 million in new local corporate sponsorship dollars for the Kings in one week. Stern immediately challenged the mayor to make the number $9 million. Which, as it turned out, was our true figure.

The Board of Governors was stunned. The owners didn't expect Johnson to become the Kings' top corporate salesman. They had heard nothing about those kinds of dollars—$7 million or $9 million—from the Maloofs, who whined about the hardships of doing business in Sacramento. One week later, the owners sent their colleague Clay Bennett of the Oklahoma City Thunder to Sacramento. He came to see the money.

LANDING IN his private jet, Bennett was whisked to a series of meetings, including one at the U.S. Bank Tower downtown, where Johnson assembled his corporate sponsors. One by one, the business executives told Bennett how much cash they were prepared to pay in new sponsorship dollars over the next two, three or four years.

The pledges topped $9 million for the upcoming season. Later that afternoon at City Hall, I sat next to Bennett as he reviewed the day's progress with Johnson. When the subject of corporate dollars came up, I thought the Oklahoma City mogul would cry. "When those guys went around the room and said how much money they would put up, well, I have never seen anything like that before in my life," Bennett said with a tone of astonishment. Nothing moves an NBA owner like $9 million in windfall sponsorships.

Johnson had resolved the question of corporate support. And he had wrecked Anaheim's chance to grab the Kings. Anaheim was still confident. The Maloofs registered the nickname "Royals" in preparation for the move, to avoid confusion with the NHL Los Angeles Kings. But Stern and Clay Bennett were now pushing for The Boys to give Sacramento one more year.

Stern knew the league almost certainly lacked the legal authority to block a move. In discussions with Johnson, the commissioner made it clear he would not engage the Maloofs in a courtroom battle over their right to relocate. The league had no desire for a federal antitrust fight over the Kings, a fight the NBA would very likely lose.

The NBA was a cartel of multiple owners, not one company running 30 teams. If David Stern tried to stop an owner from moving, a federal judge would probably say the league was practicing restraint of trade and bless the relocation.

Stern had a new strategy, based on his decades of friendship with The Boys. He would personally persuade them to stay in Sacramento, arguing that Sacramento deserved one last chance. He asked the Maloofs to give Mayor Johnson time to put together a finance plan for an arena. Stern offered a 10-month deadline.

Feeling the commissioner's pressure, The Boys agreed to stay for one more season. Among the family, there was the sense that the relocation would happen regardless. There was no way Johnson could produce a legitimate finance plan in 10 months. What was one more year? Besides, Anaheim needed time to make improvements at Honda Center. The

Maloofs phoned Stern and Johnson and said they would not file paperwork for relocation to Anaheim. Johnson had his chance to build an arena.

The mayor called a celebratory press conference in the plaza in front of City Hall. Stern was delighted. Also pleased was Tim Leiweke of AEG, who didn't want a third NBA team in the Los Angeles market competing with AEG's Staples Center. Stern set a public deadline of March 2012 for Sacramento to fund its new arena. "We are going to put all our efforts in Sacramento and make it happen and make it succeed," Stern said. "But if it can't, if this becomes the fifth or sixth or seventh (failure), it will be the last as far as we are concerned."

Funding had always been the big problem, the place where were political and public interests and the realities of the pro sports marketplace crashed and burned. The NBA wanted a maximum amount of public dollars for the arena, but wouldn't define what it meant by "maximum."

Johnson knew he couldn't tap the city's general fund, which was shrinking under the recession thanks to plunges in property tax values and sales taxes. Johnson knew he couldn't count on the state of California or surrounding cities and counties for help. As for the Maloofs, the mayor knew the family would contribute nothing.

CHRIS LEHANE went to work, hoping to soften the public for what he knew would be a fight over city assets. The arena penciled out at $387 million. Johnson insisted on keeping it under $400 million for psychological reasons. The city would likely be responsible for about two-thirds. This could only mean the sale of surplus city properties and billboard locations, the collection of user taxes, and scooping revenues from hotel and car rental taxes. General sales taxes and property taxes were off limits. Those funding sources would require a public vote.

Lehane enlisted a consultant named Jeremiah Jackson, an economics prodigy with degrees from Stanford University and Harvard Business School, to organize a community task force called "Think Big Sacramento." The task force would keep the media occupied and present a united regional front of elected officials, community leaders, business executives and labor organizations.

Think Big's job was to drown out people who opposed public dollars for pro sports facilities and flood the community with positive arena information. As might be expected from a young man with degrees from Stanford and HBS, Jackson was smart and industrious about his task.

He created an assembly line of reports about jobs and economic investment, portraying the new Entertainment and Sports Complex (the Mayor's Office stopped calling it an arena because that sounded too sports-obsessive) as a catalyst to rescue Sacramento from the recession. The reports examined every aspect of the arena and its relationship to the community.

There was a report on mass transit and the arena. On labor unions and the arena. On user fees and public lands and the arena. On local jobs and regional jobs and the arena. On public opinion polls and the arena. Jackson fed his reports to the media ("Filling the cup," as Lehane put it) to discourage reporters from poking around in Entertainment and Sports corners that weren't authorized by the Mayor's Office.

The reports were well-polished white papers that sidestepped certain financial realities. One section, the "Nexus Report," said the arena would be funded by "finding a Nexus" with "revenues from financial beneficiaries, revenues from users and revenues created or enhanced because of" the new arena. One day Lehane told reporters, "We are going to identify the delta and bifurcate the delta." Watching reporters write this down, I marveled at Chris's effortless ability to tie a silky ribbon around an abstraction.

The "Nexus Report" concluded that the funding plan "will likely be fundamentally different than approaches in other cities." Fortunately, nobody asked what all those words meant. The true answer would have been something like: well, let's see, the arena should generate new dollars for the city; beyond that, we don't exactly have a finance plan.

WE DID HAVE an abundance of creative finance offers. Almost daily, I received cold calls from sketchy middlemen (never women) eager to give Sacramento easy money for an arena. There were patterns. The callers habitually deployed cell phones with traffic noise such as trucks, horns, leaf blowers and sirens in the background.

They represented mysterious Middle Eastern or Asian interests with mountains of cash that had to be invested by lunchtime. And they always advised me not to borrow a mere $250 million or $400 million but nothing less than $1 billion. The heftier number would show we really meant business.

One promoter said he could finance the arena with funds from death benefit insurance policies. He offered to deliver a $400 million check by Friday with minimal paperwork. Another promoter said the city could immediately collect $300 million by agreeing to sponsor U.S. residency visas for wealthy Chinese nationals.

There was some truth in the death benefit and visa schemes. Chinese and Middle Eastern wealth was attracted to California. The U.S. government did have a special visa program for foreign investors who created jobs for U.S. citizens. But once the leaf blowers and sirens faded, my callers were all the same: Money hustlers offering fast loans at high interest rates. They lacked the gilded wise-guy humility of Louie Jacobs and his peanuts, but they could deliver money almost as fast.

Some of these benefactors claimed to personally know Kevin Johnson. Unfortunately, they referred to him as "KJ," his nickname among NBA fans. Nobody who really knew the mayor called him KJ. He was either Kevin or Mayor (or even Frog, if you went way back).

When Roger Craig, the former all-pro San Francisco 49ers running back, called to inquire about buying the Kings, he used the word "Mayor." Roger had a touch of intrigue about him. He represented a mysterious investor from India. But knowing Kevin's proper title was one more detail that made Roger Craig special. I never heard a leaf blower while speaking to Roger.

While I juggled the phone calls and sales pitches, Jeremiah Jackson managed the message and served as the project's rapid response police force. He took to the TV and radio airwaves and Web whenever a negative story threatened to break about the city's arena funding process. He engaged everyday fans, marshaling large turnouts for city council meetings and press conferences.

The fan groups were politically important. They reminded local elected officials and the media that the community's identity was wrapped around the Kings. Dan Barrett, the sports financing consultant hired by the city, began to piece together revenue streams from all possible sources, making the "Nexus" somewhat real.

The Dream Team joined in, rolling out designs and construction work schedules. The collaborative energies made for delirious, pep-rally staff meetings at City Hall, with one problem. There simply wasn't enough money to build a $387 million arena.

BY SEPTEMBER, Stern was growing angry over the lack of progress on the money front. Stern didn't buy the "Nexus Report." He wanted to see the public dollars that would close the funding gap and reduce the Maloofs' equity position. The family, he knew, needed its cash to pay for players and operating costs.

And while Kevin Johnson wanted the Maloofs to sell the Kings, Stern could not force a sale. In conversations with Johnson, the commissioner and NBA President Joel Litvin sounded like New York Police detectives running out of patience with a suspect.

David Stern: "We're going to have a meeting next week, but what the real question is, when are you going to stop avoiding having the real discussion? We need to know where this is going. We can have all kinds of meetings, because that's how you operate, but I only have one goal here: how can I come up with a lease that makes the Kings competitive? If we can't, we aren't going to have a deal."

Kevin Johnson: "I want our working groups to meet."

Stern: "We have wars on two fronts, revenue sharing and collective bargaining. We have problems involving transfers in Atlanta and Philadelphia. With regards to Sacramento, we need a term sheet or some kind of document in invisible ink if you wish, but if you are waiting for us to get rid of the Maloofs, it's not going to happen. I don't care how many Ron Burkles you have in your pocket."

Johnson: "Are you not OK meeting with our working group?"

Joel Litvin: "What we want is your best estimate of all funding sources other than the Kings. A schedule of funding sources other than the Kings. Can you get that?"

Johnson: "Yes. I'll meet with the commissioner on September 20, then I will get you a date for that schedule, then you will have it within a week of that."

Stern: "The owners were talking about this yesterday. You guys were 95 or 90 to 10 that it wouldn't happen, now you're maybe 60-40 it won't happen. We can have a meeting and a great sandwich and coffee or dinner, but we need a document with a number. I understand we have different strategies. You like to have meetings. You think we have a laborious style. But we have only one question we're interested in. We need to know the number. If there's a need for money other than the Maloofs, we can be allies, but you keep hiding the ball and playing games. We are your loyal servants."

Johnson: "We don't have a document."

Stern: "OK, keep dicking us around, dick around 30 owners who do this sort of stuff on the back of envelopes. That's your strategy."

Kevin had a strategy, but he didn't necessarily comprehend it. The idea was called "Parking Monetization." It was a way for cities to raise cash by leasing, selling or bonding against the revenues of two very valuable assets: parking garages and metered street parking spaces.

The strategy had mixed results in other cities. In Chicago, parking assets were used to backfill general-fund budget gaps and pay down debt, which quickly drained the parking assets. Consultant Dan Barrett, plus Sacramento Assistant City Manager John Dangberg and Treasurer Russ Fehr, dug into parking monetization. They were nudged along by private parking operations that wanted to get their hands on Sacramento's downtown garages.

The city's team found a positive outcome in Indianapolis, where parking services improved under private management and new revenue sources were tapped. Dangberg figured the strategy might work for Sacramento if the city treated its parking as a pump to inflate one economic development balloon—the arena—and not cover shortfalls for on-going expenses like police, fire and city worker pensions.

The city asked parking operators if they would be interested in bidding on the Sacramento inventory. Thirteen operators said yes. The value was unspecified, but the parking operators told the city its goal of raising $255 million was not unreasonable with long-term leases, somewhere between 30 and 50 years.

> *Joel Litvin: "We gather this parking thing is your ace in the hole. Is this really viable? I know it's been done in other places. Can you really come up with a big number?"*
>
> *Kevin Johnson: "Normally, cities need something like six months to dive deep into the parking question. We know we can't afford six months. But it's viable because this is a labor town and I've got labor leaders on Think Big, and they like this project out of self-interest. It will create jobs."*

Parking was more than Kevin's ace in the hole. It was the only way Sacramento could deliver large amounts of public money to a project that would require at least $255 million in taxpayer dollars, if not more. Without the city's parking assets, that kind of public money did not exist in Sacramento.

If Sacramento wanted a new arena, it would have to mortgage its cash cow: Parking.

Chapter Twenty-One: You Are Sitting On A Great Market

The ability to make arena dollars grow from parking held a powerful allure for the Sacramento City Council. All that money right under our noses, and we didn't even know it! But the more the council members thought about monetizing the city's parking assets, the more questions they had.

Weren't several garages already mortgaged? Would arena bonds be tax-free? What would happen if the garages weren't worth as much as the city hoped? What if the garages and arena didn't generate enough cash to repay the bonds?

Council member Bonnie Pannell rarely asked questions, unless they involved City Council District 8, her economically depressed base in South Sacramento. Now she had questions about parking monetization. John Dangberg, the assistant city manager, wrote a memo to Pannell explaining that, yes, $52 million in debt did exist on three garages, and, yes, that debt was tax free, and, yes, that tax free status might change with the arena, meaning the city might get hit with millions of dollars in tax penalties.

Dangberg tossed around the words "defeased" and "callable" and "nominal value," the sort of phrases Pannell would never use in private conversations, public appearances or city council discussions. She may not have understood the words. But Dangberg was operating at his bureaucratic best. He was addressing city council questions with a whirlwind of credible vernacular that added up to nothing too concrete.

He closed his memo with the promise, "When staff presents the Council with the proposals and options for parking monetization, the method of bond repayment will be clearly shown." This was how representative government worked in Sacramento. Many questions, many calming assurances from staff. Few solid answers.

The system was based upon layers of brightly colored tissues that obscured the greasy mechanics of municipal governance. The city council was all part-timers, other than the mayor, who worked full-time under City Charter rules. The council pretended to be in charge. But the bureaucrats ran the city. And the bureaucrats often relied on outside consultants for the tricky stuff, consultants who could bifurcate the delta while texting on their mobile phones.

Many members of the public believed the mayor had primary authority in the city. But of course he didn't. Johnson had no more power than Pannell (a fact she would not let him forget). Nobody was held accountable, except in most superficial sense during the horse race campaign blitz of election season. As long as the city had the right bureaucrats listening to the right consultants, the system worked well enough. As Jim Collins might say, it was good but not great.

The city's metered street parking spaces were part of the tissue. Under state and city law, dollars from street meters could not help finance an arena. Meter money could only be used for traffic control and parking improvements. When questions were raised about street parking dollars somehow being sneaked into the city's arena contribution, city officials had trouble providing straightforward answers.

City Treasurer Russ Fehr, who took office after Tom Friery retired, offered a beautifully obtuse response when asked about parking meter dollars by "Inside City Hall," a local watchdog blog. "We've already worked this through with the city attorney and bond counsel," Fehr said, brushing aside the question. "As part of the bond indenture, there would be a general fund contribution to the nonprofit (parking) financing authority equal to the annual profits of the parking meters."

Fehr appeared to be saying that a quick rinse cycle would resolve the problem. He signaled the city's willingness to take a liberal read on the intent of state and city laws relevant to parking meter dollars. The only trouble was, the intent was not ambiguous in those statutes. The laws were clear: meter funds go to traffic and parking.

The city's path to parking meter money was being adroitly blazed. The general fund would cover the dollars promised to the arena from parking meters. The parking meters would repay the general fund. Dollars would slide from one column to another. No meter money would go directly to the arena. It would be laundered through the general fund. The delta would be bifurcated.

Another problem was the amount of money expected from parking. In 2013, the city made about $9 million in profit from parking. To make the arena plan work, that number would have to increase to about $20 million, according to professional estimates. All of that money would have to be repaid to the general fund. Such were the parlor tricks required of a publicly financed arena.

The city, its bureaucrats and consultants began to seriously study parking dollars as a funding mechanism in October 2011. Reports to the city council would become public in early February 2012. To honor David Stern's March 1 deadline, the council would have to approve the parking money plan, conceptually, at least, on February 14. To imagine the council members that week was to see eight people huddled together on the edge of a high diving board looking down at a small tank of water. They would not have much time to decide whether to jump, much less to analyze the depth, wind and temperature.

OF COURSE, there was never a serious doubt how the majority would vote. From 1985 onward, the Sacramento City Council always acted in the best interests of the Kings. This was an important political benefit, overlooked in the "Nexus Report" and underplayed by Kevin Johnson when he spoke to the NBA owners. This was what 100 percent market share really meant.

Over the decades, several city council members staked out skeptical positions on taxpayer support for a new arena. They even held press conferences noting their opposition to welfare for millionaires. But no member wanted to be part of a city council that drove away the only game in town. The Kings meant too much to Sacramento. Even council members such as Bonnie Pannell, who disliked Johnson for his independent, imperious attitude, supported whatever idea the mayor advocated to help save the basketball team.

By February 2012, the plan was parking monetization, even though the city council didn't know how it would work or how much money it would generate. The numbers frequently changed. The path of least resistance for the city council was something called the "Public Sector Model," where the city would not lease its 12 garages and surface lots to private operators for 30 or 50 years in trade for upfront dollars, but would create a publicly controlled, nonprofit corporation to hold the parking assets and borrow $255.5 million against future earnings of garages and meters.

The nonprofit would be managed by the city. The general fund of Sacramento would be tapped as the backstop. But as John Dangberg wrote, "The risk can be mitigated by using conservative assumptions and coverage factors."

So the arena became its own sales agent. The city council and public were told garages and metered street spaces, often deserted after dark and on weekends when government office workers fled downtown for their suburban homes, would be filled with arena customers at night and on weekends throughout the year. The idea of populating an arena with non-Kings events excited Tim Leiweke, the AEG chief executive. AEG agreed to contribute $58.75 million to the arena project in exchange for operating and naming rights of 30 years.

Leiweke had three main reasons for putting dollars into the Sacramento arena. He wanted a premium Northern California venue to book AEG musical acts. He wanted to keep the Kings away from Southern California. And he wanted a larger profile in the political policy heart of California's $1.9 trillion economy. Operating an arena in the capital city was good for AEG's business. "Sacramento is a C-level market," Leiweke said. "Our executive committee can turn it into an A market. Kansas City was C-level. The building sucked, the weather is cold, never good. Sacramento is comparable, a regional gathering place." AEG turned Kansas City into an A-level concert market despite the city having lost its NBA team to Sacramento.

Leiweke was chasing the golden chalice of strategic booking, which occurs when promoters design "package bundles" for artists to appear on consecutive nights in cities linked by geography, such as Ontario, Ca., San Diego, Las Vegas, Phoenix, Los Angeles and Sacramento. "It's better for the artist, and we can bundle Seattle to L.A.," he said.

In many ways, musical events were better than sports for an arena operator. "Concerts are more a point of destination than sports," Leiweke said. "Concert fans are newbies, they park close in high-end parking and spend more money on merchandise than sports fans, who know where to park cheap and don't spend as much. Concerts provide a much better diversity between club seats and non-premiums."

Leiweke, who would leave AEG in early 2013, believed he could persuade the Maloofs to accept an inferior deal on money splits at the new arena. His confidence was based on the aborted Honda Center agreement, which was helpfully posted on a public website by the city of Anaheim for the world to examine. Leiweke digested the Anaheim document word for word. "That's really a bullshit deal," he said. "Why they did that deal, I don't know. It's a terrible deal. They are idiots."

He figured the Maloofs might have a better understanding about arena operations than some NBA team owners, if only because the Maloof family owned and operated the Sacramento arena. But Tim believed the North Natomas building was poorly managed. "You are sitting on a great market," Leiweke said, launching into a soliloquy about the art of making money in arena operations. It was a true art, requiring exquisite brush strokes by a master. The Maloofs painted with Cheetos-flaked fingers. "We need to understand what they are making, line-item. Merchandise, ticket rebates, concerts, club seats, premium seats, suites. We need to see their underwear," Leiweke said.

The financial deal took shape two weeks before Stern's March 1 deadline. The numbers hardened into place: $255.5 million from the city's parking assets, $58.75 million from AEG. Jeremiah Jackson worked on a plan to generate $3 million from sports fans. At the Mayor's Office, we often heard from local residents who wanted to give us money for the arena, $100, $20, $5, anything. I responded to dozens of calls and emails from everyday citizens who said they had a terrific idea. Why couldn't the city just buy the Kings and turn them into a community owned asset like the Green Bay Packers?

The Packers' romance with Green Bay was a dream shared by many Kings fans. I developed a boilerplate email response to the dreamers, explaining how the Packers formed as a nonprofit public company in 1923, how the world of professional sports had changed somewhat since then.

I said that while the Packers' model was a lovely relic from a more simple time in America, it would not be permitted by league ownership cartels in today's corporate sports and entertainment world. And that's assuming that a city laying-off cops and closing swimming pools could gather the half-billion dollars or so needed to buy an NBA team.

I closed the message with good news. There was a way for fans to help! They could buy personalized, engraved bricks that would be set on a plaza outside the new arena. Jeremiah researched several brick programs and realized there were a large number of people eager to see their parent's and children's names and birthdays and anniversaries and homilies stamped into bricks. The $3 million was a reasonable guess, sales reps from souvenir brick companies assured Jackson.

Beyond bricks, Jeremiah helped Mayor Johnson engage political figures on behalf of the arena. These were elected officials who rarely spoke to each other and hardly ever agreed on anything. They started with two state senators from the Sacramento region, the President Pro Tempore Darrell Steinberg, a city Democrat, and suburban Republican loyalist Ted Gaines. Steinberg was as liberal as Gaines was conservative. But they linked arms for Think Big Sacramento and the Kings.

Steinberg, whose political ambitions ran deep, had been around the arena issue for years. He was a former Sacramento city councilman who once worked as a lawyer for the Maloofs while between elections. Senators Steinberg and Gaines appeared together at press events. They hailed the arena as an economic booster rocket for the entire region.

The arena had a way of making adversaries shake hands and canoodle.

Chapter Twenty-Two: Keep Your Hands Off Our Kings

The fight to keep the Kings alive in Northern California nudged one faded local personality back onto the stage. Fan groups held several rallies in Cesar Chavez Plaza across the street from Historic City Hall in Sacramento. At one rally, Gregg Lukenbill was in the audience. Still smoking and favoring flannel shirts, Lukenbill's appearance was a surprise. When he sold his ownership in the Kings, he stepped away from public attention and wanted nothing to do with the team.

He stopped attending games and completed an undergraduate history degree at California State University, Sacramento. His professional focus shifted from real estate and basketball to aviation. Smitten by flying despite the challenges presented by his first airplane, the old BAC 1-11 Airball One from the Dick Motta days, Lukenbill started a charter air service called SkyKing. He catered to hockey teams, rock music acts and business executives. The company went bankrupt in 2010. Lukenbill reorganized and operated SkyKing from Florida. He provided charter flights to backwaters in the South Pacific and Caribbean, including Cuba. The airline went broke again in 2012.

With time on his hands, Lukenbill decided to help save the Kings. He appeared at the Chavez Plaza rally and told a reporter that Sacramento would not get another major league sports team if the Kings left town. "We have no shot at another franchise for probably generations," he said. And he called Kevin Johnson, suggesting they meet to discuss a surefire plan Lukenbill had to build the new arena.

The mayor politely declined the offer from the Kings' founding partner. Instead, Johnson asked me to follow up with Lukenbill and hear his ideas.

I phoned Lukenbill and sent an email suggesting we meet for coffee. There was no response.

One Sunday afternoon, Lukenbill walked with his dog near his East Sacramento home and realized he had a new neighbor, Mayor Kevin Johnson. The garage door was open. Lukenbill entered the yard, spotted Johnson and introduced himself. The excitement was too much for Lukenbill's dog, which yanked its leash and bit Johnson on the leg. "I can't believe he walked up to me and his dog bit me," Johnson said. The Mayor laughed off the incident, but avoided Lukenbill and his dog.

As the arena dollars fell into place, Stern acknowledged that the final chunk of money, $73.25 million, would come from the Maloofs. But The Boys weren't around. Since the summer of 2011, Stern's transactions attorney, a faithful NBA servant named Harvey Benjamin, represented the Maloofs. Harvey had assistance from NBA President of Operations Joel Litvin.

The NBA executive team hammered out the numbers with the city's consultant, Dan Barrett, along with ICON chief Tim Romani and Leiweke's crew at AEG. Benjamin and Litvin were responsible for keeping the Maloof family updated, if not sedated and silent.

This was a surgical piece of orchestration for Stern. He wanted The Boys to stay miles away from the delicate arena negotiations, knowing their capacity for breaking things. Yet he needed their consent and cash for a final agreement. The commissioner's key goals were to keep the family blissful and separated from reporters.

There had been only one Maloof outburst in 10 months, when a whimsical George Maloof complained to a reporter about being cut off from the arena talks. Johnson noted the rogue Maloof media appearance in a conversation with Stern and Litvin. The larger discussion focused on the arena-funding gap, a far more critical issue for the NBA.

> *Kevin Johnson: "Let me ask you about the Maloofs. I'm concerned about comments they made in the paper about being on the sideline, about not being consulted. Did you see that?"*
>
> *Joel Litvin: "We heard about some things George said like that."*
>
> *David Stern: "I didn't know about that, and if they said that, we should have told George to shut the fuck up. That's our bad. But you have a much bigger problem and you don't want to deal with it. You've staked out your position and we've staked out ours and we have a huge gap.*

You've moved mountains."

Litvin: "The issue is we have 25 owners who thought they had a good deal in Anaheim, and we said, wait, let's give Mayor Johnson a chance to get this done. Now it's a matter of credibility for us. How much more time are you going to ask for?"

Johnson: "OK, we'll get you in the position you need to be in March."

On February 14, 2012, the Sacramento City Council leaped off the high dive. The members voted 9-0 to begin formal work on the best way to monetize Sacramento's parking garages. The vote was not a legal commitment to build the arena, but it was the strongest possible signal of the city's intent to embrace the parking fund strategy. The next big task belonged to Stern, Litvin and Benjamin. They would have to sit down with the Maloofs, Kevin Johnson and the city's negotiating team at the All-Star game in Orlando and persuade The Boys to accept the term sheet worked out by Benjamin and Litvin, AEG and the city.

The meetings took place at the Waldorf Astoria hotel at Disney World, miles away from the All-Star commotion downtown. They lasted two and one-half days. There were painful moments. At various points, the Maloofs appeared to have not read, much less understood, any of the materials forwarded to them over the previous five months by Benjamin and NBA staff. The documents detailed the parking monetization plan and the AEG equity position.

The city's consultant, Dan Barrett, explained the parking asset idea to The Boys, telling them how the garage monetization business would work, how AEG would operate the new building for 30 years, how the city would be the landlord, how the Kings would be anchor tenants, how everybody would win. People in the room were tempted to comment on the irony of the city's consultant explaining this strange new poker game to the slack-jawed Maloofs. Discretion prevailed.

UNTIL THAT WEEKEND, city officials in Sacramento, including the mayor, had no idea how the Maloofs would pay their $73.25 million share. By all accounts, the family no longer had that kind of money. Stern resolved the uncertainty by announcing a method for the Maloofs to make their contribution. The NBA would loan the family $67 million and invest another $7 million independently as equity to close the funding gap.

This was astonishing. The league's owners, guided by the commissioner, were directly investing in Sacramento and subsidizing the NBA's poor relations—The Boys—with a hefty loan package. The money would come on top of millions of dollars the Maloofs previously borrowed from the league, about $125 million, retired City Treasurer Tom Friery estimated. The image of Stern rising from his chair, walking behind George Maloof and affirming the NBA's $7 million in faith would not be forgotten by people in the room.

Media were camped outside the hotel, waiting for news. Kevin Johnson's body language told the story. Grinning, he walked into the sunshine and hugged Stern and shouted, "It's game over! Sacramento deserves to win, and this is our chance to win. I'm so emotional, I can't even articulate it." George Maloof, who more so than his brothers, sister and mother disliked Sacramento and refused to believe there would ever be an acceptable deal for a new arena, said, "I think it's a fair deal. We gave a lot. Everybody had to give. Sometimes, you have to take chances, and we think this is worth taking." As for Gavin Maloof, he wept for the cameras.

The celebration ended almost as suddenly as it began. Gavin's tears were quickly wiped away, replaced by the anger of buyer's remorse. And George, it seemed, hadn't really meant what he said that day in Orlando. Upon reflection, George didn't think the risk was worth taking. He didn't want to roll the dice on Sacramento. Sometime between the time they left Florida and arrived home in Las Vegas, George and his brothers began to plot an escape route from the deal created for the Kings by David Stern and the NBA.

The Maloof reversal was unprecedented in NBA history. A family ownership group, once respected for its loyalty and determination to get back in the game after the death of a patriarch, was prepared to repudiate Stern's lovingly handcrafted arena agreement. And more. The family was ready to publicly embarrass the commissioner and make league owners look foolish for offering money to support a new Sacramento arena.

In the days that followed, I couldn't stop thinking about Kevin Johnson's dramatic comparison between Stern and the fictional character from Mario Puzo's vivid imagination. Would the commissioner metaphorically rub out the Maloofs? Michael Corleone surely would, and then some.

The exit strategy used by the Maloof family was a scheme of brazen revisionism. They attacked the financial projections for the Kings and the new arena, projections that had been prepared by two organizations with ultimate credibility in pro basketball and arena operations, the NBA and AEG.

The Maloofs hired a Southern California economist named Christopher Thornberg, who declared that the city of Sacramento, the NBA and AEG were too optimistic while committing dollars to the arena. On the logic that Economist Thornberg knew more about the NBA than Commissioner Stern, more about arenas than AEG (which ran arenas around the world), and more about Sacramento than Mayor Johnson and the city manager, the Maloofs said the plan they agreed to in Orlando was not viable. They formalized their retreat with a trip to New York on April 12 for the annual Board of Governor's meeting.

They met with their fellow NBA owners and continued to backpedal. The Maloofs expressed concerns about the arena projections. They said they would like to renegotiate the Orlando accord, which, the family now insisted, had only been a starting point in discussions, not a final deal.

Next, the Maloofs held a press conference where they characterized the Orlando agreement as a framework full of holes. A Maloof lawyer, Barry McNeil, told reporters, "We raised the question to the NBA: Can Sacramento really afford a new arena?" Kevin Johnson rushed out to New York, but was helpless. "I wish I had better news," Kevin said. "They are now saying they don't want to do the deal, which essentially means they don't want to be in Sacramento."

Stern held his own press conference. He was subdued, probably exhausted, but outwardly respectful toward the Maloofs. With a glimmer of sarcasm, he noted the family had thoughtfully invited to New York that day several attorneys, including one or two who specialized in antitrust litigation. Score one point for the Maloofs. But the game was just beginning.

Public relations strategist Chris Lehane wrote an "Open Letter" to Think Big Sacramento and the community at large. The letter was designed to give Lehane the bad guy role in place of Mayor Johnson. The opening sentence read, "Based on your calls, texts, tweets and emails, it's clear many are understandably upset at the conduct of the Maloof family (I have had emails referring to them as 'clowns,' 'buffoons,' the 'Three Stooges without the brains')." Near the end of the letter, Lehane wrote, "It had become abundantly clear that the Maloofs had no real interest in the deal, and therefore no real interest in Sacramento."

SACRAMENTO FAN organizations began to play a loud and sustained role on social media, with the goal of promoting community support no matter how badly the Maloofs behaved. One group was called Crown Downtown, led by community college counselor Mike Tavares. Crown Downtown printed T-shirts, organized "Save Our Kings" parties, attended city council meetings and rallied members with Facebook, Twitter and blogs.

As the community rallied, George Maloof committed more mischief. He told reporters he wanted to think about retrofitting Arco Arena, an idea that had been rejected by the NBA as a waste of money. The 1988 structure needed so much work and was so small, about 440,000 square feet, when modern NBA arenas were pushing 700,000 feet or 800,000 feet or more, that a retrofit would cost almost as much as a new building. The retrofit tease from George contradicted a statement made by Kings President Matina Kolokotronis, who wrote to the media, "Refurbishing the current Arco Arena is not an option."

Economist Thornberg warned the new arena plan "would really put the city right on the edge of potential fiscal disaster. There's a massive amount of risk for the Kings, the city and ultimately the NBA." His comments were challenged by City Manager John Shirey and ignored by the NBA and AEG, but it didn't matter. The Maloofs were out, leaving a swath of wrecked relationships behind them.

The Maloof retreat was not without some curious timing. The Boys were required to write their first check for arena predevelopment, a $3,250,000 commitment that would have locked the family into the Sacramento project. The Maloofs didn't want to write any checks. They refused to identify collateral for a rework of the $73 million loan designed by Tom Friery in 1997, an option that would have benefitted the family with lower interest rates on the borrowed money.

Without the Maloofs, the arena project was dead. Tim Romani, the ICON chief executive, had been right when he worried about paying for staff hours and plane trips between Colorado and Sacramento. The Sacramento City Council stopped its due diligence on parking monetization. Romani went back to Colorado. Leiweke returned to AEG headquarters in Los Angeles. It had all been a very nice try.

OVER THE NEXT few weeks after the New York debacle, Kevin Johnson became obsessed with catching the Maloofs in lies large and small.

He called me into his office one morning to witness a demonstration. He phoned George Maloof and asked if they could meet privately and secretly in Las Vegas, just to see if there was any hope of mending fences and getting back on track. George was polite and agreeable. Certainly, come to Las Vegas, he said. The mayor insisted that no public disclosure be made of the meeting. George agreed. Absolutely no public disclosure.

Within an hour, a public relations person working for The Boys used his Twitter account to announce Mayor Johnson was seeking an audience with Maloof in Las Vegas. The media picked up the Tweet and made Kevin look like a groveling supplicant. Johnson was more amused than mad. Maloof perjury had become a game.

"Watch this," Johnson told me as he phoned George back. "George, it's Kevin Johnson. I thought we agreed there would be no media on the Vegas meeting." George claimed he didn't know what the mayor was talking about. "Your guy has Tweeted it out," Johnson said. George hesitated and said, well, uh, yes, maybe he did mention something to a P.R. guy after all. Sorry about that! Johnson hung up. "You see? What a liar!" the mayor shouted. He went to Vegas anyway and met with George. Nothing changed.

While the arena dramatics generated headlines, curses, tears, name-calling and confusion, three related but distinctly different groups continued on their separate paths, as if oblivious to the intrigue in Sacramento. The first of these groups were the Kings themselves. Apart from Johnson's talk about jobs and economic development, the basketball team was, of course, the primary reason to build a new arena.

But the Kings were mostly absent from the arena discussions. With the community's political and business leaders preoccupied by endless arena strategizing, it was easy to forget we were talking about a basketball team, a perennial loser with a sad history, a team that hardly seemed worth all the trouble sometimes. It was difficult to admit, but the Kings were the perfect team for Clipperville, Mayor Johnson's code word for hapless direction of Sacramento, where the clocks were frozen, where people were good losers, where nothing much happened.

The Kings existed in a parallel universe, playing in North Natomas just as they had since 1985, but leaving only vapor trails and no tracks. Mayor Johnson made smiling, glad-handing appearances at many home games between 2009 and 2012, but rarely sat through four quarters or paid attention to the games. More often, he made the rounds of arena luxury suites, saying hello to political friends and financial supporters.

Sometimes he watched a quarter or two from courtside seats that belonged to local business owners. There wasn't much compelling basketball to watch, especially for a discerning NBA observer such as Kevin Johnson. The Kings were the same old team they had been since the day Joe Axelson showed up in Cincinnati and traded Oscar Robertson. They were habitual failures. And deep down Johnson couldn't shake the demons from 1987. He still disliked the franchise that drafted Kenny Smith.

In 2009, the Kings drafted guard Tyreke Evans, the NBA's top rookie that season. The next year, they acquired a new center, DeMarcus Cousins. The team seemed to be in a positive rebuilding phase, apart from Cousins, whose verbal outbursts against coaches and teammates caused him to be suspended and recommended for psychological treatment.

But if the Kings were building anything, it was a sand castle, impressive for a brief period, then washed away by the rising tides. They won 17 games in 2008-2009. It was a miserable campaign even by Kings standards. They failed to reach 30 wins the next four years. The club fired Paul Westphal, Kevin Johnson's former coach at Phoenix, and hired Keith Smart to guide the team. Smart was fired in 2013.

Reporters asked players about the arena distractions. The athletes didn't hide behind the excuse of uncertain lodgings. They said their job was to play basketball and not worry about arenas or where they might be working next year. They were getting accustomed to the endless relocation question. Even when they concentrated on basketball, the Kings weren't very good at running and jumping and playing basketball to win. And they displayed no personal loyalty to the Sacramento community.

An earlier generation of Kings players, men such as LaSalle Thompson and Harold Pressley, returned to Sacramento after their NBA careers, bought homes and started new businesses. Mitch Richmond returned in 2013 to join the investors who wanted to buy the team from the Maloof family. Chris Webber opened a restaurant in North Natomas, Center Court With C-Webb, but it closed after three years. The landlord sued Webber for $134,997 in unpaid rent. As for newest generations of Kings, Sacramento was a place to play, get paid and leave.

ANOTHER GROUP operated in a parallel universe in Silicon Valley. This was the network controlled by Vivek Ranadive, the electrical engineer whose story was almost too perfect. He arrived in the U.S. from Mumbai, India, with $50 in his pocket. From that humble debut he built a billion-dollar company, Tibco Software.

Ranadive, born in 1957, was not aware of basketball while growing up in Mumbai. Young Vivek played cricket and soccer. When he finally saw a basketball game, he thought it was silly. His father was an airline pilot, which should have been the foundation for a comfortable life. But his father was a troublesome pilot, forever complaining to governmental authorities about the precarious condition of India's planes, constantly raising questions about safety. The complaints became such an annoyance that Prime Minister Indira Gandhi had the elder Ranadive jailed to shut him up.

As a teenager, Vivek was no less stubborn than his father. After viewing a documentary program about the wonders of Massachusetts Institute of Technology near Boston, Vivek was convinced he should go there. Overseas study required government permission for the release of foreign currency in India during the 1970s. The authorities ignored Vivek's request. He camped outside the door of the chairman of the Reserve Bank of India until the funds were approved.

Young Vivek excelled at MIT. He earned two engineering degrees, undergraduate and master's, from the elite Cambridge, Mass., university, then pursued a second master's program down the street at Harvard Business School. Exceptionally educated, he made his way to Silicon Valley. He founded a software company called Teknekron, intending to resolve issues of "real time" data processing. His quest was to erase the lag time between the creation and distribution of information. He sold the company and founded another, named in whimsical fashion as an acronym for "The Information Bus Company," or Tibco.

Ranadive and his company became darlings of Wall Street, not only for the investment potential, but also for the services provided by Tibco. By 2010, almost all trading activities on Wall Street were powered by Ranadive's software. Tibco caught the eye of CBS Sportsline, which applied the Ranadive real-time philosophy to sports news.

Around 2008, Ranadive came to the attention of the writer Malcolm Gladwell, whose profiles in the New Yorker magazine led to several best-selling books based around the general theme of why certain things worked and others failed. Gladwell was captivated by Ranadive's life story and his success as a girls' youth basketball coach in Atherton, where the Ranadive family lived. Despite knowing nothing about basketball (and even less about coaching), Vivek engineered a national championship-caliber season for his team, whose players included the youngest of the Ranadive family's three children, Anjali.

The team lacked height and talent, but Vivek applied the principles of real time. Rather than follow the basketball norm, he instructed his girls to pressure their opponents, especially on the inbounds pass and while advancing across the midcourt line, two procedures that are under a timed deadline. Relentless pressure defense would mask his girls' weaknesses on offense.

Vivek did other things. He vowed to never raise his voice or appear stressed. He acknowledged that as he knew nothing about coaching or conditioning or basketball, he would need expert assistance. He enlisted Roger Craig, who knew something about sports. The girls advanced to the national championships but lost in the third round of playoffs. A referee began to whistle fouls against the girls' whirlwind defensive moves, infecting Vivek's strategy like a virus. The experience left Vivek satisfied to a point. Craig eventually became director of business development for Tibco.

Malcolm Gladwell called his New Yorker profile of Ranadive "How David Beats Goliath." The story was published in May 2009, a year before Vivek would record his next big breakthrough in basketball, becoming a limited partner in the new ownership group of the Golden State Warriors.

Ranadive would also have success in publishing. He wrote three inspirational business books between 1999 and 2011, "The Power Of Now," "The Power to Predict," and "The Two-Second Advantage." The books promoted Ranadive's theories about real-time opportunities. Ranadive's books were really about How David Beats Goliath. It was the story of his life.

As the first person from India to own part of an NBA team, Ranadive was on the forefront of a new frontier for the league and David Stern, who had worked years on ways to reach India's masses. Limited ownership was not enough. When Ranadive heard the Kings were possibly for sale, he asked Roger Craig to poke around and see what he could learn about Sacramento.

Vivek had to be careful. As a minority partner at Golden State, he didn't want to be accused of tampering with another team's affairs. He knew the Maloofs were in trouble, and knew Craig would be discreet. Roger called the Mayor's Office in Sacramento, obliquely representing a mysterious potential buyer for the Kings. The call was routed to me. We began to chat. "All I can tell you is my man hates to lose," Craig told me. Now that was a refreshing thing to hear at Clipperville City Hall.

A THIRD GROUP operated in a parallel universe around the city of Seattle. Beginning in 2010, a San Francisco hedge fund manager named Christopher Hansen pieced together support to build a new arena and bring an NBA team to the shores of Puget Sound. Hansen wanted to replace the SuperSonics, whose new owner, Clay Bennett, moved the franchise to Oklahoma City in 2008.

As with Sacramento, the major issue in Seattle was the absence of a proper, modern, arena for the team, filled with premium seating opportunities. The city, burdened with debt from baseball and football stadiums, was reluctant to negotiate with Bennett over public financing for a new NBA palace. Bennett became fed up with Seattle. He broke his lease and moved to his home state of Oklahoma, his goal from the start, detractors claimed.

Hansen was determined to resurrect the SuperSonics. He formed a partnership with three of the region's most respected business figures, Microsoft chief executive Steve Ballmer and department store heirs Peter and Erik Nordstrom. With his wealthy associates, Hansen promised to secure $290 million in private funds for the arena. He would buy and relocate an NBA team if Seattle taxpayers would contribute $200 million in bonds that, Hansen promised, would be repaid with income from the project. He would rename the team the SuperSonics, a title held in reserve for Seattle, and turn back the clock to the good old days.

With Sacramento politicians and residents focused on the Maloof family and Anaheim and the NBA Board of Governors meetings and the arena that could never get funded, Hansen quietly stalked his target. It was the Sacramento Kings.

Jeremiah Jackson, the Think Big consultant, recognized the threat. Jeremiah went on the attack in February 2012. He posted an Open Letter to Hansen, admonishing the money manager to "keep your hands off our Kings." Jackson publicly invited Hansen to Sacramento for a debate, setting out the terms in fighting language worthy of the old Harlem Globetrotters and barnstorming Rochester Pros. "Come and defend the indefensible and explain the inexplicable: your efforts to steal our jobs," Jackson wrote.

A meeting room was booked for the debate at the Oak Park Community Center, 12 blocks from Kevin Johnson's boyhood home. Jeremiah invited a dozen Kings fans, arranged for an oversized purple throne to be delivered from the downtown children's library, set up folding chairs, called the media and waited for Hansen not to appear.

Two TV stations sent camera crews and gave Jackson several minutes of positive publicity for Think Big Sacramento. While his challenge was entirely theatrical, Jackson did provide a valuable public service. His demand for a debate with Hansen was the first time anybody in Sacramento took recognition of Seattle's very real threat to steal the Kings.

Of course, Chris Hansen didn't show that day in Oak Park. The big purple chair sat empty for the cameras. After an hour of discussing the importance of keeping the Kings in Northern California, of creating jobs and opportunities for economic development, Jackson declared the event a success.

Everybody went home.

Chapter Twenty-Three: These People Have More Than Enough Money

Wednesday, January 9, 2013, broke clear and cold in Sacramento. The temperature was in the high 30s, with rain moving in from the Pacific Northwest. Seattle weather. Mayor Kevin Johnson had a light schedule. He would follow the same pattern he did most Wednesdays.

A black SUV driven by a retired Sacramento police officer pulled up to Johnson's home in East Sacramento at 7:30 a.m., collected the mayor and traveled six miles to 825 K Street, where Johnson's wife, Michelle Rhee, leased offices for her education advocacy group, StudentsFirst. Johnson enjoyed his weekly visits to StudentsFirst. It was better than starting the day at City Hall, a place he didn't like.

For five years, Johnson dreamed about becoming a strong, executive-style mayor. In his dream, the first directive by the new strong mayor was to vacate City Hall. Kevin preferred the old building next door, Historic City Hall, a century-old wedding cake with marble floors and clock tower. "We need to be physically separate from them," he said. By "them," he meant the city council, city manager and city attorney: the cabal that ran the city.

Most Wednesdays, the mayor spent half the day at 825 K, strategizing with Rhee and her staff about the couple's favorite topics: how to break the collective-bargaining process that dictated teacher workloads, tenure, seniority and accountability at public schools. Rhee, born with a gift for theatrics, announced the start of StudentsFirst on the Oprah Winfrey show. Winfrey fawned over Rhee and helped solicit memberships. When Kevin told me about StudentsFirst, he called it "a Moon shot" and predicted it would be "one of the biggest things to ever happen in education." Two years later, the Moon shot had left the launch pad but was still orbiting Earth.

Johnson and Rhee were married in September 2011 in Tennessee, where Rhee spent half her time with her two children from a previous marriage. Rhee's former husband, Kevin Huffman, was the education commissioner for the state of Tennessee. The couple wanted their daughters educated in Nashville, not Sacramento. So Rhee commuted from California to Tennessee every 10 days or so, leaving her new husband alone in Sacramento.

The love affair between Johnson and Rhee blossomed when he heard her give a lecture on education. Philosophically, they were a fine match, right down to the likelihood that their firebrand intractability made them poorly suited for serious public leadership roles. The diva style of Rhee was a hallmark of her brief tour as chancellor of the Washington, D.C. school system. Johnson was similarly miscast for many of his mayoral chores.

They could mesmerize a crowd from the stage. They could inspire. They could charm benefactors. They could lead pep rallies. But they were not effective when it came time to focus on details and realistically negotiate the compromises demanded of governance beyond their personalities. For Johnson and Rhee, details were for staff to figure out, often in the dark and with guesswork. And compromise was for losers.

After three hours of education policy at StudentsFirst, the rest of Johnson's day was light. He would meet with Ron Vrilakas, a local architect working on a new theater for Midtown Sacramento. Lunch was scheduled at the private Sutter Club with Dr. Aaron Reeves, a Sacramento children's dentist whose rapidly expanding practice intrigued Johnson. There was a photo op with staff from Benefits Connect, a company that worked with human resource departments and insurance brokers. Johnson was not thinking about the Kings. He was barely thinking about being mayor. Apart from StudentsFirst, he was bored.

Over the previous four years, Sacramento City Council members complained of Johnson's detachment from civic chores. He refused to attend most closed session meetings held by the city council, weekly gatherings where the members privately discussed personnel issues, lawsuits, real estate transactions and collective bargaining.

Most city council members enjoyed the hush-hush propriety of closed sessions. Not Johnson. He believed the meetings were a waste of time, nothing more than a chance for the city manager and city attorney to remind everybody that they—not the elected mayor—ran the city.

Kevin Johnson had no interest in being mayor of a city he couldn't run. He had been elected twice after convincing himself he could change the system by rewriting the City Charter, but change was harder than he imagined. After one four-year term, he made almost no progress. Those of us who worked in the Mayor's Office had no idea how he planned to spend his second term. He almost didn't run a second time. I had to organize the paperwork for him because nobody else would do it.

Hoping to beat the filing deadline, I spread out the second-term candidacy documents on his desk. I pointed to the dotted line. "Do I really have to sign this?" he said. "What's the point?" "You have to sign it," I said. He signed, saying, "If there was a legitimate person in the race, I wouldn't run. Seriously. But there's nobody running except a bunch of jokers. I can't do that to the city."

He easily beat the jokers and won a second term. And he quickly minimized his City Hall operation. "I won't be doing any new initiatives," Johnson said. Most of the team, including Press Secretary Joaquin McPeek, personal assistant and bodyman Daniel Lopez, assistant Charlita Anderson and the arena crew, led by Jeremiah Jackson, plus interns Alex Kasner, Daniel Ajise, Raihane Dalvi and Benny Aziz, left City Hall and moved to other projects. Our gifted young political operative, Ryan Garner, had quit earlier to join a Washington, D.C., campaign firm. I left, too, and soon started work on this book.

Another mayoral staffer, Lisa Serna, was the daughter of the late Sacramento Mayor Joe Serna. Lisa departed under unfortunate circumstances. She was arrested and convicted of abusing her city-issued credit card with iTunes, lunches and a family trip to Disneyland. Lisa was the staff member most devoted to Kevin Johnson. Her downfall embarrassed the mayor and tarnished Serna's famous family, but Kevin supported Lisa in his public comments.

Johnson hired two part-time retired annuitants from the city manager's office to handle his council business and old initiatives. One month into his second term, the mayor had checked out. Other than education and charter reform, there was only one topic that interested Kevin Johnson: the Kings and their arena. And on that subject, there was nothing to talk about on January 9, 2013.

UNKNOWN TO Johnson, the Kings were talking about Sacramento that day. The Maloof family was ready to sell and move the team. Unlike the flirtation with Anaheim in 2011, The Boys were serious this time. Hedge fund manager Chris Hansen, Steve Ballmer and the Maloofs were putting together an agreement to sell the Kings to Hansen's Seattle group, 65 percent for $341 million. The Maloof Boys, who vowed to never sell the Kings, who said the biggest mistake of their lives was to unload the Houston Rockets in 1982 after their father's death, were cashing out.

They were selling to an investor who wanted to pull the franchise 750 miles north. The Boys made no effort to engage Ron Burkle or Vivek Ranadive other potential buyers who might keep the team in Northern California. They didn't call the mayor and ask him to find local investors. Like an embittered jilted lover, they struck back in punishing fashion. If we can't have the Kings, neither can you. Liz Salmi, a Kings fans and green tech entrepreneur in Sacramento, went to social media and created a new action verb for the family's behavior: Maloofed.

There were warning signs. For several months in 2012, the Maloof family talked to officials from Henderson, Nev., a Las Vegas suburb, and Virginia Beach. The Henderson discussions didn't get much past the introductory stage. But in Virginia Beach, where Mayor Will Sessoms hoped to improve his city's status with big league sports, the talk grew serious.

The courtship was coy. The Kings were not publicly acknowledged as Sessoms's target. And there was no finance plan for an NBA arena in Hampton Roads, Va. Smaller than Sacramento, Virginia Beach would need tax dollars from its state legislature. Local political leaders were skeptical. On January 8, the arena chatter stopped when Mayor Sessoms said, "The city doesn't see a clear opportunity at this point and, as such, it's not something we're aggressively going after. The city is kind of withdrawing."

The prospective Virginia Beach deal had one complication that didn't exist in Seattle. The Maloof family would have owned the team in Virginia Beach. That would have been a problem. The Boys appeared to lack the financial capacity to compete in the NBA. Accounts of massive debt against the Kings suggested the Maloofs could be leveraged to sell. Media estimates had the debt at between $100 million and $150 million, with the majority owed to the NBA.

A deal to relocate the team would have to include settlement of the $73 million loan from the city of Sacramento, making a move even more expensive. Chris Hansen was a professional money manager. He knew the numbers. He was not going to risk his funds and reputation on a new arena in Seattle and leave The Boys in charge.

Hansen and Ballmer needed control, so they plied the Maloofs with the tonic the family so desperately needed: cash. The strategy worked. Twelve days after the surrender by Virginia Beach, the Seattle group publicly announced it had reached a deal to buy the Kings.

Having co-opted the Maloofs, Hansen next focused on a quick, decisive end to the Kings' Sacramento narrative. He didn't want Kevin Johnson to mobilize investors, resurrect the 2012 rail yards arena plan and lobby NBA owners with a story about scrappy little Sacramento, the city that could. This time, David would not beat Goliath.

But Hansen's quick-kill strategy carried a monumental risk. When they agreed to buy the Kings before the team was relocated, Hansen and Ballmer threw away the Maloof family's strongest leverage point with the NBA. They gave up the unilateral right to move to Seattle without the NBA's blessing—a right backed by the threat of a federal antitrust lawsuit.

While this point was overlooked in the voluminous media coverage in Sacramento, Seattle and across the country, it set the tone for the next five months. And it handed David Stern mastery over the Kings' future. By seeking to transfer ownership in the team before it relocated, the Maloofs, Hansen and Ballmer turned themselves into spectators along for the ride. Stern was at the wheel.

Whenever an NBA team is sold or moved, the league's owners are required to first meet, confer and vote. Such inner workings are normally rubber-stamp affairs, with the details settled days before the vote. The procedures are so mundane that the media and public often regard a sale and move as parts of a linked equation. But they are vastly different. They require two separate votes. The difference between a team sale and relocation is critical. It's a matter of federal law. U.S. district judges know the difference.

Under the law, the NBA Board of Governors has an absolute right to determine whom it allows into the league. But once a new team owner is admitted, the league has essentially no right to stop that brother or sister from moving their team to another city. This is why the Maloofs made a point of bringing antitrust lawyers to the Board of Governors press conference in 2012, after the Orlando accord fell apart.

The Maloofs could have moved to Anaheim in 2011 and the NBA would have sat back and watched. There would have been relocation fees and grumbling from the Lakers and Clippers and their friends, but that would have been that. The Anaheim Royals would have been a reality if the Maloofs so desired. Seattle was no different. The Maloofs could have move north at any point, if they were serious about it.

Pro sports leagues have argued for decades that they deserve something called single entity treatment, which means to be treated by the courts as one organization with a single ownership. Federal courts have consistently denied this argument, pointing out the inconvenient truth that sports leagues are cartels, a group of independent and competitive owners. (Major League Baseball is the exception, having been given a pass by the U.S. Supreme Court in 1922.)

Tulane University Law School professor Gabriel Feldman, writing in the April 2012 UC Davis Law Review, described the five standard legal pleas sports leagues make for single-entity treatment, which he called the Shangri la of everlasting antitrust immunity: "All of these arguments ... have been rejected, either by the courts, Congress or both," he wrote.

In the 1980s, after Al Davis moved the Oakland Raiders to the Los Angeles Memorial Coliseum against the NFL's wishes, the NBA began to treat its relocation approval as window dressing and use the commissioner's charm and persuasion, not threats, to keep teams in place. This laissez-faire philosophy resulted in almost two decades of stability after a hostile move by the San Diego Clippers to Los Angeles and the friendly move by the Kansas City Kings to Sacramento.

Princeton professor of politics and public affairs Michael Danielson called the Raiders' suit "the most successful antitrust litigation affecting the location of a professional sports team." The NFL couldn't stop the Raiders. So the NBA knew it was boxed in by the Sherman Antitrust Act. The ever charming and persuasive Commissioner Stern decided to make the best of it.

When Hansen and Ballmer announced they had bought the Kings and would move the team, the media and public paid no attention to the order of battle presented by Hansen and Ballmer. The Seattle opportunists would buy first and move second. The order didn't seem to matter.

But to David Stern (and those federal judges), the order was everything. And Hansen and Ballmer had it all wrong. They were doing it backwards. Once the NBA allowed Hansen and Ballmer into the league, the NBA would be powerless to stop them from relocating the Kings to Seattle. What was the solution to save Sacramento's team? Stern would make a calculated gamble by getting his owners to deny the move before Hansen and Ballmer gained control of the team.

Simply and brilliantly, Stern reversed the agenda. The Seattle men anticipated that their approval as NBA owners would be the first order of business. But Stern had the Board of Governors vote on the move first, before anything else, while the Maloofs still technically owned the Kings.

When the NBA Board of Governors denied the move, the board's vote was almost certainly an illegal action that would not have withstood antitrust litigation. But collectively, the Maloofs, Hansen and Ballmer could not sue. The Seattle men were not validated owners. They had no standing with the NBA.

And if Hansen and Ballmer helped the Maloofs relocate to Seattle under the threat of an antitrust action, they would never be voted into the league. "When you buy a team, you consent that the league has final say," said NBA TV legal expert Mike McCann. To put it succinctly: Checkmate.

The consequences of the timing, of attempting to buy the Kings in January, before the team relocated, could not have escaped Hansen and Ballmer and their lawyers. Judging by their actions, Hansen and Ballmer seemed to believe they could fix the deal with dollars. Thus the January sale announcement and a $30 million non-refundable deposit paid to the Maloofs.

A more patient strategy, which would have had the Seattle group waiting on the sideline while the Maloofs moved to Seattle, then buying the Kings in a year or two, after the dust settled, would be the stuff of speculation over beers.

For the first five months of 2013, few people beyond a small circle understood that the chess match was over, that the Maloofs had squandered their leverage in January and David Stern controlled the game. The outcome wasn't completely ordained. Sacramento still needed a viable new ownership group and a real financing path to an arena. But Stern was able to give Kevin Johnson and Sacramento the running room they needed to keep the Kings.

CRISIS BROUGHT out the fighter in Kevin Johnson. It brought out Oak Park. The mayor began making phone calls after news broke that the Maloof family had agreed to sell the team. The Kings hurt Kevin twice before, on Draft Day 1987 and when the Maloofs walked away from the arena agreement in 2012. He would not get burned again. "He's totally obsessed with it. There's no point in even talking to him about other stuff," Vice Mayor Angelique Ashby said.

Kevin called Darius Anderson, the lobbyist who introduced Ron Burkle to the Sacramento arena drama in 2011. Anderson represented the 24 Hour Fitness gyms and knew the company's founder, Mark Mastrov, who tried and failed to buy the Golden State Warriors in 2010. Mastrov was still interested in becoming an NBA owner. And Mastrov knew another Bay Area man interested in the Kings: Vivek Ranadive.

By late January, Johnson was ready to announce a press conference and introduce 20 Sacramento area residents who each pledged $1 million toward the Kings. Beyond the local money, he said he was assembling "whales," a catchy label appropriated from Las Vegas as shorthand for high rollers. The whales would swim in, buy the Kings and build the arena. Burkle and Mastrov were Kevin's whales, revealed at the mayor's annual "State of the City" speech. "Come April or before, we're going to submit a fair and competitive offer," Johnson said. Stern had given Kevin a road map and a flashlight. The mayor was using both.

Kevin was not a born dealmaker. In private meetings, his style was short and dictatorial, pure Alpha Dog. And the "State of the City" speech was spoken in error. Burkle and Mastrov would never be Sacramento's whales. But Kevin was the perfect cheerleader. In this role, he would walk a traditional mayoral path.

In 1958, Los Angeles Mayor Norris Poulson was instrumental in directing the appeals for the Brooklyn Dodgers to move west. Poulson made sure the right people were in the room and prevented Los Angeles from needlessly giving away assets. "We wanted desperately to get the team, but made it clear we would have to come up with a plan that wouldn't get us all run out of the city," Poulson said. The Dodgers built their own stadium in Chavez Ravine after the city helped the team acquire land. Dodger Stadium would be one of the most profitable sports palaces in U.S. history.

While Poulson shook hands and twisted arms, New York Mayor Robert Wagner treated the Dodgers as something beneath his dignity. He ended up losing two teams in 1957, the Dodgers and the Giants. Wagner finally appointed a blue-ribbon baseball commission (not called Think Big New York), which led to the creation of the Mets for America's largest city.

Other mayors learned from Poulson's success in L.A. In Baltimore, Mayor (and eventually Governor) William Schaefer drove tough bargains with the Orioles. Pittsburgh Mayor Richard Caliguiri linked private investors with public money to keep the Pirates in 1985. Kevin Johnson had good company.

WITH MAYOR Johnson busy on TV and pep rallies, the Sacramento investment group was taking shape away from the stage. The low-keyed dealmaker was Vivek Ranadive, ready to beat another Goliath. By February, bolstered by faith and dollars from Silicon Valley, Sacramento was no longer acting like Clipperville. The Silicon Valley group had serious money, enough to make Sacramento competitive against Hansen, Ballmer and Seattle. Ranadive studied the data and calculated his position. He would need two deals: one to buy the team, one to build an arena.

Ron Burkle was first to study the real estate play. He knew the downtown rail yards were Mayor Johnson's first choice for an arena site, but Burkle liked bargains and there were no blue-light specials at the rail yards. The property owner, Inland American, wanted a premium price for land around the arena. So Burkle retreated from the project. The focus shifted to the Downtown Plaza, a troubled shopping mall two blocks south of the train depot. The Plaza included 1.16 million feet of retail space, but was in steep decline for the last six years. By 2012, the Downtown Plaza suffered an occupancy rate of about 50 percent.

A year earlier, the mall was bundled for sale with other dying properties by its owner, Westfield Group, the Australian shopping center giant with 105 malls and $40 billion in retail sales. Johnson visited Westfield CEO Peter Lowy and asked him to sell the Sacramento center to a buyer of the mayor's choice. Lowy didn't care about Sacramento, but he liked Johnson. Westfield unloaded the Downtown Plaza to a Northern California hospitality and lifestyle firm, JMA Ventures, represented by Darius Anderson and supported by Johnson.

JMA paid $21.7 million for the mall. It was a fire sale that underscored the decline of downtown Sacramento property values. The mall underwent a $157 million remodel in 1992, with about $14 million from public redevelopment dollars. It was worth around $200 million in 2006. Now Westfield was practically throwing it away.

With JMA owning Downtown Plaza, the prospective Kings' investors figured the mall would be an ideal place to invest more public dollars, this time for an arena. The city and its $258 million parking monetization (plus surplus land assets and electronic billboards) would be essential. The investors announced they would demolish the mall and build a $448 million arena in partnership with the city. "We won't get another chance like this in Sacramento," Anderson said. Within months, the Plaza's ownership transferred from JMA to Vivek Ranadive.

It was Spring 2013. The Sacramento group had site control at a new arena location. City funding was identified. One big question remained: who would own the Kings? Thanks to Chris Hansen and Steve Ballmer, a bidding war billowed around the team. The Kings had rocketed to the highest sale price in NBA history, with a total value of about $550 million.

A consortium would be required, exactly what Vivek Ranadive had in mind a year earlier when Roger Craig phoned the Mayor's Office to discreetly inquire about the Kings. "We have a group," Roger said. "These people have more than enough money."

Ranadive knew his moment had arrived. He understood Stern was obsessed with keeping the Kings in Northern California. And he knew the commissioner was eager to raise the league's profile in India. The Mumbai native called the commissioner and formally announced his determination to buy the Kings. Stern pushed Kevin Johnson for an introduction to all the right people in Sacramento. "A lot of people called us," Stern said, trying to downplay his Kingmaker role. "We directed everybody to the mayor." The deal was coming together.

Suddenly, there was an ecumenical mix of Silicon Valley money, Southern California money and local money lined up for Sacramento. Mark Friedman, a key Kevin Johnson supporter and developer whose family owned the prosperous Arden Fair shopping mall in Sacramento, joined the investors. He would manage the Plaza arena project.

Ranadive brought in more friends: the Jacobs brothers of San Diego, Paul, Jeff and Hal, whose father founded Qualcomm, the satellite communications company. Along with the brothers came a former Facebook executive, Chris Kelly. Ranadive expanded his network, triggering the strategy he had plotted for years. Into the investment group swam whales Raj Bhathal, a Southern California swimwear manufacturer, venture capitalist Arjun Gupta and tech entrepreneurs Andy Miller and Katrina Garnett.

Ranadive, the electrical engineer whose minimally talented girls basketball team pressured its way into the national playoffs, was now coaching the whales to an NBA victory, contesting every inbounds play from Seattle. The Seattle quick-kill strategy was in ruins. Goliath, as played by Hansen and Ballmer, decided to throw more dollars at the deal. They raised their bid by $25 million. Three weeks later, they pushed in another $75 million, a total of $100 million in sweeteners. The potential valuation of the Kings stood at $625 million.

For six decades of NBA history, a premium of $100 million would have immediately closed the deal with the Board of Governors. But things were different in 2013. It wasn't just about the money.

The NBA had an incumbent city and mayor to protect, a vagrant franchise to anchor and a renegade ownership to punish—and expel. David Stern was months from retirement. The commissioner was in full command of the organization he had devoted his intelligence, his energy, his life to since 1966. Nobody could get in his way now.

Basketball had no moment like this, but opera did: the last grand aria, where the maestro stands perfectly still and for the final time in his career hits the top C, the note that approximates the human cry, the note that makes us weep, then leaves the theater for good.

Chapter Twenty-Four: The Appropriate Outcome

Chris Hansen and Steve Ballmer knew David Stern didn't like relocations. They knew the commissioner had a special relationship with Kevin Johnson. They thought more money would work because they had plenty of money and money always worked. But there was another factor playing against Seattle. David Stern was determined to expel the Maloofs on terms not dictated by The Boys. Picture Michael Corleone in the commissioner's chair.

When the Maloofs abandoned and ridiculed the 2012 Sacramento arena deal, a plan devised by Stern and partially funded by the NBA, the family broke its bond with the league. While the Maloofs figured they could still negotiate terms over their sale to Hansen, Stern had another idea. Unconditional surrender.

The shift in Stern's attitude was monumental. Before the Maloofs walked away from the 2012 arena deal, the commissioner had taken the opposite viewpoint. He was a massive ally for The Boys. He pushed hard for maximum arena dollars on the family's behalf. He wanted public money from Sacramento to ease the Maloof's pain.

In a 2011 phone conversation, Stern was angry with Johnson for being vague about the city's financial contribution to the arena. Stern did not want Sacramento to short change the Maloofs.

> *David Stern: "That's your strategy, to make all these other deals and cram the Maloofs with a suppository. You take care of the doughnut and forget the hole. You have got to be kidding me. You are proceeding at your own risk, and I want to make that very clear. You are negotiating*

with everybody so there are no moving parts left by the time you get to the Maloofs."

Kevin Johnson: "No, we're talking about structure. We're not negotiating."

Stern: "I told them they would get a great deal. But by the time you get around to negotiating with them, they will be gone and everything else will be irrelevant. There's only one subject I'm interested in, and that's the amount of money not from the Maloofs."

By 2013, everything was different. Stern would deploy the suppository. When Hansen and Ballmer aligned with the Maloofs, they stood with outcasts.

FOUR MONTHS after the sale to Hansen, the Seattle media began to complain that Stern was helping Sacramento. Fans piled on with blogs, Tweets, Facebook attacks and endless social media entries defaming the commissioner. Many NBA fans and Seattle media commentators believed Stern was vindictive after Seattle's acrimonious divorce from the NBA in 2008. They didn't understand that by 2013, Seattle was just a side player in an intense family purge.

Stern was delaying Hansen's purchase, claiming the deal was unprecedented and complicated and the league needed more time for study. Basketball fans in Seattle were convinced the stall was designed to give Sacramento a chance to solidify its finances. That was true enough.

But from the league's perspective, Seattle forfeited the SuperSonics by failing to muster the political will to resolve the need for a new arena several years before 2008, under the ownerships of Howard Schultz and eventually Clay Bennett.

To the NBA, arena resolutions were measured by political support and public dollars. None of that was abundant in Seattle. No matter, a battalion of SuperSonics loyalists saw themselves as victims of David Stern. A public Twitter exchange in May 2013 between Miami Heat owner Micky Arison and a SuperSonics fan named Danny told the story:

Arison: "U don't get it. We are voting to leave or not Sac. I love Sea and will support team there but honestly u r making it harder to support u. Done."

Danny: "Again Mr Arison I'm not trying to harass u. I want a NBA team back. 2008 was so painful and so is now. If u tell me what I need to do to get ..."

Arison: "U don't want 2understand. The question b4 the committee is has sac done all it should to keep the team. The answer is yes. Not a vote abt sea."

Danny: "Well if Sac got 10 years to try we'd have arena too. We r bein shunned again after all this. Ppl in Sac r celebrating..."

Arison: "If sea especially local politicians had done what sac's did a move to okc would never have been approved. I want a team in sea just not sacs."

Danny: "I don't think the NBA understands the pain this has caused Seattle! If u want Sac to stay, fine. Expansion. We at least earned that."

Arison: "Sorry but u r wrong. Ballmer never stepped up in 08 & the issue was the turning dwn of the arena project to shultz then bennett over a many yrs."

Not quite Shakespeare, but a fair summary of the NBA's position on Seattle.

THE NBA SAID the Kings' sale and move would be voted up or down at the Board of Governors meetings April 18 and 19 at the St. Regis Hotel in New York City. Then Stern declared those dates weren't firm. He asked Chris Hansen and Kevin Johnson to come to New York two weeks before the meetings and present arguments to NBA ownership committees. After each representative spoke, Stern said the situation was so complex that more meetings were required. He would drag the process into May.

The commissioner, who once admonished Kevin for "dicking us around" and claimed the NBA had "30 owners who do this sort of stuff on the back of envelopes," now required an exhaustive, protracted process for a sale and move for a franchise that had been sold six times and moved among five cities. "This will be by far our most extensive review of anything like this in the league's history," Stern said. No scribbling on the back of envelopes now. David Stern was buying time for Sacramento.

"A bad look for David Stern as Seattle-Sacramento battle for Kings drags out," read the Seattle Times headline above an April 19 column by Jerry Brewer. The writer commented on an exchange between KING5-TV reporter Chris Daniels and Stern after Daniels inferred the commissioner was helping Sacramento. "It was no surprise what the fight was over: The widespread perception that Stern is fighting alongside Sacramento—and against Seattle, again—in this tug-of-war over the Kings franchise," Brewer wrote.

The Maloof family never cited favoritism by Stern. The family argued basic economics, saying the Sacramento dollars didn't match Hansen and Ballmer. In a strict sense, the family was right. The Maloofs wanted to take the money and run. They sent a letter to the NBA claiming the Sacramento offer was "deficient economically."

Stern was not impressed. Both bids "are in the same ballpark with respect to the net result to the selling family," the commissioner said. Complications such as relocation fees and the $73 million owed Sacramento for the Jim Thomas loan of 1997, plus the millions of dollars the Maloofs had borrowed from the NBA, made the two offers difficult to compare.

Concerns about Stern favoring Sacramento were proved prescient on April 29, when the NBA Relocation Committee, a group of seven owners who influenced the other 23, conducted a two-hour conference call. The conversation ended with a unanimous vote to deny the move to Seattle.

The committee's recommendation stunned Hansen and Ballmer. Ranadive had to catch his breath before he Tweeted his astonishment. "I'm speechless," he wrote as Goliath lay dying. Stern was marginally surprised by the unanimous outcome. He figured the Maloofs would get at least one or two votes.

The news reached Kevin Johnson as he ate lunch. He was pleased but warned against early celebrations. "It's not over yet," he said. "I feel like we have won a round in the playoffs. There is still work to be done." Dick Motta would have been proud of Kevin's temperance before the fat lady sang.

Ballmer, unaccustomed to seeing his wealth rejected, went on a Seattle radio show and said, "I'm horribly, horribly disappointed." Hansen took the longer view. He wrote a statement for his website: "We have a binding transaction to purchase the Kings for what would be a record price for an NBA franchise ... a much higher price than the yet to be finalized Sacramento Group, and have placed all of the funds to close the transaction into escrow."

What Hansen's statement didn't say was that binding transaction or not, the Maloofs still owned the Kings. The NBA had not approved the sale. By denying the move to Seattle, the NBA dared the Maloofs to challenge the Board of Governors in federal court. If the Maloofs filed an antitrust lawsuit and went ahead with relocation, the sale to Hansen and Ballmer would never be approved. The NBA was playing hardball. And the game was over.

TWO WEEKS later, on May 15, 2013, representatives from 30 NBA teams and the Seattle and Sacramento prospective ownerships trekked to the Hilton Anatole Hotel in Dallas for a final vote on the Maloof application to relocate the Kings to Seattle. Hansen spoke for 45 minutes. Johnson, Ranadive and Mark Friedman followed. The league owners deliberated for two hours. Then they voted 22-8 to deny the relocation.

Twenty-four hours later, the Maloof family agreed to sell its 65 percent share of the Kings to Ranadive and partners for $347 million. At the last minute, Ranadive agreed to sweeten his offer by $6.5 million. After deducting about $140 million in debts, the Maloof family and partner Bob Hernreich took home around $206 million, plus the $30 million nonrefundable down-payment from Hansen and Ballmer. The Seattle men swallowed their defeat in a manner familiar to Sacramento fans, though Hansen admitted to a Seattle radio station, "It kind of made me sick to my stomach." This time, Hansen and Ballmer, not Sacramento, played the role of good losers.

But time would prove that the loser was not so good. A month after the Dallas vote, Hansen secretly funded a political campaign to harass, confuse and derail the work by Ranadive and the city of Sacramento to build a new arena. Anonymously shoveling $100,000 into an anti-arena petition drive, Hansen was revealed after his operatives failed to file campaign disclosure documents in July 2013. Josh Wood, executive of a Sacramento advocacy group, Region Builders, exposed the violations.

Humiliated, Hansen emerged from the shadows and apologized. He said, "This is clearly a decision I regret." Hansen promised no further interference and paid a $50,000 fine. Finally, Sacramento saw how bad losers from other cities behaved.

The most eloquent summation of the decision to keep the Kings in Sacramento was made by David Stern. He called it, "The appropriate outcome." The words burrowed deep into the righteous high ground. The outcome was simple. The NBA protected a small, incumbent city that had demonstrated political, corporate and public support. It expelled a negligent and incompetent owner. That was what the NBA stood for in 2013, nine months before Stern stepped into retirement.

The decision was not an indictment of Hansen and Ballmer. If anything, it was a rejection of Seattle and that city's political attitude toward the NBA. Political support for the NBA was tepid at best in Seattle.

Corporate dollars came late to the game. There were loyal NBA fans in Seattle, but how many were corporate titans willing to buy premium packages and lobby for support from elected officials?

By 2013, the league had matured past the point where dollars dictated every executive committee decision. Dollars were still crucial, of course, but the NBA fell for a community's love in Sacramento. Seattle and other hungry cities were left to chew on that appropriate outcome.

When Johnson returned from Dallas, he stepped off a plane at Sacramento International Airport wearing a rumpled plaid shirt, blue jeans and eyeglasses the 47-year old mayor never wore in public. He hadn't had a decent night's sleep for days. He accepted congratulations and made remarks to several TV cameras. Later that afternoon, he rode with his wife in the black police SUV to Oakland, where the Golden State Warriors were playing San Antonio Spurs in a Western Conference semifinal game.

In the midst of the contest, Johnson received a message saying the Maloof family had agreed to sell the Kings to Vivek Ranadive. Kevin knew the commissioner was at the game in Oakland, and went to find him. When Johnson told Stern the deal was completed, Stern smiled and said it was old news. The Kings were staying in Sacramento? Why, of course they were. "You didn't think I knew that?" Stern said.

All the years of fighting with the Maloofs, of dealing with threats from Kings owners, of worrying about offers from cities, none of that mattered anymore. It was time to dig a hole and bury the past, every day of it, even the decision by Bill Russell to draft Kenny Smith over Kevin Johnson in 1987. A deep hole would be needed. But it was time.

That night in Oakland was a moment to savor. Yet Stern knew the hardest part was still ahead: clearing the Downtown Plaza and constructing an arena with public and private dollars under the limitations of time, transparency and budgets. One lawsuit had already been filed against Johnson and City Manager John Shirey for their support of the arena with public dollars. The NBA was imposing a deadline of 2017 for the new building. Same as it did with Gregg Lukenbill in 1987.

And the maestro had a message for his student. "Be careful what you ask for," David Stern told Kevin Johnson that night in Oakland.

THE NEXT day, I called Roger Craig to congratulate him on the appropriate outcome, Vivek Ranadive's acquisition of America's most nomadic sports team, the Vagrant Kings. Craig laughed and reminded me how he could not mention Ranadive's name because of his equity stake in the Warriors, which would soon be sold. "Remember when we talked last year? We had this whole thing figured out last year," Roger joked.

We talked about Stern and Johnson and Ranadive and Sacramento and saving the Kings and building a new arena. We talked about how these astonishing events would change the "good loser" attitude of the city, improve its image and enliven the downtrodden central core.

Roger told me the new arena would be the most technologically sophisticated building in the NBA. And the Kings would emerge as a model franchise with players and staff who were hungry and determined to win. The team's new CEO would be Chris Granger, a star at NBA headquarters and personal favorite of David Stern. Even in retirement, Stern would have a hot line to the back stage in Sacramento.

These attributes would reflect the new owners, smart people who could do other things but chose to spend their energy, time and money on a losing basketball team in a one-horse town, Clipperville. Along the way, they beat Seattle and the hedge fund manager and the CEO of Microsoft with all his billions of dollars. What a remarkable story.

Roger Craig was infectiously optimistic. Once he began to talk about the Kings and Sacramento, it was hard to make him stop. I had heard similar enthusiasms before, from Sacramento people, among them Gregg Lukenbill, going back to 1985.

This time, the words were not from a Sacramento promoter who could be expected to say such things, or from a concession genius driven to sell peanuts, or a Los Angeles real estate developer who lived in Bing Crosby's house and was the best high school free-throw shooter in Cleveland, or a family of silver-spoon gamblers from Las Vegas.

The enthusiasm came from Roger Craig, who was born in Davenport, Iowa, played college football for Nebraska and helped the San Francisco 49ers win three Super Bowls. Craig knew almost nothing about Sacramento. Neither did his boss, Vivek Ranadive, who came from Mumbai, was educated at Cambridge, Mass., and ran his business in Silicon Valley. They arrived with no history of Sacramento, no illusions, no prejudice. They believed in the place. They wanted to stay and build. That was what really mattered.

The romance of an unbreakable link between a place and its team had never been savored by the Kings since the day they switched from being the Rochester Pros to the Royals, when Lester Harrison handed young Richard Paeth a $100 victory bond for winning the name-our-team contest. And Harrison could never be sure about Rochester. Once the Royals stopped winning, Rochester stopped buying Royals tickets. The link was broken early.

In Sacramento, the community based its patronage upon spirit and attitude, not victories. As long as the owners, coaches and players seemed to work hard while sincerely caring about the team and the community, customers came and bought tickets, even when the product failed. Few pro teams in any sport could claim that kind of loyalty. In Sacramento, the link held firm over decades. That's what David Stern meant when he spoke the words, "The appropriate outcome."

DR. JAMES NAISMITH, the Canadian theologian, coach, physician and teacher who invented basketball, lived another 48 years after writing his famous 13 Rules in 1891. He witnessed the game as it grew through its first phase, from creation to the barnstorming days to the formation of pro leagues.

He didn't enjoy watching basketball. It was a game to be practiced and played, Dr. Naismith believed. As a coach at the University of Kansas, he didn't even care about the score. His only concern was the true effort by his players. He ignored opportunities to make money on basketball. He refused to patent his invention. He disliked people who used his game for profit.

More than anything, Dr. Naismith loved to find evidence that his creation had stirred imaginations in unexpected locations, places that were mundane and nothing special, where the sight of basketball hoop was something remarkable. One day he wrote down what made him happy.

"I am sure that no man can derive more satisfaction from money or power than I do from seeing a pair of basketball goals in some out of the way place. Deep in the Wisconsin woods, an old barrel hoop nailed to a tree. High in the Colorado mountains, a pair of crude backstops; halfway across the desert, a crude iron ring fastened to a weather-beaten barn. All are constant reminders that I have at least partially accomplished the objective that I set up."

Before the Kings, that was Sacramento. Then it was home.

Chapter Notes

Preface: In Sacramento, Dying May Be Redundant

1. Telephone calls to David Stern's Office: Author, as Special Assistant, 2009-2012.
2. September 16, 2011, phone call: Author, Ibid., Transcript, conference call, September 16, 2011.
3. Biggest athletic event before the Kings: John Schumacher, The Sacramento Bee, "What was the biggest event in Sacramento sports history?" February 8, 2009.
4. "The appropriate outcome": Stern press conference, Dallas, May 15, 2013.
5. Sacramento population: U.S. Census Bureau.
6. Sold out 17 of 28 seasons: Author, Ibid.
7. Stern christened two arenas: Author; Ibid., 2012 Sacramento Kings Media Guide, p. 174.
8. Johnson despised the Kings: Author, Ibid.
9. "In 12 years," Author, Ibid.
10. "Thank you; you've ended my honeymoon," Author, Ibid., Transcript, conference call, September 16, 2011.
11. John Sutter: Joseph McGowan and Terry Willis, "Sacramento: Heart of the Golden State," p. 11.
12. William Sherman: Sherman, "Memoirs of W.T. Sherman," p. 60.
13. Leland Stanford: Stanford University, "The Birth of the University."
14. Joan Didion: Didion, "Where I Was From," p. 14.
15. Herb Caen, San Francisco Chronicle, October 1, 1975.

16. Tom Hanks: David Garner, "The Tom Hanks Enigma," p. 60.
17. Ronald Reagan: Reagan, "An American Life," p. 156.
18. Arnold Schwarzenegger: Evan Halper and Michael Rothfeld, Los Angeles Times, "This puts your commute to shame," March 7, 2008.
19. Made almost $30 million: Basketball-Reference.com, "Kevin Johnson."
20. In January 2013: Bob Condotta, The Seattle Times, "Stern doesn't expect both Seattle and Sacramento to get NBA teams," February 16, 2013.
21. Ballmer and his team: Author, Ibid.
22. Only one similar transaction had been rejected: The New York Times, "NBA settles suit over Timberwolves," May 31, 1995.
23. Offer $100 million less: Ryan Lillis, Tony Bizjak and Dale Kasler, The Sacramento Bee, "Seattle pumps up its offer," May 11, 2013.
24. Made fortune in Silicon Valley by applying real-time strategies: Malcolm Gladwell, The New Yorker, "How David beats Goliath: When underdogs break the rules," May 11, 2009.
25. "A lot of people think I'm crazy": Author, Ibid.
26. Atlanta Hawks history: 2012 Atlanta Hawks Media Guide, p. 114.
27. "I do feel sorry for Sacramento": Ailene Voisin, The Sacramento Bee, "Jackson says he's sorry - for the Kings," June 7, 2002.
28. Jackson would join: Cork Gaines, Business Insider, "By blocking Kings move to Seattle, the NBA also blocked Phil Jackson's return to NBA," May 21, 2013.

Chapter One: A Distant Memory

1. Friery funeral described: Author, as Special Assistant, 2009–2012.
2. When he was not at work: Ibid.
3. Pompous city council member: Ibid.
4. "It's really not that big of a deal": Ibid.
5. Johnson performed surprisingly well: Martin McNeal, The Sacramento Bee, "KJ relishes turnaround," June 15, 1993.
6. NBA Finals ended: Ibid., "Three the hard way," June 21, 1993.
7. Moon shots: Author, Ibid.
8. Signed professional contract with Oakland A's: Jim Van Vliet, The Sacramento Bee, "One more sleepless night won't bother Kevin Johnson," June 19, 1987.
9. Auerbach thought Cousy was too small: John Taylor, "The Rivalry," p. 26.
10. Many NBA teams were intrigued: Van Vliet, Ibid.

11. Family rented three motel rooms: Van Vliet, Ibid, "Cavaliers Surprise Johnson - and everyone else," June 23, 1987.
12. Boos were heard at Felt Forum: Ibid.
13. Russell should have known: S.L. Price, The Sacramento Bee, "Kings make a point with Smith," June 23, 1987.
14. "Kings are still the same team": Author, Ibid.
15. In modern history of American professional sports: Michael Danielson, "Home Team," p. 307.
16. By early 2013 the Kings were prepared to move: Editorial Board, The Sacramento Bee, "Maloofs need to come clean on plans," January 10, 2013.
17. Among the most bitter: Jim Brunner and Ralph Thomas, Seattle Times, "Ballmer's Sonics offer runs out soon," March 11, 2008.
18. Defeated the New York Knickerbockers: Barry Rubinstein, NBA.com, "Their Royal Highnesses."
19. Most controversial playoff games in NBA history: Chris Sheridan, ESPN.com, "2002 Lakers-Kings Game 6 at heart of Donaghy allegations," June 11, 2008.
20. Ralph Nader: Nader, Open Letter, "Dear Mr. Stern," June 4, 2002.
21. Tim Donaghy, who told a federal court: Sheridan, Ibid.
22. Lawrence Pedowitz ran the inquiry: Pedowitz, "Report to the Board of Governors of the National Basketball Association," October 1, 2008.
23. Pedowitz, nba.com, "Larry Pedowitz Teleconference Transcript," October 2, 2008.
24. Donaghy convicted: Associated Press, "Donaghy sentencing in betting scandal moved to April," January 24, 2008.

Chapter Two: Would Have Been Real Problems

1. Threatened to move the Kings: Author, as sportswriter, The Sacramento Bee, "Thomas forcing city to decide," January 18, 1997.
2. Responsible for upkeep: Martin McNeal, Ibid., "Kings owner pleads case," January 19, 1997.
3. Eli Broad: Steven Magagnini, "Kings owners, partner have big building ideas," December 21, 1992.
4. Losing $5 million per year: Tony Bizjak and Gary Delsohn, Ibid., "How Kings deal came to be," February 23, 1997.
5. A series of 30-year bonds: Ibid.
6. "I won't say anything is ironclad": Author, as sportswriter, 1997.

7. Friery was so confident: Bizjak, Ibid., "Council to get loan revision," September 3, 2010.
8. A self-made entrepreneur: Author, as Special Assistant, Ibid.
9. City government faced a $200 million deficit: Editorial Board, The Sacramento Bee, "Talk about bad timing," August 11, 2008.
10. He would be viewed with suspicion: Mary Lynne Vellinga, Ibid., "Labor groups divided," October 3, 2008.
11. Upgrade the city's outdated, small-town style of government: Lillis, Ibid., "Council members miffed," December 13, 2008.
12. Johnson wanted to do many things: Editorial Board, Ibid., "Kevin Johnson has this priority straight," December 1, 2008.
13. Withdrew her support: Lillis, Ibid., "Honeymoon may be over at City Hall," January 16, 2009.
14. "Everyone told me not to take on": Author, Ibid.
15. Johnson knew Maloof family: Ibid.
16. Since around 2000: McNeal, Ibid., "Granik: Much discussion before Kings could move," January 18, 1997.
17. The alert said the NCAA: Johnson blog, kevinjohnson.com, "Devastating and embarrassing," September 23, 2009.
18. "Did you see this?": Author, Ibid.
19. He formed a "blue-ribbon" task force: Bizjak, Ibid., "Mayor recruits arena team," November 20, 2009.
20. Friery funeral described: Author, Ibid.
21. The Maloof family had walked away: Ken Berger, CBSSports.com, "Sacramento arena deal absolutely dead," April 13, 2012.
22. One call stood out: Author, Ibid.
23. Roger Craig was coy: Ibid.
24. He took to calling Sacramento by a codename: Ibid.
25. Friery funeral described: Ibid.

Chapter Three: We Got A Franchise

1. Games were social events: Kevin Cook, Rochester History Journal, "The Rochester Royals, The Story of Professional Basketball," Winter 1996.
2. "You'd see some people with diamonds": Barry Rubinstein, NBA Encyclopedia, NBA.com., "Their royal highnesses."
3. Neighborhood around the old building: Nothnagle Realtors, "Rochester home listings," February 2013.

4. Goals were bigger than basketball: Kevin Johnson, U.S. Bank Tower speech, "Rules of the Game," October 29, 2009.
5. Cops laid off, fire stations closed: Ryan Lillis, The Sacramento Bee, "Memos offer severe city cuts," April 28, 2010.
6. Chris Lehane background: Adam Nagourney, The New York Times, "Two character models for a single cinematic point," December 7, 2011.
7. Data from economic development studies: Capitol Public Finance Group, Sacramento, "The Economic Engine Report," June 30, 2011.
8. Lehane's playbook: Author, as Special Assistant, 2009-2012.
9. "Always make it about protecting": Ibid.
10. Grow in value from $25,000: Cook, Ibid.
11. Lobbied the political leaders: Ibid.
12. Financial demands of big city arena operations: Michael Danielson, "Home Team," p. 24.
13. Won two championships: Cook, Ibid.
14. Made money and lost money: Ibid.
15. Who appreciated the supremacy of the guard position: Michael Schumacher, "Mr. Basketball," p. 110.
16. Tried to contact the person: Author, as columnist, 1998-2007.
17. Old man was ignored: Ibid.
18. Game was sold as entertainment: Neil Isaacs, "Vintage NBA," Kindle.
19. In large cities: Ibid.
20. Game became a popular activity: Ibid.
21. His was a pure brand: Danielson, Cook, Ibid, p. 110.
22. Large cities were different: Isaacs, Ibid.
23. Encouraged brutal play: Schumacher, Ibid, p. 91.
24. In the 1970s: Author, as sportswriter, 1972-1997.
25. Civic minded local business owners: Schumacher, Ibid, p. 127.
26. Featured African-American players: John Taylor, "The Rivalry," p. 27.
27. Serious, highly skilled: Taylor, Ibid, p. 102.
28. Physically rough and slow paced: Taylor, Ibid, p. 35.
29. Benevolent corporate sponsors: Cook, Ibid.
30. Three corporations: Ibid.
31. Harrison was a basketball man: Ibid.
32. Outstanding player at Rochester East: Ibid.
33. Revived liquor industry: Ibid.
34. Fruit and vegetable company: Ibid.

35. Merged Ebers with the Seagram's: Ibid.
36. Hiram Edgerton: Monroe County (N.Y.) Library Pathfinders, "Rochester City Hall Photo Lab, Aldridge and Edgerton."
37. Western House of Refuge: Ibid., "The Western House of Refuge."
38. Originally the prison Drill Hall: Ibid.
39. Conditions became so notorious: Ibid.
40.Challenges from the biggest newspaper in town: Cook, Ibid.
41. A dry new title: Rochester Pros: Ibid.
42. Many games were sold out: Ibid.
43. NBL franchise was offered to Rochester: Danielson, Ibid., p. 24.
44. Crowning alliterative image: "2012 Sacramento Kings Media Guide," p. 130.

Chapter Four: One Of My Few Mistakes

1. Esoteric clutch of future stars, Chuck Connors: Connors, Ourchuckconnors.com, "Sports Career, Chuck played basketball for two teams: the Rochester Royals and Boston Celtics."
2. Otto Graham: Kevin Cook, Rochester History Journal, "The Rochester Royals, The Story of Professional Basketball," Winter 1996.
3. Del Rice: Ibid.
4. "We must have played 100 exhibition games": Ibid.
5. Eliminate general admission tickets: Ibid.
6. Maurice Podoloff: John Taylor, "The Rivalry," p. 30.
7. Ice under the court melted: Terry Pluto, "Tall Tales," p. 30.
8. NBL and BAA completed their merger that day: Schumacher, Ibid., p. 142.
9. Two years later, Royals were champs: Barry Rubinstein, NBA Encyclopedia, NBA.com., "Their royal highnesses."
10. Facing humiliation: Louis Effrat, The New York Times, "Royals top Knicks for crown 79-75," April 21, 1951.
11. "I remember he had a set of gold": Rubinstein, Ibid.
12. NBA was slowly strangling the Harrison Brothers: Cook, Ibid.
13. Twenty-four second shot clock: Schumacher, Ibid., p. 239.
14. Relinquished coaching chores: Cook, Ibid.
15. Fan threw a knife at Lakers center George Mikan: Mikan, NBA.com, "Greetings from Rochester," December 12, 2007.
16. He blamed: Cook, Ibid.
17. Harrison said he lost $23,600: Ibid.
18. Royals did not draft Russell: Taylor, Ibid., p. 68.
19. "We found out later": Cook, Ibid.

20. William "Dolly" King: Aram Goudsouzian, "King of the Court," p. 65.
21. First African-American player: Irwin Silber and Lester Rodney, "Press Box Red," p. 201.
22. Leery of their brutal travel schedule: Goudsouzian, Ibid., P. 64.
23. Guards were keys to championships: Schumacher, Ibid., p. 110.
24. "One of my few mistakes": Cook, Ibid.
25. "We were really selling out the place": Ibid.
26. Harrison spoke with two businessmen in Kansas City: The New York Times, via Associated Press, "Royals seek new home," March 14, 1957.
27. Built in 1949 for $3 million: Steve Watkins, Cincinnati Business Courier, "The beat goes on at history-rich Gardens," November 24, 2008.
28. He announced the Royals were moving: The New York Times, via United Press, "Royals' quintet shifts franchise to Cincinnati," April 4, 1957.
29. "From a survey made": Cook, Ibid.

Chapter Five: A Gross Miscarriage Of Justice

1. Johnson running late: Author, as Special Assistant, 2009-2012.
2. Stories circulated: Author, as sportswriter, 1972-1997.
3. Friendly and relaxed: Author, as Special Assistant, Ibid.
4. "Oscar Robertson Triple-Double Award": NBA.com, "Isaiah Thomas wins Kings 2012 Oscar Robertson Triple-Double award."
5. "It's a shame": Author, Ibid.
6. "You'll notice": Ibid.
7. Gold medal in basketball: Newsday, "The 'original' Dream Team, 1960 Rome Olympics," April 12, 2012.
8. Leader of the NBA players union: Oscar Robertson, The New York Times, "NBA should honor its history and learn from it," December 24, 2011.
9. "They still call it": Author, Ibid.
10. Wrote an autobiography and a book on basketball: Oscar Robertson, "The Big O" and "The Art of Basketball."
11. Charities: Oscar Robertson, thebigo.com, "Biography."
12. "I'm no hero": John Johnston, Cincinnati Enquirer, "Big O: All-star family man," October 9, 1997.
13. "This is the kind of stuff": Author, Ibid.
14. "Do you know": Ibid.
15. "I noticed that watching": Ibid.
16. "It's OK": Ibid.

17. "Why are you so grumpy": Ibid.
18. Cincinnati was like that: Kevin Cook, Rochester History Journal, "The Rochester Royals, The Story of Professional Basketball," Winter 1996.
19. Reds baseball club dominated the market: baseball-almanac.com, "Cincinnati Reds."
20. Mohawks struggled: Ken Grave, "Cincinnati on Field and Court," p. 94.
21. Harrison found two prospective buyers: Cook, Ibid.
22. The price matched: Rich Westcott, "The Mogul," p. 248.
23. The NBA Board of Governors: Cook, Ibid.
24. "The team was moved": "2012 Sacramento Kings Media Guide," p. 130.
25. Jacobs, called Louie: John Underwood and Morton Sharnik, Sports Illustrated, "Look what Louie wrought," May 29, 1972.
26. "I did what any man": Ibid.
27. Part owner of Cincinnati Gardens: Oscar Robertson, "The Big O," p. 165.
28. "Anytime you want more than $3 million": Ibid.
29. Listen rather than talk: Ibid.
30. "We're in business to sell peanuts": Ibid.
31. The Jacobs operation began: Joe Jares, Sports Illustrated, "Their business is peanuts," January 17, 1966.
32. By 1960: Underwood and Sharnik, Ibid.
33. The brothers invested: Ibid.
34. Airports became key: Ibid.
35. Louie was among: Ibid.
36. Tom Wood: Robertson, Ibid.
37. "Arguing against": Ibid, p. 166.
38. "Pepper Wilson": Ibid.
39. "And for all intents": Ibid.
40. The Royals reached the NBA semifinals: "2012 Sacramento Kings Media Guide," p. 145.
41. The priorities of Louie: Underwood and Sharnik, Ibid.
42. Royals games were scheduled: Robertson, Ibid., p. 246.
43. Jacobs involvement with Moe Dalitz and Jimmy Hoffa: John Smith, Las Vegas Review-Journal, "Moe Dalitz," February 7, 1999.
44. Federal prosecutors established: Underwood and Sharnik, Ibid.
45. Making matters worse: Ibid.
46. "Not only was Emprise": Ibid.
47. "Reopen our inquiry": Ibid.

48. "A gross miscarriage": Ibid.
49. Maurice Stokes raced to the basket:
John Edgar Wideman, "Hoop Roots," p. 204.
50. "I feel like I'm going": Ibid.
51. "I was the only one there": Douglas Martin, The New York Times, "Jack Twyman, NBA star known for off-court assist, dies at 78," May 31, 2012.
52. "He gave me a lot more": NBA TV, "Maurice Stokes and Jack Twyman, NBA greats," September 21, 2012.

Chapter Six: Left To The Professionals

1. Manipulation was overseen: Oscar Robertson, "The Big O," p. 226.
2. "A guy nobody had ever heard of": Robertson, Ibid.
3. Young Joe graduated: Stephen Magagnini, The Sacramento Bee, "Is this just a rebound romance? Joe Axelson takes his best shot," February 1, 1987.
4. He would tell people: Ibid.
5. "I think I know as much": Ibid.
6. "I liked what I was doing": Ibid.
7. Brought in retired Celtics great Bob Cousy: Robertson, Ibid.
8. They paid him the extraordinary salary: Sam Goldaper, The New York Times, "Cousy is signed for $150,000 pact at $150,000," May 10, 1969.
9. Auerbach wasn't impressed: John Taylor, "The Rivalry," p. 29.
10. As the draft reached: Ibid.
11. Did manage to identify: NBA.com, "Complete Bio of Nathaniel Archibald."
12. Royals fans hated: Taylor, Ibid, p. 119.
13. Red Auerbach once chased: Taylor, Ibid.
14. Axelson had more important concerns: Robertson, Ibid, p. 247.
15. Axelson announced the relocation: The New York Times, via Associated Press, "Kansas City to get Cincinnati Royals," March 15, 1972.
16. A small crowd watched the final game: The New York Times, Ibid., "4,022 see Royals go," March 25, 1972.
17. Attendance: "2012 Sacramento Kings Media Guide," Ibid.
18. Axelson would be a partner: Robertson, Ibid, p. 246.
19. A new Kansas City building: Robertson, Ibid., p. 247.
20. Nine Kansas City investors: Robertson, Ibid., p. 246.
21.Bob Cousy was pushed into retirement: Robertson, Ibid., p. 247.
22. Lost to the Houston Rockets:
"2012 Sacramento Kings Media Guide," Ibid., p. 163.
23. "I was ready to sign him": Magagnini, Ibid.

24. "We believe that ownership": Associated Press, Fort Scott, Kan., Tribune, "Kings announce change in ownership," May 12, 1982.
25. Terry Furlow: Eric Woodyard, Flint, Mich., Journal, "Friends, family remember Flint legend 33 years after tragic death," May 23, 2013.
26. Walter Davis: Bruce Newman, Sports Illustrated, "Risen again," February 27, 1989.
27. Micheal Ray Richardson: Sam McManis, Los Angeles Times, "The troubling career of Micheal Ray Richardson," February 28, 1986.
28. Lewis Lloyd: Sam Goldaper, The New York Times, "Lloyd and Wiggins of Rockets banned for drug use," January 14, 1987.
29. Mitchell Wiggins: Ibid.
30. One person in place: E.M. Swift, Sports Illustrated, "From corned beef to caviar," June 3, 1991.
31. "If you had 30 minutes with a prospective sponsor": Ibid.
32. It would come from the West: S.L. Price, The Sacramento Bee, "Building a kingdom: how Gregg Lukenbill & Co. plan to turn the Kings into a Sacramento institution," November 10, 1985.
33. The young man: Joe Davidson, The Sacramento Bee, "G Force, Heee's got the talent and the longevity," April 26, 1999.

Chapter Seven: We Foresaw The Reality

1. Westcore Properties: Hudson Sangree, The Sacramento Bee, "$600 million property sale," December 21, 2012.
2. Anonymous boxes: Author, as Special Assistant, 2009-2012.
3. Largest industrial real estate transaction: Sangree, Ibid.
4. Maidu definition of Natoma, A.L. Kroeber, "California place names of Indian origins," University of California Publications in Archaeology and Ethnography, Vol. 12, June 15, 1916.
5. In the late 1970s: S.L. Price, The Sacramento Bee, "Building a kingdom: How Gregg Lukenbill & Co. plan to turn the Kings into a Sacramento institution," November 10, 1985.
6. In theory: Ibid.
7. Benvenuti figured: Author, as sportswriter, 1972-1997.
8. Under the rules: Ibid.
9.Between 2006 and 2012: Sangree and Phillip Reese, The Sacramento Bee, "On housing-busted street, a few have found a way to stay," July 15, 2012.
10. Joe Benvenuti was a real estate speculator: Price, Ibid.

11. His angel investor: Ibid.

12. Every city had stories: Joseph McGowan and Terry Willis, "Sacramento: Heart of the Golden State," p. 21.

13. A property tax bill: Amy Chance, The Sacramento Bee, "North Natomas is land of conflicting dreams," December 29, 1985.

14. "We're going through": Ibid.

15. Most angry: Price, Ibid.

16. Anne Rudin: Jim Sanders, The Sacramento Bee, "Anne Rudin: a different style in City Hall," September 16, 1987.

17. "The sports issue and the land issue": Price, Ibid.

18. He managed to place an initiative: Price, Ibid, "Lukenbill's egg has hatched," January 22, 1985.

19. "Most of the people": Price, Ibid.

20. The 1950s home plate: Author, Ibid.

21. He also thought the NFL: Bill Conlin, The Sacramento Bee, "Al Davis pays a visit," July 9, 1989.

22. Move to Los Angeles: Oakland Raiders, raiders.com, "Timeline."

23. CBS paid the league: InsideHoops.com, "NBA TV contracts,"

24. An entrepreneurial attitude: Jason Belzer, Forbes, "NBA Renaissance man," May 7, 2013.

25. Joe Hamelin: Author, Ibid.

26. Broker a sale for the Pacers: Gary Delsohn, The Sacramento Bee, "Mr. Relentless wins grudging respect," October 30, 1988.

27. Within 72 hours: Price, Ibid.

Chapter Eight: People Have Raised Valid Concerns

1. A fluid number: Scott Price, The Sacramento Bee, "Lukenbill's egg has hatched," January 22, 1985.

2. Benvenuti began to boast: Author, as sportswriter.

3. Axelson made the pretense: Stephen Magagnini, The Sacramento Bee, "Is this just a rebound romance? Joe Axelson takes his best shot," February 1,1987.

4. Transfer was swiftly approved: Price, Ibid, "Here come the Kings," April 17, 1985.

5. "We were the No. 5 sports franchise": Author, The Sacramento Bee, "A city remembers," February 23, 1997.

6. "We identified about eight": Ibid.

7. Gary Sage: Ibid.

8. Temporary arena: Amy Chance, Ibid, “Planning, politics revolve around the sport of the Kings,” October 25, 1985.
9. County board of supervisors: Ibid.
10. News finally broke: Price, Ibid.
11. The last game: Price, Ibid, “Kings fans burn bridge, Axelson,” April 15, 1985.
12. Mike Randall: Ibid.
13. “It isn’t a good basketball town”: Price, Ibid, “Kings entertain at Kemper for final time,” April 14, 1985.
14. “There’s something about being the first major-league team”: Price, Ibid, “It’s official, the Sacramento Kings,” April 17, 1985.
15. League could buy the team: Ibid.
16. “The Kings are coming”: Price, Ibid, “Dutch and crew works on the house fit for Kings,” April 24, 1985.
17. “Hey, at least we didn’t name it Preparation H Arena”: Jaime Diaz, Sports Illustrated, “The Kings and their court,” March 31, 1986.
18. Opening night 1985: Joe Hamelin, The Sacramento Bee, “Coronation clipped at last, city’s day in court,” October 26, 1985.
19. Eliminated in three straight games: Dan Vierria, The Sacramento Bee, “Rockets bench helped team get rid of all the jinxes,” April 23, 1986.
20. Lukenbill pushed the Sacramento City Council: Sanders, Ibid, “Stadium, arena win city council’s OK,” October 29, 1986.
21. Council members heard: Ibid.
22. The vote that evening: Ibid.
23. Allied Bank of Texas: Sanders, Ibid, “Deal linking pension fund to new arena ends,” May 6, 1988.
24. Removed $8 million: Ibid.
25. Pension fund would earn: Ibid.

Chapter Nine: They Appear To Be Open To My Approach

1. Land values leaping: Amy Chance, The Sacramento Bee, “N. Natomas buildup may cost $1 billion,” June 16, 1985.
2. The team that delighted: Joe Hamelin, The Sacramento Bee, “Kings finalize deal for Clippers’ Smith,” August 20, 1986.
3. “If you knew the game”: Author, as sportswriter, 1972-1997.
4. The Kings agreed to pay Smith: Hamelin, Ibid.
5. Smith injuries: Hamelin, Ibid.

6. “The moves Joe has made”: S.L. Price, The Sacramento Bee, “Now, Axelson doesn’t go hunting unarmed,” October 5, 1986.
7. “The worst part is the burden”: Author, The Sacramento Bee, “Derek’s King-sized problem,” December 18, 1988.
8. Phil Johnson: Author, as sportswriter, 1972-1997.
9. “I have never seen anything like that”: Price, Ibid, “For quarter, Kings shoot nothing but blanks,” February 5, 1987.
10. “I can jump”: Author, Ibid, November 22, 1987.
11. Smith death: Mitch Lawrence, New York Daily News, “Death of a driven man,” September 1, 1996.
12. Players rushed to the bank: Author, Ibid.
13. One-year extension: Price, Ibid, “NBA grants five wishes,” April 23, 1987.
14. Most unenjoyable year: Price, Ibid, “Coach Russell fit for Kings,” April 29, 1987.
15. Reaching out to the greatest of them all: Ibid.
16. The details of Russell’s coronation: Jack McCallum, Sports Illustrated, “The King at his new court,” November 16, 1987.
17. The flirtation between Russell and the Kings: Price and Jim Van Vliet, Ibid, “Kings, Russell still conducting talks,” April 25, 1987.
18. Met at Aldo’s restaurant: McCallum, Ibid.
19. “It’s been a terrible year”: Price, Ibid, “Coach Russell fit for Kings,” Ibid.
20. Russell did not win: Author, Ibid.
21. Russell spent three years: Ibid.
22. The 21st century deification: Ibid.
23. It was coincidental: Ibid.
24. “Second Wind”: Bill Russell and Taylor Branch, “Second Wind: The Memoirs of an Opinionated Man,” Random House, September 1979.
25. “That’s nice”: Author, Ibid.
26. My first assignment: Author, Ibid.
27. He always politely said, “No thanks”: Author, Ibid.
28. “The players understand,” Author, Ibid, “Game only a piece of Russell puzzle: There’s much more to Kings coach than basketball,” November 5, 1987.

Chapter Ten: He Felt Relieved By The Whole Thing

1. We went to Alaska and Montana: Author, as sportswriter, The Sacramento Bee, “Weary road trip ahead for Kings,” October 22, 1987.
2. “I don’t sign autographs”: John Taylor, “The Rivalry,” p. 364.

3. Great Alaskan Bush Company: Author, Ibid,
"Kings fishing for Alaska's lure," October 27, 1987.
4. "When you travel": Author, Ibid.
5. "Bill is a very private person": Author, Ibid,
"Accessibility not a priority for Russell," October 4, 1987.
6. "Don't you ever wonder?": Author, Ibid.
7. "We needed an extra pot of coffee": Author, Ibid.
8. Larry the Painter: Author, Ibid,
"He paints a picture for Kings tickets," April 30, 1993.
9. Russell and media: Taylor, Ibid., p. 361.
10. "I am not a racist sports writer": Ibid.
11. He sent a letter: Bill Russell, "Dear Bob," November 6, 1989.
12. The letter: Author, Ibid.
13. Willis Reed: Author, Ibid.
14. The Kings second assistant coach: Author, Ibid.
15. "I didn't know I was lying around":
16. There was one person who knew: Author, Ibid.,
"Hadnot stood out being a good guy," August 7, 1998.
17. "Don't worry about it": Ibid.
18. Smith never found his footing: McCallum, Ibid,
"A dream come true," March 22, 1993.
19. "From high school to college": Van Vliet, Ibid,
"Kenny Smith, rookie on the run," November 5, 1987.
20. Ten years before he arrived in Sacramento: McCallum, Ibid.
21. "Horizontal game": Murry Nelson, "Bill Russell, a Biography," p. 56.
22. Most Kings players did try to appreciate: Author, Ibid.
23. Russell refused to call time out: Author, Ibid.,
"Kings endure Los Angeles horror show," December 24, 1987.
24. The Kings' annual visit to the cathedral: Author, Ibid,
"Russell's visit to Boston rekindles bad memories," January 17, 1988.
25. Kings center LaSalle Thompson: Author, Ibid.
26. "It proves the Celtics are a very good team": Author, Ibid.
27. The change in scenery: Frank Deford, Sports Illustrated,
"The Ring Leader," May 10, 1999.
28. More leaks were made: Author, Ibid,
"Kings trade No. 1 pick Ellison in NBA-record time," June 26, 1990.

29. What are you doing in Texas? Darryl Matsuda, Ibid., "Another embarrassing chapter," December 27, 1988.
30. Finally, Axelson admitted: Tom Jackson, Ibid., "Kings use imagination to redefine 'sellout,'" February 10, 1989.
31. Russell's personality hurt attendance at Boston Garden: Taylor, Ibid., p. 365.
32. "I talked to Bill": Author, Ibid., "Kings fire Russell in major shakeup," December 20, 1989.
33. Favorite show was "Jeopardy": Deford, Ibid.

Chapter Eleven: They Have To Learn To Pay Their Dues

1. Danny Ainge: Author, as sportswriter, 1972-1997.
2. "Can you come over": Ibid.
3. "You see what's going on": Ibid.
4. Players on bad teams: Robert Lipsyte, "Accidental Sportswriter," p. 38.
5. He was already considered: Author, The Sacramento Bee, "Coping with Motta's non-star system," January 29, 1990.
6. Celtics wanted Kings center Joe Kleine: Author, Ibid., "Kleine, Pinckney dealt for Ainge, Lohaus," February 24, 1989.
7. Dick Motta: Leigh Montville, Sports Illustrated, "Two for the ages," February 3, 1997.
8. "The opera isn't over": John Papanek, Sports Illustrated, "They're first, at long last," June 19, 1978.
9. That was the kind of stuff he asked me to write: Author, Ibid.
10. The latitude granted sports writers: Lipsyte, Ibid, p. 214.
11. Most sports teams realized: Jimmy Breslin, "Can't Anybody Here Play This Game?" p. 40.
12. By the early 2000s: Lipsyte, Ibid.
13. He provided insight and candor: David Halberstam, "Playing For Keeps," p. 413.
14. Pushing Motta could be tricky: Montville, Ibid.
15. "Tell him if he doesn't like it here": Author, Ibid.
16. His first speech: Ibid.
17. "We felt sorry for coach": Ibid.
18.The Kings lost 43 consecutive games: Author, Ibid., "Kings losing streak was almost incomparable," November 24, 1991.
19. Washington Generals: Tim Crothers, Sports Illustrated, "The general whose army never wins," February 20, 1995.

20. Motta stripped off his clothes: Author, Ibid., "Tisdale gets grip on this game ball," November 24, 1991.
21. "This is going up in my trophy case": Ibid.
22. Died at age 44: Sports Illustrated, "Wayman Tisdale 1964-2009," May 25, 2009.
23. Airball One: Author, Ibid., "Kings will stick with Airball One," July 26, 1991.
24. "They have to learn": Ibid.
25. Lukenbill hoped to help pay: Ibid.
26. Motta was fired: Martin McNeal, Ibid., "Motta's reign as Kings coach over, probably this week," December 24, 1991.
27. Traded to Portland: Author, Ibid., "Ainge gets a one-way ticket home," August 2, 1990.
28. In a reminder: Gary Washburn, Boston Globe, "Celtics' Danny Ainge facing critical summer," May 12, 2013.
29. Another connection to the Jacobs era: The Sacramento Bee, "Axelson ends career as Kings executive," May 21, 1990.
30. For all his bluster: Author, Ibid.
31. The Kings constantly changed subjects: Ibid.
32. Ricky Berry: Author, Ibid., "Berry prepared to fight his way into lineup," January 5, 1989.
33. Bought at $360,000 house: Dale Maharidge, Ibid., "Berry suicide bewilders friends, fans," August 15, 1989.
34. Then something happened: Ibid.
35. Johnson arrived on Keane Drive: Ibid.
36. "I know his wife": McNeal, Ibid., "Forever unanswered, a year after Berry's suicide, friends wonder," August 14, 1990.
37. "If you look at his life": Ibid.

Chapter Twelve: Am I Going To Die?

1. Bobby Hurley: Martin McNeal, The Sacramento Bee, "Kings begin paring their seven options," May 26, 1993.
2. Daniel Wieland: Ramon Coronado, Ibid., "DA charges driver who hit Hurley," January 14, 1994.
3. Hurley's new Toyota: Tim Layden, Sports Illustrated, "The long road back," May 23, 1994.
4. Spotted Dr. Richard Marder: Author, as sportswriter, 1972-1997.
5. A renowned trauma physician: Layden, Ibid.

6. "Think of it this way": Author, Ibid.
7. Two criminal trials: Coronado, Ibid., "Witness: Headlights off in car that hit Hurley," September 24, 1994.
8. The second jury: Edgar Sanchez, The Sacramento Bee, "Driver guilty in Hurley collision," December 30, 1994.
9. A painful, courageous: Layden, Ibid.
10. Writing newspaper stories: Author, Ibid.
11. "Don't worry": Ibid.
12. I was unable to run: The Sacramento Bee, "Polynice grabs and threatens Bee columnist," November 4, 1995.
13. "It's assault and battery": Author, Ibid.
14. "You're not a referee": Ibid.
15. Hintz doubted: Ibid.
16. Despite vast land holdings: Ilana DeBare, The Sacramento Bee, "City threatens foreclosure over Natomas debt," June 2, 1990.
17. Missing payments of $381,968: Ibid., "City cleared to foreclose on Sports Association land," April 13, 1994.
18. Bob Cook sued Lukenbill: Sam Stanton, Ibid., "Co-owner sues Lukenbill to stop Kings sale," March 25, 1992.
19. Work stopped on the baseball stadium: Gary Delsohn, Ibid., "Lukenbill's stadium dream in limbo," January 6, 1991.
20. The bank took a severe haircut: Mary Lynne Vellinga, Ibid., "Quick action marks stadium deal," March 6, 1994.
21. The real estate men: Delsohn, Ibid., "Anderson buys stadium," June 4, 1992.
22. Davis backed away: Delsohn, Ibid., "How the Raiders deal collapsed," March 16, 1990.
23. "I sincerely and honestly believe": Deb Kollars, Ibid., "Plenty of uses for bonds sold to lure Raiders," February 16, 1992.
24. Donated the unfinished stadium: Author, Ibid., "An offer city can't refuse," March 26, 1995.
25. In came Jim Thomas: Steve Wiegand and Stanton, Ibid., "Tentative deal for control of Kings," March 19, 1992.
26. "You know, we never really got along": Author, Ibid., "Kings partners changing courts," August 10, 1994.

Chapter Thirteen: No Reason To Doubt Their Sincerity

1. Jim Thomas bought the Kings: Steve Wiegand and Sam Stanton, The Sacramento Bee, "Tentative deal for control of Kings," March 19, 1992.
2. Now they had a strange new species: Author as sportswriter, 1972-1998.
3. There was not much else: Ibid.
4. It would be Sacramento's sad fate: Ibid.
5. Thomas and his partner Rob Maguire: Stephen Magagnini, The Sacramento Bee, "Kings owner, partners have big building ideas," December 21, 1992.
6. Paid tribute to the potential: Stanton, Ibid., "Buyers say Kings only move is up as winner," April 1, 1992.
7. "We'd be interested": Magagnini, Ibid.
8. They posed for pictures: Stanton, Ibid.
9. Paid relatively little: Gary Delsohn, Ibid., "Final papers signed on $140 million sale of Kings, arena," April 7, 1992.
10. Controlling interest pieces: Stanton, Ibid.
11. Bob Cook filed a lawsuit: Stanton, Ibid, "Co-owner sues Lukenbill to stop Kings sale," March 25, 1992.
12. Move the Kings to Anaheim: Author, The Sacramento Bee, "How can the Kings move south? Let us count the ways," March 20, 1992.
13. "They have verbally given us assurance": Stanton and Wiegand, Ibid., "Buyers of Kings say teamwork will bring success," March 28, 1992.
14. Dunk the ball as a teenager: Magagnini, Ibid., "Habitual winner nurtures high hopes for his lowly Kings," December 21, 1992.
15. Owned Bing Crosby's old house: Author, Ibid, "Kings owner keeps them on their toes," September 21, 1993.
16. Consecutive wins of 58 and 56 points: "2012 Sacramento Kings Media Guide," p. 182.
17. Gary Gerould would describe: Debbie Arrington and Marcus Crowder, The Sacramento Bee, "Meet the fans who define 'fanatic," April 16, 2013.
18. Losing about $5 million per year: Author, Ibid., "Thomas has had it rough in NBA," February 5, 1997.
19. The Maloof family: Delsohn, Ibid., "Meet the Kings' new co-owners, Maloof family returns to NBA," January 15, 1998.
20. Old man's principle: Hugo Lindgren, The New York Times Magazine, "The flying Maloof brothers," February 15, 2004.
21. The Maloof family is famous: Ibid.

22. "We don't try to outsmart anyone": Ibid.
23. New Mexico bank that was slipping: Ibid.
24. Small casinos in Central City, Colo., and North Las Vegas: Ibid.
25. Acquired stock in another bank: Ibid.
26. A $265 million hipster haven: Las Vegas Sun, "Details announced on Maloofs' new Las Vegas hotel-casino," October 25, 2000.
27. Sold the Fiesta for $185 million: Lindgren, Ibid.
28. Bought the Houston Rockets in 1979 for $9 million: Ibid.
29. George Sr.'s two sisters: Ibid.
30. Rockets were sold in 1982: Delsohn, Ibid.
31. San Antonio Spurs: Ibid.
32. Tampa Bay Lightning: Ibid.
33. Invested in second-tier pro football: Lindgren, Ibid.
34. Gambling was a conflict of interests: Ibid.
35. "The Boys": Author as Special Assistant, 2009-2012.
36. Stern filled the air with curses: Ibid.
37. With a matchmaker's touch: Author, Ibid.
38. "The new owners are responsible": Author, Ibid.
39. Palms opened two months after September 11, 2001: Architectural Studies Library, University of Nevada, Las Vegas, casino timeline, library.unlv.edu.

Chapter Fourteen: People In Sacramento Have A Sense Of Humor

1. Rap productions, skateboards and the MTV reality show: Hugo Lindgren, The New York Times Magazine, "The flying Maloof brothers," February 15, 2004.
2. Made space for a Playboy Club: Steve Green, Las Vegas Sun, "Palms says Playboy Club to close, ending partnership," March 15, 2012.
3. Midweek $69 packages: Author, as Special Assistant, 2009-2012.
4. They could blow: Lindgren, Ibid.
5. After a game at Arco Arena: Author, as columnist, 1997-2007, "After $100 thank-you, everyone's eager to give Maloof a cigarette," April 17, 2002.
6. "Real Housewives of Beverly Hills": Lauren Beale, Los Angeles Times, "Adrienne Maloof of 'Real Housewives' sells Beverly Hills manse," October 23, 2012.
7. She found new romance: Jill Heller, International Business Times, "Adrienne Maloof steps out in lingerie with Sean Stewart," March 25, 2013.

8. The value of Palms collapsed: Oskar Garcia, The Associated Press, Bloomberg Businessweek, "Shuffle leaves Maloofs 2 percent of Palms," June 21, 2011.
9. Sold its legacy business: Kelly Johnson, Sacramento Business Journal, December 7, 2009.
10. Colleen and Joe unloaded mansions: Dale Kassler, The Sacramento Bee, "Maloofs sell beer distributorship," December 8, 2009.
11. "We want to concentrate": Ibid.
12. George Jr. was arrested: Jackie Valley, Las Vegas Sun, "Report released in DUI arrest of Palms owner George Maloof," October 26, 2010.
13. TPG confirmed it would remove a marquee: John Katsilometes, "Rebranding of the Palms has turned Joe Magliarditi into a quick-change artist," Las Vegas Sun, August 24, 2012.
14. "That's only because": Ibid.
15. Insisting they would never sell: Editorial Board, The Sacramento Bee, "Local bidders deserve a shot at the Kings," January 10, 2013.
16. Near victory over the Lakers: Marcos Breton, Ibid., "It's do or die: In grinding brawl, the Lakers tie the series," June 1, 2002.
17. Hire his friend Rick Adelman: Ailene Voisin, Ibid., "Can Adelman reshape Kings as he did Blazers?" October 4, 1998.
18. Adelman was difficult to categorize: Phil Taylor, Sports Illustrated, "Long live the Kings," February 19, 2001.
19. Success came quickly: Ibid.
20. The Lakers were insulting them: Voisin, Ibid., "Jackson says he's sorry—for the Kings," June 7, 2002.
21. "You're talking about some semi-civilized Sacramentans": Ibid.
22. "I'm not worried about the Sacramento Queens": Martin McNeal, Ibid., "Shaq's latest outburst fails to faze Kings, much," October 11, 2002.
23. They finished with 55 wins: "2012 Sacramento Kings Media Guide," p. 198.
24. The Kings won 61 games in 2001-2002: Ibid., p. 200.
25. Webber fell and tore the meniscus: Jack McCallum, Sports Illustrated, "Chris Crossed," April 4, 2004.
26. "That was the Titanic": Voisin, Ibid., "Q and A with the Maloofs," July 24, 2010.
27. Arco Arena was on borrowed time: Terri Hardy and M.S. Enkoji, Ibid., "City's goal: public vote on arena in March," July 23, 2004.
28. "This isn't the kind of project": Mary Lynne Vellinga, Ibid., "Hail Kings! But an arena?" May 20, 2002.

29. Kings fans enjoyed the Arco Arena experience: Mark Kreidler, Ibid., "Arco Arena intimacy big for Maloofs," December 20, 2003.
30. Palace of Auburn Hills opened: NBA.com, "The Palace of Auburn Hills."
31. Bradley Center in Milwaukee: BMOHarrisbradleycenter.com, "Arena highlights."
32. "No, it's finished": Author, as sportswriter, Ibid.
33. When the Maloof family first toured: Ibid.
34. Metropolitan Chamber of Commerce: Hardy, Ibid, "New task force to tackle arena," January 3, 2004.
35. "We're not in favor of this": Hardy and Enkoji, Ibid.
36. "It's about more than an arena": Tony Bizjak, Ibid., "Fargo ponders best timing for vote on railyard plan," July 7, 2002.
37. "They lied to us": Hardy, Ibid, "Maloofs: City sabotaged arena," October 29, 2003.
38. "I don't think they have done a very good job": Voisin, Ibid., "Mayor throws in towel on arena vote," October 25, 2003.
39. A group of Natomas property owners: Vellinga, Ibid., "Blanas plan would fund arena," September 4, 2004.
40. The downtown rail yards: Morris Newman, The New York Times, August 11, 2009.
41. Theodore Judah surveyed: Stephen Ambrose, "Nothing Like It in the World," p. 19.
42. Goss and Lambard Iron Works: Kevin Hecteman, "Sacramento's Southern Pacific Shops," p. 8.
43. "Sacramento was a railroad town": Ibid., p. 9.
44. Union Pacific bought Southern Pacific in 1996: Ibid.
45. The Boys placed themselves in a remarkable position: Vellinga, Ibid., "Arena effort quietly resumes," April 22, 2006.
46. Asked voters to approve a $1.2 billion sales tax: Ibid.
47. The Maloof family's obligation: Hardy and Vellinga, Ibid., "Some say lost arena bid was calculated," November 9, 2006.
48. Appear in a Carl's Jr. television commercial: Ibid.
49. "I said, 'People in Sacramento have a sense of humor'": Vellinga, Ibid., "Arena details to remain secret," October 18, 2006.
50. The votes were counted: Hardy and Vellinga, Ibid.
51. "Although I have a full-time job": Hardy, Ibid., "Stern takes lead in arena talks," November 16, 2006.

Chapter Fifteen: Had To Go Oak Park On Him

1. On the rare occasions when he drove: Author, as Special Assistant, 2009–2012.
2. He found the games boring: Ibid.
3. "You've got to keep your foot on the pedal": Ibid.
4. Kevin was focused on education: Laurel Rosenhall, The Sacramento Bee, "Kevin Johnson on state boards," June 1, 2006.
5. Johnson memorized data: Ibid.
6. The solution, Johnson believed, was charter schools: Rosenhall, Ibid, "Winfrey's show spotlights Sac High," April 12, 2006.
7. A camera crew from the Oprah Winfrey show: Ibid.
8. "Education is the 21st Century": M.S. Enkoji, Ibid., "Oprah to spotlight hometown star's quest," March 30, 2006.
9. Oprah would interview: Enkoji, Ibid.
10. Joan Didion would view: Didion, "Where I Was From," p. 164.
11. He created Stand Up: Standup.org, "About Stand Up."
12. A $500,000 grant from a foundation: Diana Lambert, The Sacramento Bee, "Improving youth education is goal of nonprofit agency," December 19, 2009.
13. He disliked asking for money: Author, Ibid.
14. Johnson took great pride: Ibid.
15. After Johnson was elected: Ibid.
16. Was 16 when she became pregnant: Wil Haygood, "Kevin Johnson's winning streak," The Washington Post, March 10, 2010.
17. Raised by grandparents: Ibid.
18. George and Georgia were white: Ibid.
19. Stories about his grandfather's experiences: Author, Ibid.
20. Challenge Johnson at a Town Hall event: Ibid.
21. "Did you see me get after": Author, Ibid.
22. "Going Oak Park": Ibid.
23. "The bus would take me": Ibid.
24. Averaged 34.2 points: Joe Davidson, Maxpreps.com, "Kevin Johnson leads 30th class," March 2, 2012.
25. "I was the only one in the room": Author, Ibid.
26. Kevin worked hard to find a place: S.L. Price, The Sacramento Bee, "New Sun determined to shine," February 27, 1988.
27. Six current and former players had been indicted: Author, Ibid., "Ex-King, nine others indicted in drug probe," April 18, 1987.

28. The Cavaliers didn't explain: Price, Ibid.
29. An experienced NBA scout: John Walters, Sports Illustrated, "Barzin Arizona," January 29, 1996.
30. The criminal accusations were exaggerated: Author, Ibid, "County DA drops charges against Bratz," July 29, 1987.
31. Unloaded one-third of his roster: Bruce Newman, Sports Illustrated, "... Risen Again," February 27, 1989.
32. "I think most people in Phoenix": Ibid.
33. "There's a train leaving at midnight": Ibid.
34. Neither Colangelo nor Johnson realized it: Author, Ibid.
35. "If he needed money": Author, Ibid.
36. One of the grandest recoveries in NBA history: Newman, Ibid.

Chapter Sixteen: Bring It On. I'm Running

1. He began to mentor teens: Phoenix Police Department, report No. 61165388.
2. Never locked his home: Author, Ibid.
3. Girl later identified as "Amanda": Terri Hardy and Dorothy Korber, The Sacramento Bee, "Report details Johnson sex case," April 16, 2008.
4. The therapist, Kristan Larson: Phoenix Police, Ibid.
5. "Looking at it different": Hardy and Korber, Ibid.
6. A lawyer, Kent Turley: Paul Rubin, New Times, "The Summer of '95," May 8, 1997.
7. New Times: Ibid.
8. Bee sent a reporter: Author, Ibid.
9. If there is one category: Nick Pappas, "The Dark Side of Sports," p. 71.
10. Claimed she had been groped: Hardy and Korber, Ibid.
11. "I really don't know how many different ways": Ryan Lillis, The Sacramento Bee, "Chief outlines Johnson probe," May 1, 2008.
12. St. HOPE misused $847,673: Sam Stanton, The Sacramento Bee, "Gerald Walpin, ex-inspector general: Johnson settlement didn't end controversy," July 12, 2009.
13. Walpin had been appointed: Ryan Lillis and Melody Gutierrez, Ibid, "St. HOPE probe: Beltway bloggers abuzz," June 16, 2009.
14. To describe Obama and Kevin as friends: Author, Ibid.
15. Kevin campaigned: Ibid.
16. Johnson loved to tell: Ibid.

17. Lawrence Brown made a deal: Editorial Board, The Sacramento Bee, "Johnson, city can move ahead," April 10, 2009.
18. Evidence suggested he was a slumlord: Hardy and Phillip Reese, Ibid., "Neglect taints a star's legacy," October 14, 2007.
19. A brick wall collapsed: Ibid.
20. Butchered sheep and goats: Ibid.
21. Amassed 73 code violations: Ibid.
22. Johnson had enemies: Author, Ibid.
23. Three statements: Hardy and Reese, Ibid.
24. "I didn't get any sense": Hardy and Reese, Ibid, "Johnson given deadline by city," October 19, 2007.
25. A Sacramento bounty hunter: Hardy and Korber, Ibid, "Report details Johnson sex case," Ibid.
26. "Part of the ugly and dirty": Vellinga, Ibid., "Johnson: Forget scandal, talk issues," April 30, 2008.
27. "Sacramento needs to have a healthy discussion": Ibid.
28. Fargo wanted Johnson arrested: Author, Ibid.
29. "I heard they were saying": Ibid.
30. Stern devised a plan: Hardy, Ibid., "Stern takes lead in arena talks," November 16, 2006.

Chapter Seventeen: There Is No Plan B On The Table

1. "Well, I didn't smoke it yet": Terri Hardy and Kevin Yamamura, The Sacramento Bee, "Stern touts fund plan: NBA chief talks up a statewide arena agency," December 6, 2006.
2. They talked inside the governor's smoking tent: R.J. Middleton, KNTV San Jose, "Tour Arnold's smoking tent before it disappears," December 22, 2010.
3. Outdated by decades: Author as Special Assistant, 2009–2012.
4. Schwarzenegger used his smoking tent: Bill Ainsworth, San Diego Union-Tribune, "Critics are fuming over governor's smoking tent," May 13, 2005.
5. The filled the room with the aroma: Author, The Sacramento Bee, "Governor thinks he has Capitol idea: making patio a cigar bar," January 26, 2004.
6. The embarrassing defeat of two Sacramento County ballot measures: Hardy and Mary Lynne Vellinga, Ibid., "Some say lost arena bid was calculated," November 9, 2006.

7. Statewide authority to support the construction: Michael Danielson, "Home Team," p 284.
8. Challenges in Los Angeles: Sam Farmer, Los Angeles Times, "Philip Anschutz committed to bringing NFL back to LA," April 2, 2012.
9. Oakland: Bill Shaikin, Los Angeles Times, "Bud Selig on A's stadium situation: "I would like to move faster," October 24, 2012.
10. San Jose: Danielson, Ibid, p. 273.
11. Santa Clara: Mike Rosenberg, San Jose Mercury News, "Levi's Stadium: 49ers' new Santa Clara home gets a name in $220 million deal," May 8, 2013.
12. Civic leaders had tried and failed: Hardy and Vellinga, Ibid.
13. Astonishing suburban expansion: Crystal Carreon, Ibid., "Growing pains in a suburban boomtown," February 10, 2007.
14. Other states used governmental entities: Danielson, Ibid., p. 283.
15. Create thousands of jobs: Danielson, Ibid., p. 105.
16. Schwarzenegger wasn't willing to spend political currency: Frank Girardot, Pasadena Star News, "Even as Schwarzenegger kills their lawsuit, NFL stadium protesters march on," October 22, 2009
17. Kill an environmental lawsuit: Ibid.
18. You must stand down and do nothing: Vellinga and Hardy, Ibid., "Stern takes arena helm: NBA boss arrives in capital, says he'll take the helm to build Kings a new home," December 6, 2006.
19. His plan had two elements: Ailene Voisin, Ibid., "Maloofs alter their game in court of public opinion," September 19, 2007.
20. John Moag: Hardy, Ibid., "Expo's arena moment: earlier plans for a sports facility have flopped, but now NBA leads the charge," September 26, 2007.
21. Major League Baseball went 50 years: Danielson, p. 176.
22. The NBA grew roots for 16 years: Mike Lessiter, nba.com, "The names of the games."
23. New arenas were planned in Orlando and Brooklyn: Mark Schlueb, Orlando Sentinel, "Orlando's new arena opens after years of talk, millions of dollars," September 30, 2010.
24. The auditoriums in Oakland and Manhattan: Rusty Simmons, San Francisco Chronicle, "Warriors' owners scout arena ideas in New York," June 1, 2012.

25. Runner for state Senate president: Jon Morgan and William Zorzi, Jr., The Baltimore Sun, "Mover Moag comes out of hiding," November 7, 1995.
26. Sports facilities almost never turned a profit: Danielson, Ibid., p. 107
27. Find less stressful way: Danielson, Ibid., p. 286.
28. The tricks behind financing sports facilities: Ibid.
29. Needed to make his work seem mysterious: John Steadman, "From Colts to Ravens," p. 9.
30. The beating heart of Moag's work: moagandcompany.com, "About."
31. One truly big deal: Ruth Thaler-Carter, Baltimore Business Journal, "A conversation with John A. Moag, Jr.," September 6, 1999.
32. No comparable organization in California: Hardy and Yamamura, Ibid.
33. The Maloof boys had been ordered by Stern: Voisin, Ibid., "Hope is not lost for new arena," September 30, 2007.
34. The NBA commissioner and his consultant: Danielson, Ibid., p. 121.
35. His job was to bring an NFL team: Farmer, Ibid., "Rose Bowl joins forces with Moag," August 13, 2002.
36. "Purposefully and intentionally blindsided us": Gary Scott, Pasadena Star News, "Sports broker goes toe-to-toe with owners to land LA team," June 2, 2003.
37. A better arena site than the downtown rail yards: Vellinga, Ibid., "Kings arena at Cal Expo? In blow to city's rail yard plan, NBA is said to prefer fairground for its open land and parking lots," September 5, 2007.
38. Running up $40 million in deferred maintenance: Daniel Weintraub, Ibid., "Does arena plan add up for public?" March 15, 2009.
39. Disneyland North: Tony Bizjak, Ibid., "Cal Expo seeks boost at gate," June 30, 2010.
40. In 1975 and 1979 consultant studies: Hardy, Ibid., "Expo's arena moments: Earlier plans for an arena have flopped," September 26, 2007.
41. "There's a lot of discussion that has to go on": Vellinga, Ibid.
42. Huddled in a cramped meeting room: Author as broadcast journalist, 2007–2009.
43. Here was the plan: Weintraub, Ibid.
44. "There is no Plan B on the table": Vellinga and Hardy, Ibid, "Arena talks OK'd: Cal Expo, NBA to seek a deal at fairgrounds that avoids new taxes," September 29, 2007.
45. Team made headlines: Melody Gutierrez, Ibid., "Coach could face range of penalties," October 24, 2006.

46. Eric Musselman: Ryan Lillis and Sam Amick, Ibid., "Kings new coach busted," October 22, 2006.
47. Suggestive photos: Bobby Caina Calvan and Gutierrez, Ibid., "Kings dancers' misstep: salacious photos crop up online," February 15, 2008.
48. Theus was fired: Amick, Ibid., "Kings fire head coach Reggie Theus," December 16, 2008.

Chapter Eighteen: And I Apologize To Hustlers And Scam Artists Around The World

1. Diet Coke thrown by spectator John Green: ESPN.com News Services, "Fan details strides since brawl," November 20, 2009.
2. "Shocking, repulsive and inexcusable": Mark Kreidler, The Sacramento Bee, "4 players in brawl benched by NBA," November 21, 2004.
3. "I can be reckless at times": Sam Amick, Ibid., "Artest is trying to regain normalcy," March 21, 2007.
4. Artest pleaded no contest: Art Campos, Ibid, "Artest will do public service," May 4, 2007.
5. "I know he's working on other things": Amick, Ibid., "Suspended, then defended," July 15, 2007.
6. "The photos of the Sacramento Kings Dance Team": Calvan and Gutierrez, Ibid.
7. Gensler Architects: Tony Bizjak, Ibid., "Arena plan unveiled: Big on vision, light on details," February 28, 2009.
8. Just 1.5 million feet: Ibid.
9. "The whole country is cutting back": Mary Lynne Vellinga, Ibid., "Blueprint for 'village' still under wraps; arena plan likely in 90 days," October 22, 2008.
10. Dollars would come from private developers: Ibid.
11. "It comes as no surprise": Bizjak, Ibid., "Arena plan called workable," July 24, 2009.
12. Gerry Kamilos: Bizjak, Ibid., "Downtown arena proposal puts spotlight on Kamilos," January 10, 1010.
13. When Kamilos spoke: Author as Special Assistant, Ibid.
14. No project frightened Kamilos: Bizjak, Ibid.
15. "Operation Grand Slam": Ian Fleming, "Goldfinger," p. 163.
16. This is how Convergence worked: Bizjak, "Cal Expo decision: Sell or stay," February 24, 2010.

17. Macquarie Capital: Dale Kasler and Bizjak, Ibid., "Would-be arena financier is no stranger to big deals," January 22, 2010.
18. Pacific Coast Capital Partners: Ibid.
19. Building restrictions in North Natomas: Vellinga and Matt Weiser, Ibid., "Levee report shocks city: Feds plan tough restrictions that could halt building in Natomas," January 16, 2008.
20. Cal Expo board, which knew nothing: Bizjak, Ibid., "Cal Expo decision," Ibid.
21. Johnson didn't like Kamilos: Author as Special Assistant, Ibid.
22. Johnson barely mentioned: Author as broadcast journalist, 2007–2009.
23. Most residents couldn't identify: Author as Special Assistant, Ibid.
24. Council members developed great skill: Ibid.
25. Johnson wanted to be in charge: Lillis, Ibid., "Johnson's sure capital is ready for strong mayor, but opposition builds, says plan goes too far," July 4, 2009
26. NCAA said it was removing: Lillis and Bizjak, Ibid, "Mayor: Get arena going, team may pack up, he says, as NCAA rejects Arco bid," September 23, 2009.
27. He began making phone calls: Author, Ibid.
28. "Rules of the Game": Lillis and Bizjak, Ibid., "Mayor seeks clear path to sports and entertainment site," October 30, 2009.
29. "Sacramento First": Bizjak, Ibid., "Arena effort taps expert in hardball," December 23, 2009.
30. Twelve members: Ibid.
31. We couldn't rig: Author, Ibid.
32. Seven groups made proposals: Bizjak, Ibid., "Mayor: No site yet an arena winner, city, NBA may differ on pick," January 16, 2010.
33. Second media event was taking place: Ibid.
34. "The Convergence plan has the guys": Ibid.
35. "I knew I shouldn't have trusted": Author, Ibid.
36. "Shooting air balls": Suzanne Hurt, Sacramento Press, "Council members, NBA upset over arena task force comments," February 3, 2010.
37. "Your friend Lehane": Author, Ibid.
38. No point in having Sacramento First review: Lillis and Bizjak, Ibid., "Mayor, council members cross swords," February 15, 2010.
39. "Is this what you're asking about?": Author, Ibid.

40. A public execution: Bizjak and Lillis, Ibid., "Cal Expo rejects Arco site for fair, critical blow is dealt to land-swap plan," September 25, 2010.

Chapter Nineteen: Trying To Cut A Deal To Leave

1. Kevin Johnson surrounded himself: Author, as Special Assistant, 2009–2012.
2. Johnson required the staff to read: Ibid.
3. Assigned an armed police driver: Kim Minugh and Ryan Lillis, The Sacramento Bee, "Detectives shifted to protect mayor, budget cuts hit reserve cops, so elite officers guard Fargo," September 18, 2008.
4. "No joke. This dude is not normal": Author, Ibid.
5. Stern spent almost five decades: nba.com, "Careers, executives."
6. Stern was juggling many crucial issues: Harvey Araton, The New York Times, "The hardening of Easy Dave," November 8, 2011.
7. Believed in the Sacramento market: Sam Amick, USA Today, "David Stern holds the key to Sacramento Kings' future," April 12, 2013.
8. When he was in a good mood: Author, Ibid.
9. Reveal detailed knowledge: Ibid.
10. New arena would be built at the rail yards: Tony Bizjak, The Sacramento Bee, "Mayor upbeat on railyards after meeting new owners," November 10, 2010.
11. About 65 percent: Lillis, Ibid., "Think Big gets bigger agenda," July 4, 2012.
12. "You need to create": Author, Ibid, "Transcript, conference call," July 18, 2011.
13. Fourteen months after Stern was promoted: nba.com, Ibid.
14. Stern disliked franchise relocations: Amick, Ibid.
15. Dollars came from premium seats: Michael Danielson, "Home Team," p. 64.
16. Kevin Johnson represented a special box of intrigue: Author, Ibid.
17. "The big thing that came through": Ibid.
18. Stern tipped off Johnson: Ibid.
19. Dave Bing: Mary Williams Walsh, The New York Times, "Making the case for Detroit's future," September 23, 2011.
20. Bill Bradley: Barton Gellman and Dale Russakoff, The Washington Post, "In the Senate, prepping for the presidency," December 16, 1999.
21. Taught him to fear and love the commissioner: Author, Ibid.
22. He refused to touch a basketball: Joe Davidson, The Sacramento Bee, "Mayor hopes hoops remain relevant here," March 8, 2011.

23. Goal was to change the Sacramento City Charter: Lillis, Ibid., "Johnson's sure capital is ready for strong mayor, but opposition builds, says plan goes too far," July 4, 2009.
24. "I'm an executive": Author, Ibid.
25. Stalled by the city council: Lillis, Ibid., "Charter review committee: panel rejects strong mayor," November 4, 2009.
26. "As long as we can say": Author, Ibid.
27. Kevin Johnson was nervous: Ibid.
28. "I want a document": Transcript, Ibid.
29. The collapse of the Convergence: Bizjak and Lillis, Ibid., "Cal Expo rejects Arco site for fair," September 25, 2010.
30. Lehane wanted to simplify: Author, Ibid.
31. The idea of creating the "Dream Team": Lillis, Ibid., "Arena's viability will be studied; council picks developer, builder for jobs," February 9, 2011.
32. Promised the Dream Team an exclusive path: Author, Ibid.
33. Majority of council members to play along: Lillis, Ibid.
34. Urban Land Institute: uli.org, Urban Land Institute, "Using the Railyards redevelopment to revitalize the urban core," January 25–28, 2011.
35. Matina Kolokotronis, Author, Ibid.
36. The Maloof strategy was revealed: Bizjak, Ibid., "Stern: Kings discuss move; he says Maloofs have talked to Anaheim's rep," February 20, 2011.
37. The Boys were ready to relocate in Anaheim: Ailene Voisin, Ibid., "Stern's remarks should raise fears," Ibid.
38. "This means one thing": Bizjak and Dale Kasler, Ibid., "Kings ask for more time; NBA will consider extending deadline for a move request," February 25, 2011.
39. Secondary tenants at the Honda Center: Lance Pugmire, Los Angeles Times, "Honda Center eyes NBA with project," February 9, 2012.
40. No dollar amount: City of Anaheim, "Agreements and Amendments contingent upon the relocation of an NBA team to the Honda Center," March 29, 2011.
41. One word he used to describe the Maloof boys: Transcript, AEG meeting, June 1, 2011.
42. The NBA Board of Governors heard from two California mayors: Kasler and Lillis, Ibid., "Rivals trek to NBA summit; Sacramento, Anaheim will talk to board," April 14, 2011.

43. Darius Anderson: Kasler, Lillis and Bizjak, Ibid., "Capital still has a shot; billionaire says he'll buy team for Sacramento; Maloofs vow not to sell," April 15, 2011.
44. The Anaheim group: Ibid.
45. The Sacramento message: Ibid.

Chapter Twenty: OK, Keep Dicking Us Around

1. The commissioner told Johnson: Author, as Special Assistant, 2009–2012.
2. Never been a major consideration: Michael Danielson, "Home Team," p. 64.
3. The Brooklyn Dodgers: Danielson, Ibid, p. 138.
4. Owner Al Davis: Danielson, Ibid., p. 117.
5. The commissioner explained: Author, Ibid.
6. Johnson said he could prove: Ibid.
7. "You will have to prove that": Ibid.
8. Johnson insisted on secrecy: Ibid.
9. "You have Burkle": Ibid.
10. First challenge was to prove: Ibid.
11. Found 29 businesses willing to pay $9.2 million: Tony Bizjak, Ryan Lillis and Dale Kasler, The Sacramento Bee, "League reps to verify pledges by business," April 26, 2011.
12. Found major companies: Ibid.
13. "The one thing I don't want": Author, Ibid.
14. At the NBA meetings: Kasler, Lillis and Bizjak, Ibid.
15. Many NBA owners knew Romani: Cindy Brovsky, The Denver Post, "Stadium may have name by Jan. 28," December 15, 2000.
16. "That got their attention: Author, Ibid.
17. "Burkle's dramatic emergence": Kasler, Lillis and Bizjak, Ibid.
18. Didn't believe the former all-star: Author, Ibid.
19. Bennett was whisked: Bizjak and Lillis, Ibid., "Crucial visit to capital; pair to asses city's case for keeping Kings," April 21, 2011.
20. "When those guys went around the room": Author, Ibid.
21. Registered the nickname "Royals": Bizjak and Kasler, Ibid., "Maloofs put dibs on 'Royals' if they move to Anaheim," March 17, 2011.
22. Lacked the administrative authority: Daniel Lazaroff, Fordham Law Review, "The antitrust implication of franchise relocation in professional sports," volume 53, 1984.

23. Stern had a new strategy: Bizjak, Lillis and Kasler, Ibid., "City wins, Kings to stay, but a new arena finance deal must come by March," May 3, 2011.
24. Ten-month deadline: Ibid.
25. The Maloofs phoned Stern and Johnson: Ibid.
26. "We are going to put all our effort": Ibid.
27. Funding had always been the problem: Think Big Sacramento, "Public synergies report," July 28, 2011.
28. Chris Lehane went to work: Author, Ibid.
29. Assembly line of reports: Think Big Sacramento, "100 day report," September 2011.
30. "Filling the cup," Author, Ibid.
31. "Finding a nexus," Think Big Sacramento, Ibid.
32. "We are going to identify": Author, Ibid.
33. Received cold calls: Ibid.
34. One promoter said: Ibid.
35. Visa program for foreign investors: Ibid.
36. Roger Craig: Ibid.
37. Dan Barrett: Kasler, Ibid, "Arena bid may hinge on private parking," September 12, 2011.
38. Stern was growing angry: Author, Ibid.
39. "We're going to have a meeting": Transcript, conference call, September 16, 2011.
40. Parking monetization: Kasler, Ibid.
41. The city asked parking operators: City of Sacramento, "Entertainment and Sports Complex, staff report," March 6, 2012.
42. "We gather this parking thing": Transcript, Ibid.

Chapter Twenty-One: You Are Sitting On A Great Market

1. The more questions they had: City of Sacramento, Desmond Parrington memo to Bonnie Pannell, "Background Information on Parking RFQ Response," February 14, 2012.
2. Council member Bonnie Pannell: City of Sacramento, John Dangberg memo to Bonnie Pannell, "Parking Bonds (Loans) Repayment," March 13, 2012.
3. Dangberg tossed around the words: Ibid.
4. "When staff presents": Ibid.

5. Based on layers of brightly colored tissues: Tony Bizjak and Ryan Lillis, The Sacramento Bee, "Funds sought for city arena push, staff seeks $555,000 for consultants, other work," September 23, 2011.
6. Nobody was held accountable: Lillis, Ibid., "Strong mayor defeat reveals power plays, unions and post-election politics turn the tide," June 24, 2010.
7. Metered street parking: Sacramento City Code, 10.40.130, "Use of parking meter and machine funds. The money required to be deposited in parking meters and pay-by-space/pay-and-display machines as provided by this title is hereby levied and assessed as fees to provide for the proper regulation and control of traffic upon the public streets, to provide for public vehicular off-street parking facilities and to cover the cost of the supervision, inspection, installation, maintenance, control and use of the parking spaces and regulating parking of vehicles in the meter zones."
8. "We're already worked this through": Craig Powell, Inside City Hall, Inside Publications, "It's all about the money: city treasurer on the arena deal, municipal finances and more," April 24, 2013.
9.Path to parking meter money was cleverly blazed: City of Sacramento, Dangberg, staff report, Entertainment and Sports Complex Update and Parking Monetization, "Under current California law, parking meter revenue and operations cannot be included in the monetization. Meter revenues may only be expended on maintenance, safety and security of the rights-of-way, and parking facilities of garages (including debt). Staff is exploring the viability of using parking meter revenue to refinance the above referenced tax-exempt debt on garages with new taxable debt, which is permissible use of the funds," December 13, 2011.
10. Seriously study parking dollars in October 2011: Ibid.
11. Never a serious doubt: Lillis, Bizjak and Kasler, Ibid., "Arena financing plan wins council approval, 7-2 vote seen as first step in complex project," March 7, 2012.
12. Members staked out skeptical positions: Ibid.
13. By February 2012: City of Sacramento, Dangberg, staff report, "Entertainment and Sports Complex," March 6, 2012.
14. "The risk can be mitigated": Ibid.
15. AEG agreed to contribute: Ibid.
16. "Sacramento is a C-level market": Transcript, AEG meeting, June 1, 2011.
17. "It's better for the artist": Ibid.
18. "Concert fans are newbies": Ibid.

19. "That's really a": Ibid.
20. "We need to understand": Ibid.
21. The financial deal: City of Sacramento, Dangberg, Ibid.
22. Responded to dozens of calls: Author, Ibid.
23. The Packers' romance with Green Bay: William Povletich, "Green Bay Packers: Trials, Triumphs and Traditions."
24. Personalized, engraved bricks: Bizjak, Kasler and Lillis, Ibid., "City arena share put at 65%, team, operator, fundraising drive would pay rest of $391million cost," March 1, 2012.
25. Two state senators: Ted Gaines and Darrell Steinberg, The Sacramento Bee, "Nexus Plan provides roadmap to fund entertainment arena," September 7, 2011.
26. He once worked as a lawyer: Author, The Sacramento Bee, "Time running out on Steinberg's deal to help Maloofs in arena talks," August 28, 2006.

Chapter Twenty-Two: Keep Your Hands Off Our Kings

1. Gregg Lukenbill was in the audience: Ailene Voisin, The Sacramento Bee, "Rally to keep Kings in capital likely a lost cause," April 5, 2011.
2. The company went bankrupt: John Chambliss, Lakeland, Fla., Ledger, "Sky Kings Airlines files for bankruptcy," September 20, 2012.
3. "We have no shot at another": Voisin, Ibid., "Preserve the dream, urges Lukenbill," March 13, 2011.
4. Lukenbill walked his dog: Author as Special Assistant, 2009–2012.
5. "I can't believe he walked up to me": Ibid.
6. Executive team hammered out the numbers: Ibid.
7. He wanted The Boys to stay miles away: Lillis and Kasler, Ibid., "City, NBA, developer today start detailed arena talks in Dallas," October 5, 2011.
8. "Let me ask you about the Maloofs": Author, Ibid, Transcript, conference call, October 13, 2011.
9. On February 14, 2012: Lillis, Bizjak and Kasler, Ibid., "Council OKs arena parking plan talks," February 14, 2012.
10. Waldorf Astoria Hotel: Lillis, Bizjak and Kasler, Ibid., "Elation now, votes next, intense talks bring an arena agreement but hurdles remain," February 28, 2012.
11. There were painful moments: Author, Ibid.
12. Barrett explained the parking asset idea: Ibid.

13. The family no longer had that kind of money: Howard Beck, The New York Times, "Foreboding in Sacramento as the Kings whither away," April 9, 2011.
14. The NBA would loan: Kasler, Bizjak and Lillis, Ibid., "Maloofs pull out of arena accord; project dead for now, charges of blame traded," April 14, 2012.
15. "It's game over: Lillis, Bizjak and Kasler, Ibid.
16. "I think it's a fair deal": Ibid.
17. He wept: Ibid.
18. Embarrass the commissioner: Richard Sandomir, The New York Times, "NBA solidifies one ownership issue, but another takes a wrong turn," April 13, 2012.
19. Economist named Christopher Thornberg: Kasler, Bizjak and Lillis, Ibid.
20. Maloofs held a press conference: Ibid.
21. "We raised the question": Ibid.
22. "I wish I had better news": Ibid.
23. Stern held his own press conference: Ibid.
24. "Based on your calls, texts, Tweets and emails": Sam Amick, SI.com, "Head of Sacramento group issues scathing account of Maloofs' faults," April 16, 2012.
25. Sacramento fan organizations: Mike Tavares, crowndowntown.org.
26. Retrofitting Arco Arena: Kasler, Bizjak and Lillis, Ibid., "NBA cuts off arena efforts after rejection," September 29, 2010.
27. "Would really put the city right on the edge": Ibid.
28. Write their first check: City of Sacramento, Ibid., March 6, 2012.
29. Halted its due diligence: Bizjak, Ibid, "Huge site still a priority, even without arena, it will transform city," April 23, 2012.
30. Phoned George Maloof: Author, Ibid.
31. "Watch this": Ibid.
32. Johnson made smiling and glad-handing: Ibid.
33. DeMarcus Cousins: Sam Amick, USA Today, "DeMarcus Cousins divides opinions of Sacramento Kings," December 29, 2012.
34. They failed to reach 30 wins: "2012 Sacramento Kings Media Guide."
35. They said their job was to play basketball: Jake Appleman, The New York Times, "Kings continue to call Sacramento home, for now," November 22, 2012.
36. An earlier generation: Ibid.

37. Landlord sued Webber: M.S. Enkoji, The Sacramento Bee, "Webber sued for millions for failed venture, ex-Kings star shut restaurant last fall," March 2, 2010.
38. Vivek Ranadive: Malcolm Gladwell, The New Yorker, "How David beats Goliath," May 11, 2009.
39. Elder Ranadive jailed: Ibid.
40. Study required government permission: Ibid.
41. Tecknekron: Alicia Jessop, Forbes, "Why the Kings are staying in Sacramento: Meet Vivek Ranadive," May 28, 2013.
42. Tibco: Ibid.
43. Limited partner in new ownership: Rusty Simmons, San Francisco Chronicle, "Owner Ranadive pushes technology for Warriors," January 30, 2012.
44. As the first person from India: Jessop, Ibid.
45. Vivek had to be careful: Author, Ibid.
46. "All I can tell you": Ibid.
47. Hansen wanted to replace the SuperSonics: Christine Willmsen and Steve Miletich, Seattle Times, "The man who would bring the NBA back to Seattle," April 13, 2013.
48. Bennett became fed up with Seattle: Percy Allen, Seattle Times, "Bennett is first in line for OKC, NBA says," January 5, 2008.
49. He formed a partnership: Willmsen and Miletich, Ibid.
50. Jeremiah Jackson: Author, Ibid.
51. "Keep your hands off the Kings": CBS13, "Open Letter to Chris Hansen from Think Big," February 13, 2012.
52. A meeting room was booked: Author: Ibid.
53. Two TV stations: Ibid.
54. Chris Hansen didn't show: Ibid.

Chapter Twenty-Three: These People Have More Than Enough Money

1. Wednesday, January 9: Author, Mayor's Calendar, January 9, 2013.
2. For five years, Johnson dreamed: Author as Special Assistant, 2009–2012.
3. "We need to be physically separate": Ibid.
4. Most Wednesdays: Ibid.
5. "Moon shot": Ibid.
6. Johnson and Rhee were married: Ibid.
7. The love affair: Ibid.

8. After three hours of education policy: Author, Ibid.
9. Over the previous four years: Ibid.
10. No interest in being mayor: Ibid.
11. "Do I really have to sign": Ibid.
12. "I won't be doing any new initiatives": Ibid.
13. Another mayoral staffer: Sharokina Shams, KCRA3, kcra.com, "Daughter of former Sac mayor pleads guilty to stealing money from city," March 11, 2013.
14. Agreement to sell the Kings: Nick Eaton, Seattle Post-Intelligencer, "Report: Chris Hansen close to buying Sacramento Kings for $500 million," January 9, 2013.
15. Henderson, Nev.: Alan Snel, Las Vegas Review-Journal, "Henderson arena deal failed because Sacramento Kings went elsewhere, developer says," February 4, 2013.
16. "The city doesn't see a clear opportunity": Aaron Applegate, The Virginian-Pilot, "Va. Beach mayor says arena project is dead for now," January 9, 2013.
17. Took a remarkable gamble: Author, Ibid.
18. Threat of a federal antitrust suit: Ibid.
19. Under the law: Gabriel Feldman, UC Davis Law Review, "Antitrust versus labor law in professional sports," Number 45, April 2012, p. 1221.
20. Professional sports teams have argued: Feldman, Ibid.
21. Given a pass by the U.S. Supreme Court: Michael Danielson, "Home Team," p. 97.
22. Stern reversed the agenda: Author, Ibid.
23. Would not have withstood a federal court challenge: Feldman, Ibid.
24. "When you bid for a team": Dale Kasler and Tony Bizjak, The Sacramento Bee, "NBA deal gets green light," May 20, 2013.
25. Talking points over beers: Author, Ibid.
26. Crisis brought out: Ibid.
27. "He's totally obsessed": Ibid.
28. "Come April of before": Andria Borba, KTXL Fox 40, "Mayor Johnson reveals 19 members of local ownership group," January 22, 2013.
29. He drove public opinion: Author, Ibid.
30. Los Angeles Mayor Norris Poulson: Danielson, Ibid, p. 263.
31. "We wanted desperately": Ibid.
32. Other mayors: Ibid., p. 265.

33. Wanted a premium price: Author, Ibid.
34. Westfield unloaded the Downtown Plaza: Kelly Johnson, Sacramento Business Journal, "JMA purchase of downtown mall was the third proposal," August 15, 2012.
35. JMA paid $21.7 million: Bizjak, Kasler, Ryan Lillis, Ibid., "New Kings ownership to buy Downtown Plaza arena site," May 21, 2013.
36. "We won't get another chance": Author, Ibid.
37. Roger Craig phoned the Mayor's Office: Ibid.
38. Ranadive knew Stern: Ibid.
39. "A lot of people called us:" Kasler, Bizjak and Lillis, Ibid, "NBA sets arena cutoff," June 1, 2013.
40. Mark Friedman: Bizjak, Kasler, Lillis, Ibid.
41. Other owners: Gregory T. Huang, xconomy.com Boston, Interview with Andy Miller, May 20, 2013.
42. A $100 million sweetener: Bob Condotta, Seattle Times, "Chris Hansen ups ante with NBA," May 10, 2013.

Chapter Twenty-Four: The Appropriate Outcome

1. Family broke its relationship: Author, as Special Assistant, Ibid.
2. Stern pushed hard for maximum arena dollars: Author, Ibid.
3. "That's your strategy": Author, conference call transcript, September 16, 2011.
4. Fans piled on: Author, Twitter account, twitter@REGraswich.
5. A public Twitter exchange: Tom Ziller, sactownroyalty.com, "Heat owner Micky Arison to Sonics fan: This isn't about Seattle, it's about Sacramento," May 9, 2013.
6. The NBA said the Kings' sale: Condotta, Ibid., "NBA needs more time to vote on Kings," April 16, 2013.
7. The commissioner, who once admonished: Author, Ibid.
8. "This will be by far": Jerry Brewer, The Seattle Times, "A bad look for David Stern as Seattle-Sacramento battle for Kings drags out," April 19, 2013.
9. "A bad look for David Stern": Ibid.
10. "Deficient economically": Sports Business Daily, "Stern gives no indication of potential outcome of NBA Kings saga," April 22, 2013.
11. "In the same ballpark": Ibid.
12. Unanimous vote to deny the move: Condotta, Ibid., "NBA panel votes to keep Kings in Sacramento," April 29, 2013.
13. "I'm speechless": Vivek Ranadive, Twitter@vivek, April 29, 2013.

14. “It’s not over yet”: KOVR, CBS 13, sacramento.cbslocal.com “NBA relocation committee blocks Kings move to Seattle,” April 29. 2013.
15. “Horribly, horribly disappointed”: Mitch Levy, KJR sports radio Seattle, April 29, 2013.
16. “We have a binding transaction”: Chris Hansen, sonicsarena.com, “To the Sonics faithful,” April 29, 2013.
17. Voted 22-8 to deny the relocation: Percy Allen, Seattle Times, “Chris Hansen vows quest to bring NBA back to Seattle will continue,” May 20, 2013.
18. Sell its 65 percent share: Allen, Ibid., “Sacramento Kings sale complete,” May 31, 2013.
19. Took home around $206 million: Ibid.
20. “It kind of made me sick to my stomach”: Steve Miletich, Jim Brunner, Lynn Thompson, Seattle Times, “Hansen’s Calif. donation could hurt NBA hopes here,” August 16, 2013.
21. Hansen secretly decided to fund a campaign: Ibid.
22. “This is clearly a decision I regret”: Ibid.
23. Paid $50,000 fine: Thompson, Ibid., “Chris Hansen, consultants fined $50,000 for failing to disclose contribution,” September 9, 2013.
24. “The appropriate outcome”: David Stern, press conference, Dallas, May 15, 2013.
25. Stepped off a plane: Author, Ibid.
26. Received a message: Kevin Johnson, press conference, Sacramento City Hall, May 17, 2013.
27. Stern said it was old news: Ibid.
28. “You didn’t think I knew that”: Ibid.
29. “Be careful what you ask for”: Ibid.
30. “Remember when we talked last year”: Author, Ibid:
31. We talked about Stern and Johnson: Ibid.
32. Similar enthusiasms before: Ibid.
33. Roger Craig history: Roger Craig, rogercraig33.com, “Bio.”
34. Dr. James Naismith history: Rob Rains, introduction by Hellen Naismith Dodd Carpenter, “James Naismith, The man who invented basketball,” p. xiv.
35. “I am sure that no man”: Ibid.

Select Bibliography

Books and Journals:

Ambrose, Stephen. "Nothing Like It in the World: The men who built the Transcontinental Railroad." New York: Simon and Schuster, 2000.

Auerbach, Red, and Joe Fitzgerald. "Red Auerbach." New York: Putman, 1977.

Breslin, Jimmy. "Can't Anybody Here Play This Game?" New York: Viking, 1963.

Cook, Kevin. "Rochester History Journal," Winter 1996.

Cousy, Bob, with John Devany. "The Killer Instinct." New York: Random House, 1975.

Danielson, Michael. "Home Team: Professional Sports and the American Metropolis." Princeton: Princeton University Press, 1997.

Didion, Joan. "Where I Was From." New York: Vintage, 2004.

Feldman, Gabriel. "Antitrust versus Labor Law in Professional Sports." Davis: University of California, Davis, Law Review, No. 45, April 2012.

Fleming, Ian. "Goldfinger." New York: Signet, 1959.

Gardner, David, "The Tom Hanks Enigma." London: John Blake, 2007.

Goudsouzian, Aram. "King of the Court." Berkeley: University of California Press, 2010.

Grace, Kevin. "Cincinnati on Field and Court." Charleston: Arcadia, 2002.

Harris, Merv. "The Fabulous Lakers." New York: Lancer Books, 1972.

Havill, Adrian. "The Last Mogul." New York: St. Martin's Press, 1992.

Hecteman, Kevin. "Sacramento's Southern Pacific Shops." Charleston: Arcadia, 2010.

Isaacs, Neil. "Vintage NBA." Graham, Texas: Masters Press, 1996.

Kroeber, A.L. "University of California Publications in Archaeology and Ethnography." June 15, 1916.

Lazaroff, Daniel. "The Antitrust Implications of Franchise Relocation in Professional Sports." New York: Fordham Law Review, Vol. 53, 1984.

Lipsyte, Robert. "Accidental Sportswriter." New York: HarperCollins, 2011.

McGowan, Joseph, and Terry Willis. "Sacramento: Heart of the Golden State." Woodland Hills: Windsor Publications, 1983.

McPhee, John. "A Sense of Where You Are." New York: Farrar, Straus and Giroux, 1965.

Pappas, Nick. "The Dark Side of Sports." Maindenhead, England: Meyer & Meyer Sport, 2012.

Pluto, Terry. "Tall Tales." New York: Simon and Schuster, 1992.

Povletich, William. "Green Bay Packers: Trials, Triumphs and Traditions." Wisconsin Historical Society, 2012.

Rains, Rob. "James Naismith: The Man Who Invented Basketball." Philadelphia: Temple University Press, 2009.

Reagan, Ronald. "An American Life." New York: Simon and Schuster, 1990.

Reynolds, Jerry, with Don Drysdale. "Reynolds Remembers." Champaign, Ill.: Sports Publishing, 2005.

Robertson, Oscar. "The Big O." Emmaus, Pa.: Rodale, 2003.

__________. "The Art of Basketball." Cincinnati: Oscar Robertson Media, 1998.

Russell, Bill, and Branch, Taylor. "Second Wind: The Memoirs of an Opinionated Man." New York: Ballantine, 1980.

Salzberg, Charles. "From Set Shot to Slam Dunk." New York: Bantam Doubleday, 1987.

Schumacher, Michael. "Mr. Basketball." New York: Bloomsbury, 2008.

Sherman, W.T. "Memoirs of W.T. Sherman." New York: Literary Classics of the U.S., 1990.

Silber, Irwin, and Rodney, Lester. "Press Box Red." Philadelphia: Temple University Press, 2003.

Steadman, John. "From Colts to Ravens." Centreville, Md.:

Taylor, John. "The Rivalry: Bill Russell, Wilt Chamberlain and the Golden Age of Basketball." New York: Random House, 2005.

Rich Westcott. "The Mogul." Philadelphia: Temple University Press, 2008.

Wideman, John Edgar. "Hoop Roots." New York: Mariner Books, 2003.

Newspapers and Magazines:

Arizona Republic
Baltimore Business Journal
The Baltimore Sun
Boston Globe
Cincinnati Business Courier
Cincinnati Enquirer
Forbes
Fort Scott Tribune
Inside Publications (Sacramento)
International Business Times
Kansas City Star
Las Vegas Sun
Las Vegas Review-Journal
Newsday
New Times (Phoenix)
Oakland Tribune
Omaha World-Herald
Orlando Sentinel
The New Yorker
The New York Times
Lakeland Ledger
Los Angeles Times
Pasadena Star News
The Sacramento Bee
Sacramento Business Journal
Sacramento Union
San Diego Union-Tribune
San Francisco Chronicle
San Jose Mercury News
The Seattle Post-Intelligencer
The Seattle Times
Sports Business Daily
Sports Illustrated
USA Today
The Virginian-Pilot
The Washington Post

Websites:

fox40.com
insidepublications.org
kcra.com
NBA.com
news10.net
sacramento.cbslocal.com
SacramentoPress.com
sactownroyalty.com
sonicsarena.com
SI.com

Index

H

J

K

L

M

T

U

V

W

Y

Z

Acknowledgements

In the summer of 2009, when I went to work for Kevin Johnson at the City of Sacramento Mayor's Office, we discussed collaborating on a book about his experiences as a former NBA star turned politician. He had another story in mind, something about his influence on the breakthrough of moderate politics in California.

This book is none of those things.

By late 2012, when I left Kevin's office, the mayor and his team had just spent three years working a new arena for the Kings. We'd gotten nowhere. It seemed likely that Sacramento's only major league team would move. Maybe to Virginia Beach. Maybe Las Vegas. Maybe Anaheim. Maybe Seattle.

The Kings were already the most migratory sports franchise in America. Surprisingly, the story of how their ready-to-wear status was achieved had not been written. The tale lent itself to a low-concept operatic narrative, with a hero (David Stern), a reluctant prince (Kevin Johnson), a ghost (Les Harrison), a visionary (Gregg Lukenbill), a wandering merchant (Vivek Ranadive) and clutch of supernumeraries. That is this book. My thanks go to every participant.

People have been helping me with this book (often without trying to) for three decades. The assistance began at The Sacramento Bee, where Executive Editor Gregory Favre put me on the Kings' beat after his talented protégé Scott Price moved to the Miami Herald. Bee colleagues Tom Negrete, Dan Vierria, Steve Blust, Jim Jenkins, Steve Nishimura, Bob Sylva, Bill Menton, Jane Hughes, Skip Shuman, Dick Schmidt, Owen Brewer, Dan McGrath, Bob Kohn, Joe Davidson, Kent Pollock, Mort

Saltzman, Marty McNeil and Sam Amick filled essential roles as I survived many nights with the Kings and three decades at the paper. Some of those colleagues are gone and missed: Bill Conlin, Marco Smolich, Jim Rattie and Ben Swesey.

Living with the Kings for so many years was a challenge requiring acts of patience and collegiality among people I reported on. Many were extraordinarily generous, indulgent and forgiving: Jerry Reynolds, Don Drysdale, Tom Peterson, Phil Johnson, Mike Bratz, Willis Reed, Dick Motta, LaSalle Thompson, Joe Kleine, Anthony Bonner and Danny Ainge. And those who are gone: Wayman Tisdale, Derek Smith and my great friend Bill Jones.

Kitty O'Neal, Alan Eisenson, Judy Farah, Scot Murdoch, Elliott Troshinsky, Bruno Cohen, Whitey Gleason, Peter Roney, Steve Charlier, Dave Manoucheri, Richard Sharp, David Benick, Rob McAllister and Pallas Huppe provided support as I blundered through the broadcast world. And my work at the Mayor's Office would not have been sustainable without Raihane Dalvi, Ryan Garner, Jeremiah Jackson, Alex Kasner, Adrianne Hall, Ronnie West, John Dangberg, Rivkah Sass, Gus Vina, Nicole West, Jennifer Berbower, Andrea Corso, Kunal Merchant, Daniel Lopez, Benny Aziz, Daniel Ajise, Joaquin McPeek, Jay Schenirer, Angelique Ashby, Steve Cohn, Lauren Hammond, Sam Jackson and Robbie Waters. Other friends, notably Kathleen Watt, Shane Singh, Brent Meyer, Bert Terry, Simon Chan, David Townsend, John McGinness, Stephanie McGann, Rick Lobley, Melissa Sanchez, Randy Paragary, Rusty Areias, Bob White and Chris Lehane gave help, insight and inspiration.

It's essential to note that the majority of material in this book has been hidden in plain sight for decades, waiting for somebody with the time and (minimal) intelligence to look. Examination of these materials would not have been possible without retrieval systems and archival collections of local, regional and national newspapers, magazines and journals. Special thanks are owed to the Sacramento Public Library, California State Library, Monroe County (N.Y.) Library System, the Public Library of Cincinnati and Hamilton County (Ohio), Kansas City Public Library, Omaha Public Library and the City of Rochester Parks Department and Mayor Thomas Richards.

And finally, thanks to the person whose enthusiasm transcended all eras of the Sacramento Kings for as long as he lived, Tom Friery.

R.E. Graswich, Sacramento, September 2013